Seven Steps to Mastering Business Analysis

Barbara A. Carkenord, MBA, CBAP

J.ROSS PUBLISHING

Copyright © 2009 by B2T Training

ISBN 978-1-60427-007-5

Printed and bound in the U.S.A. Printed on acid-free paper
10 9 8 7 6 5 4 3 2 1

Library of Congress Cataloging-in-Publication Data

Carkenord, Barbara A.
   Seven steps to mastering business analysis / by Barbara A. Carkenord.
      p. cm.
   Includes bibliographical references and index.
   ISBN 978-1-60427-007-5 (pbk. : alk. paper)
  1. Business analysts. 2. Business planning. 3. Organizational
effectiveness. I. Title.
   HD69.B87C37 2008
   658.4′01—dc22
                          2008030941

Direct all inquiries to J. Ross Publishing, Inc., 5765 N. Andrews Way, Fort Lauderdale, Florida 33309.

Phone: (954) 727-9333
Fax: (561) 892-0700
Web: www.jrosspub.com

DEDICATION

This book is dedicated to my Mom and Dad, Joann and Joseph Carkenord. My Mom taught me to be organized and always plan ahead. My Dad's lifetime commitment to education gave me a love of learning, and taught me the discipline of hard work. Organization, planning, learning, and hard work are essential skills for mastering business analysis. In addition, my parents always told me that there wasn't anything that I couldn't do!

CONTENTS

CHAPTER 2
KNOW YOUR AUDIENCE

FOREWORD

I became a business analyst almost by accident. When I graduated from university, I went out into the workforce with a vague plan to find work as a technical writer. Unfortunately, my inexperience with software development derailed that plan, and I ended up working at a management consulting firm. I started by doing desktop publishing work, then ended up rewriting and eventually just writing the reports the firm did for its clients. When I left, I expected to find work as a consultant or project manager—but I lacked the credentials for those positions. Instead, I got offered a job as a business analyst at the mortgage division of a major bank. I took that job and found myself having to figure out what a business analyst did.

It turned out I wasn't the only one who had that problem. Most of my co-workers had been pulled into the job from other roles in the business and had no formal background in the profession either. The bank had put the fate of a $20 million project in the hands of a bunch of people who had no real training in the role they were supposed to execute, and in my case in the hands of someone who didn't understand the business either! Somehow, we muddled through, and the project went live. In fact, it's still in use as I write this, a decade later, although at least one attempt to replace it has failed.

Several years later, I got involved as a volunteer with the International Institute of Business Analysis (IIBA™), a professional association of business analysts. The IIBA was formed with the goal of helping to define the business analysis profession and develop a certification program so that people coming into the profession, like myself and my colleagues, would have somewhere to go to find out what the job actually entailed.

However, in order to do that, the IIBA needed some people to figure out what business analysis actually is. One of the reasons my co-workers and I had had so much trouble figuring out what was expected of us when we first became business analysts was that nobody agreed on what exactly a business analyst does or what business analysis is. Pretty much everybody agreed that requirements were an important part of the picture, but that was about all they agreed on. Some viewed it as a junior project manager, others as a developer with an understanding of the business, and still others as a tester. The IIBA needed to reconcile all of those conflicting views before it would be possible to achieve its other goals, and so the Body of Knowledge Committee was formed, with Barbara and me as two of its earliest members.

In the four years since that group of people first met, we've come a long way. We've seen business analysis emerge from the shadow of project management, development, and testing and become accepted as a discipline in its own right. We've seen business analysts and their employers learn that business analysis is the critical link between business strategy and the implementation of new policies, processes, and information systems.

Barb's place in the development of our profession is secure, as she led the creation and development of two knowledge areas in both version 1.6 and version 2 of *The Guide to the Business Analysis Body of Knowledge®*. But as version 2 of the *BABOK®* nears completion (at the time I write these words, we are finishing the public and practitioner reviews), we can see that there's still a lot more to learn. In *Seven Steps to Mastering Business Analysis*, Barb has gone beyond what we discuss in the *BABOK* to address the real challenges business analysts face in the workplace.

There are lots of books out there that can tell you how to write a use case, how to develop a process diagram, how to facilitate sessions with your stakeholders, and how to take all of that information and craft a requirements document. Certainly, those are skills that every business analyst needs to master. However, most of those books are written with the implicit premise that business analysts are working in a vacuum. They pretend that every business analysis effort starts with a clean slate—that you can walk into a room with your stakeholders and sketch a bright new world on your white board, with no concern for what came before.

The reality is, of course, very different. *Seven Steps to Mastering Business Analysis* recognizes that a business analyst has to work in a *context*. We have to work effectively as part of a team, understanding the roles and needs of each person involved in making a change happen. The project isn't something that we do because it seemed interesting—

it's being done because we are trying to achieve certain business goals, and unless those goals are achieved, the project may not be worth doing. The project itself will change how the business works on a day-to-day basis and has to be implemented within a technical infrastructure that is already in place.

When we walk into that room with our stakeholders, even at the beginning of a project, many of the most important decisions have already been made. That's the reality of a business analyst's work. In order to master business analysis, you need to understand those decisions, understand the context in which you're working, and help your stakeholders to find the solutions that will be most effective in that context.

Those analysis techniques that most other books spend all of their space on? Well, they're in here, but they are discussed only after looking at the needs of the stakeholders, the project, and the business and technical environment. And that's the way it should be, because the fine points of a diagramming notation are much less important than understanding the people, the goals of your project, and the business environment in which it takes place. If a solution isn't right for a business, it doesn't matter how well drawn the pictures are.

When I walked on to that project ten years ago, I didn't know what my job was or what I was supposed to do there. I, and the other business analysts, had to figure it out as we went along. If we'd had access to *Seven Steps to Mastering Business Analysis* back then, we'd have had a much easier time of it. I'm sorry it wasn't available to us back then, but I'm glad that business analysts today have the opportunity to benefit from Barb's expertise!

Kevin Brennan, CBAP
Vice President, Body of Knowledge
International Institute of Business Analysis

PREFACE

THE PURPOSE OF THIS BOOK

The purpose of this book is to describe the breadth of the business analysis professional role and to offer concrete strategies for working effectively in this arena. This role is frequently misunderstood. The individuals who perform business analysis work have varying titles: systems engineer, product manager, requirements engineer, business systems analyst, project manager, developer, system architect. Throughout the book, the title *business analyst* will be used to represent the business analysis professional. It is critical for business analysts to understand the larger context within which they work: the enterprise, the project, and the technical environment. A business analyst is expected to completely understand the business domain which he or she represents, understand how this business area fits into the enterprise as a whole, and understand how current and future technology can support the work of the business, along with helping to develop ideas for improvement of the business processes. This is a tall order. When new business analysts begin to understand the expectations of the role, they are often overwhelmed. This is not a profession where one becomes an expert overnight. Knowledge and skills can be continually updated and improved, making the analyst more effective and valuable to an organization.

There are many books available that describe various approaches to eliciting and analyzing quality requirements. This book includes a brief overview of key analysis techniques, along with excellent resources recommended to learn techniques like developing business models, data models, workflow diagrams, and UML diagrams. However, it is not the purpose of this book to teach every technique. Techniques and approaches for which good resources are not available are described in more detail. This book strives to give business analysis professionals a solid foundation and springboard upon which to build their skill sets. It provides a detailed understanding of the work of business analysis, a profession which is complex and often difficult to define.

INTENDED AUDIENCE

This book is intended for people who are performing business analysis work. As mentioned previously, their titles and roles are varied. Examples include business analyst, project manager, systems analyst, quality analyst, product manager, developer, tester, system architect, and data analyst among many others. It is also intended to help executives, managers, and human resource professionals who are working to establish business analysis job descriptions and career paths in their organizations.

Read this book cover to cover if you are a *new analyst*. It will explain the fundamental concepts of business analysis in a language that you will understand. This book will also be useful for *project managers* who are expected to perform business analysis work. Other project team members performing analysis and critical thinking, like *systems analysts, quality analysts, testers, and developers,* will gain insights that will improve the quality of their work. In addition, *product managers and business development professionals,* who are always gathering requirements and working to meet them, will also benefit from the concepts presented in this book.

If you are *considering business analysis* as a profession or are new to this role, this book will help answer the question: Is this the right job for me?

The book will be a reference for *experienced analysts.* Each chapter includes detailed explanations and descriptions of business analysis tasks, strategies, and recommended techniques. Each chapter also includes examples of successful and less than successful project situations from which you can learn.

If you are *managing, working with, or are responsible for hiring business analysts,* this book will give you a good understanding of what business analysts are and how they work. Since the work of business analysis is very complex and broad, managing professionals in this area can be challenging. The more you understand their responsibilities and tasks, the better you will be able to support them and evaluate their success.

Note to hiring managers: Business analysis is not a job; it is a profession. A person who does not feel passionate about this role will not excel. Since business analysts need an understanding of the business, many organizations look for candidates from among their current employees. Many of the skills necessary to be a successful business analyst are found in other professions. To recognize potential business analysts, look for people who don't simply do what they are told, but ask *why*. They often suggest process changes that are simple yet effective. This book will help to identify the right people in your organization to consider for business analyst positions.

Many organizations have put individuals into business analysis roles who do not have the aptitude and/or passion to be successful in the business analysis profession. This sometimes occurs due to a lack of understanding of the skills and the role. If requirements are thought of as simply "documentation" and the business analyst as a "documenter" or "requirements specifier" (IBM's Rational Unified Process®), the organization will continue to have problems with projects even after implementing a formal business analysis position. Be careful with titles vs. roles. Titles are important. Business analysis professionals should not have titles like "procedure writer" or "documentation specialist." Titles should reflect the scope of the job. The title business analyst is very popular in the profession because it uses two words that accurately describe the work: *business* (focus on understanding and advocating for business stakeholders) and *analysis* (critical thinking skills).

BOOK ORGANIZATION

This book is divided into chapters based on seven steps to mastering business analysis:

- ◆ Chapter 1: Possess a Clear Understanding of Business Analysis
- ◆ Chapter 2: Know Your Audience
- ◆ Chapter 3: Know Your Project
- ◆ Chapter 4: Know Your Business Environment
- ◆ Chapter 5: Know Your Technical Environment
- ◆ Chapter 6: Know Your Analysis Techniques
- ◆ Chapter 7: Increase Your Value

Each chapter, or step, covers a significant skill area for the successful business analysis professional. The chapters do not need to be read in order; they can be referred to as needed.

ABOUT B2T TRAINING

B2T Training was established in 2000 by Barbara Carkenord and Tina Joseph to provide educational experiences focused on developing individuals into master business analysts. The company offers a full complement of courses and products designed to equip business analysis professionals with a wide range of skills, techniques, and approaches. The comprehensive curriculum is supported by useful templates, a reference manual for guidance beyond the courses, mentoring opportunities, and online resources. In addition, B2T Training offers certification for those who can demonstrate a thorough understanding of business analysis knowledge areas and the ability to successfully apply that knowledge.

The company's vision is to deliver the highest quality training available in order to provide business analysis professionals with strong foundational skills to fully perform their role, as well as additional offerings to help individuals mature in their career. Organizations that promote the continued development of business analysts benefit by being able to gather better project requirements, which leads to improved business processes and technology solutions. These benefits help meet the demands of stakeholders and overall organizational goals.

B2T Training developed the first comprehensive business analysis training program in North America, which has served as a model for other training organizations. To remain as the top in the field, the company continues to focus solely on business analysis rather than branching out to related topics. B2T Training is a founding partner of the

International Institute of Business Analysis (IIBA™), formed in 2004 to promote the profession, establish standards, and create an industry certification. The company is extensively involved in the development of *The Guide to the Business Analysis Body of Knowledge®* (BABOK®), a document of business analysis standards, and has chaired various committees and held board positions within the IIBA.

B2T Training is excited about the growing recognition of the role of business analysis professional and continues to serve as an advocate for the profession. It is our goal, with this book, to equip business analysts with a reference and critical insight into the complexity of mastering the business analyst's role.

ABOUT THE AUTHOR

 **Barbara Carkenord**, President, B2T Training, has over 25 years of experience in business analysis. She earned an MBA from the University of Michigan and is a Certified Business Analysis Professional™ (CBAP®). She began her career in the information technology area as a programmer, systems analyst, business analyst, and project manager. Ms. Carkenord is a frequent speaker at industry conferences and has authored many articles and white papers on business analysis. She is the main editor and contributor of *the bridge*, B2T Training's business analysis magazine. Actively involved in the IIBA and a core team member of the IIBA BABOK creation committee, she is regarded as a thought leader in the industry and is highly respected by her peers and competitors. She has been instrumental in the recognition and growth of the profession.

Ms. Carkenord possesses detailed knowledge and experience in many structured approaches and methodologies. She is the primary writer of B2T Training course materials, which bring together proven techniques with real-world experience. Her areas of expertise include business analysis, high-level design, quality assurance, and project management. Her experience covers many industries, including insurance, banking, and manufacturing. She conducts formal and informal training sessions and consistently receives excellent student evaluations.

ACKNOWLEDGMENTS

Writing a book is not a solitary activity. Yes, I spent many hours alone drafting and revising, but this book would never have been completed if not for the dedicated work and encouragement of my team at B2T Training. Martha Scott, our Director of Marketing, diligently contacted publishers, working to make sure that we selected an organization that believed in business analysis with the same passion that we do. Angie Perris, our *VP of everything*, was my main subject matter expert for this project. Angie's extensive business analysis, project management, and software development experience, along with her passion for research and learning, provided me with the support and feedback that I needed to make this book a useful resource for business analysis professionals. Dennis Perkins, our Director of Course Development, produced all of the graphics in the book with infinite patience. His attention to detail and commitment to excellence show through in this work, just as it does in our course curriculum. Thanks to Ian King and Jonathan "Kupe" Kupersmith for their time reviewing and their helpful suggestions.

Finally, I am most indebted to my business partner, our CEO, Tina Joseph. This book is just one of the ways that Tina has shown her commitment to furthering the profession of business analysis. Her work in helping to establish the IIBA and its local chapters has resulted in a strong organizational foundation upon which the profession will be built.

On a personal note, I would like to thank my friend Dolores Zabroske, whose constant support and confidence in my abilities have seen me through many challenges. Her love of books and love of life are a wonderful inspiration to me.

Free value-added materials available from
the Download Resource Center at www.jrosspub.com

At J. Ross Publishing we are committed to providing today's professional with practical, hands-on tools that enhance the learning experience and give readers an opportunity to apply what they have learned. That is why we offer free ancillary materials available for download on this book and all participating Web Added Value™ publications. These online resources may include interactive versions of material that appears in the book or supplemental templates, worksheets, models, plans, case studies, proposals, spreadsheets and assessment tools, among other things. Whenever you see the WAV™ symbol in any of our publications, it means bonus materials accompany the book and are available from the Web Added Value Download Resource Center at www.jrosspub.com.

Downloads available for *Seven Steps to Mastering Business Analysis* consist of business analysis white papers and business analysis planning templates that can be customized to fit each organization's needs.

POSSESS A CLEAR UNDERSTANDING
OF BUSINESS ANALYSIS

This book is intended to help business analysis professionals master their profession. In order to master business analysis, you must first possess a clear, complete understanding of the essential skills of a business analyst (BA). Business analysis involves very complex and sophisticated thinking patterns and advanced communications. Describing and defining the role is very difficult. What is it that makes a BA successful?

◆ Is it being an expert on workflow diagrams?
◆ Is it having a strong technical programming background so as to be able to design software that will meet business needs?
◆ Is it being a strong facilitator, in order to lead requirements elicitation sessions with large groups of people?

Yes and no. A successful BA is all of these things and something more. There is something special and rare about the people who can combine technical knowledge, business acumen, analytical skills, and the communication skills necessary to be successful in this role. Excellent BAs bring value to their organizations by understanding true business opportunities, making realistic recommendations, and facilitating the successful implementation of these solutions. This chapter will give you insights into the skills and knowledge that successful BAs share.

WHAT IS BUSINESS ANALYSIS?

The International Institute of Business Analysis (IIBA™) defines business analysis as "the set of tasks and techniques used to work as a liaison among stakeholders in order to understand the structure, policies, and operations of an organization, and recommend solutions that enable the organization to achieve its goals" (www.theiiba.org).

Business analysis involves:

◆ Identification of business problems and opportunities
◆ Elicitation of needs and constraints from stakeholders
◆ Analysis of stakeholder needs to define requirements for a solution
◆ Assessment and validation of potential and actual solutions
◆ Management of the "product" or requirements scope

BAs elicit, analyze, communicate, and validate requirements for changes to business processes, policies, and information systems. The business analysis professional understands business problems and opportunities in the context of the requirements and recommends solutions that enable an organization to achieve its goals.

The business analysis discipline has emerged from work previously done by project managers (gathering high-level business requirements) and systems analysts (designing functional requirements for software behavior). Currently, in many organizations there is still an unclear differentiation between the work of business analysis and project management. Chapter 2 of this book will discuss these unique roles. Business analysis builds on many of the same techniques used in *systems* analysis but focuses more heavily on business goals and less on the technology designs. Business requirements are elicited and analyzed at a much more detailed level than traditionally done during systems analysis. Business analysis also places more emphasis on understanding user groups and business environments and designing highly usable applications. The discipline of business analysis is useful for solving business problems and taking advantage of opportunities by helping business people design procedures, structures, and technology to support and enhance their work. Many solutions include a significant software component because most business areas benefit extensively from software automation and it is often the most complex piece of a solution.

Most of the projects in which business analysis professionals are involved include a software or IT solution, but the profession and role are not limited to software development. The work of business analysis focuses on helping to elicit, analyze, document, and validate requirements and implement solutions to business problems. The same skills that are useful for helping with software development projects often translate well to other types of business solutions. Frequently, an effective solution to a business problem involves a software component along with procedure changes and possibly job responsibility changes. It is rare to find a business unit that is not using software and technology to perform its work. BAs help to design solutions, not just software. The profession and the IIBA are working to use the word *solution* when possible instead of limiting discussions to software systems.

Business Analysis vs. Software Development

When talking about software development methodologies and approaches, it is important to recognize how business analysis relates to these processes. Most software development methodologies have been created by software developers to help organizations more efficiently build application systems. Very few of them include or even acknowledge the primary work of business analysis. Using the Rational Unified Process® (RUP) as an example, it mentions business models and business modeling as an activity that happens *before* project initiation. This has a very important implication: the assumption is that when a software development project is started, the business model has already been developed (and hopefully documented) and the solution determined to best support the business is software. When RUP's assumptions are accurate—the business is well understood and solution evaluations have already resulted in a conclusion—RUP works well. The software can be designed and created following the business needs and will fulfill user expectations.

Unfortunately, many organizations do not understand RUP's underlying assumptions. Truly analyzing and understanding the business is not done before project initiation. In these situations, business analysis professionals are assigned to the team to gather business requirements in the context of a methodology that has no time allocated for this work. RUP uses the word "analyze" as one of its phrases, but this is *software* analysis, not *business* analysis. Business analysis professionals who are assigned to work on these projects often find themselves helping to design software functionality while they are trying to understand the business (other methodologies have similar constraints, as discussed in Chapter 5). This slows the process of eliciting requirements, causing developers to be waiting for business analysis deliverables. Planning time for eliciting business requirements before functional or software requirements is the best way to prevent this confusion and delay. Business requirements may be developed before project initiation or as a first step of a project as long as time is allocated for this important work.

The Role of the Business Analyst

The business analysis profession has emerged and continues to grow mainly because of the need for people who can translate business needs into software technology and organizational solutions. Individuals who have both strong communication skills and analytical aptitude (the critical foundational skills) can be taught to use analysis documentation and presentation techniques. People who can clearly communicate and who can think logically will always be valuable to the success of their organizations. This unique combination of soft and analytical skills is the key to the BA role.

Business analysis work is being done by professionals with titles as varied as developer, project manager, systems analyst, systems engineer, requirements engineer, etc. More and more organizations in the United States and around the world are recognizing business analysis as a distinct profession and developing career paths for people who are interested in specializing in this area. Gartner Research predicts BA staffing at one BA per major business process (Morello and Belchar, 2005). This means there could be hundreds of thousands of BAs! Another interesting comparison is to developers. Currently, many organizations have BA to developer ratios like one to six, but that ratio is rapidly increasing. With the sophistication of developer tools and the speed at which code components can be assembled, the ratio will swing toward more BAs. It takes more time to perform thorough analysis and clearly understand a business problem (and design a solution) than it does to build software. In the next couple of decades, the ratio may be much more like two to one or even three to one BAs to developers.

Even as the role of the BA is still being defined, specializations in this profession are already emerging. There are business analysis professionals who specialize by industry, by software application, by technology, and by level of experience. Gartner, Inc. projects that one BA type is not going to meet all the needs of an organization (Morello and Belchar, 2005) and recommends that each organization develop a pool of BAs with different expertise and experience. This is great news for those in the business analysis profession. The more recognized the role is, the more opportunities there will be. It is also critical that individuals within the profession specialize so they can focus on particular types of business problems or solutions.

Business analysis is a complex, broad area that will continue to grow like other professions. The profession is still young; BAs often are expected to "know it all," like the early years in the legal and medical professions. Originally, a lawyer dealt with everything from copyright protection to personal wills. Now there are lawyers who specialize in corporate software contract negotiations and others who specialize in high-wealth individual estate planning. In the medical profession, as medical research continually uncovers new diseases and treatments, general practitioner doctors and nurses are unable to maintain expertise in every area. The medical profession has specialties like cardiology, podiatry, and nephrology. New technology, pharmaceuticals, and procedures also drive many medical professionals to choose a specialty and focus on it. Patients benefit from this specialization because a specialist can stay abreast of new discoveries in his or her area of expertise. BAs also will become specialized and focus on a particular area of the work where there is a special interest and proficiency.

Business Analyst Traits

Most people who are drawn to the business analysis profession have traits in common. Analysts enjoy learning new things and have a natural curiosity. In addition, BAs have a rare combination of the ability to see the big picture (conceptual thinking) while being very detail oriented. This combination of traits results in a very successful BA.

The "people" skills necessary to be a successful BA are many and varied. They include strong listening skills, both verbal and non-verbal. They include the ability to ask good questions and probe deeper for very detailed information. They include leadership abilities—running successful meetings, encouraging team members, and supporting corporate goals. The real secret to all of these skills is knowing the individuals with whom you are working because every human being communicates slightly differently.

The technical awareness needed to be a successful BA includes software development approaches, organizational IT standards, data design and storage strategies, and software usability principles. Business analysis professionals must stay abreast of current trends and capabilities and be able to communicate effectively with the technology team.

Since the role of BA requires so many different skills, most individuals in this role are constantly working on improving and increasing their skill sets. The effective BA is always stretching himself or herself to learn new techniques and improve his or her use of analysis tools.

The extent of the responsibilities of the BA changes on every project and may even change during the course of a project. Since the BA is bridging a gap between groups of people who speak different languages, he or she must be able to span the gap, regardless of its width. Refer to Figure 1.1. Assume the length of the line to be the extent of the gap. When a BA is working with an individual or group of subject matter experts (SMEs) who are very knowledgeable about their business and have worked on IT projects in the past, the gap is narrow. On the other side, when a BA is working with technical people who

FIGURE 1.1. Short Bridge for Business Analysts to Span

are strong communicators and knowledgeable about the business, the gap is narrowed. In this ideal scenario, the BA is easily able to span the gap by bringing the two groups together. Ideally, these are the types of project situations to which a new BA should be assigned.

When a BA is working with an individual or group of SMEs who are not experienced with IT project work, have never provided or reviewed requirements, and/or who are inexperienced in the business domain, the gap widens. On the other side, when a BA is working with an individual or group of technical professionals who have weak communication skills, little or no industry or business knowledge, and/or limited experience in developing software, the gap widens further. In this more challenging scenario, the BA stretches himself or herself to the maximum he or she can to bring the groups together to develop effective business solutions. This requires a more experienced, adaptable BA. Figure 1.2 shows this wider gap.

Most projects fall somewhere between the two extremes. An experienced BA assesses this gap soon after being assigned to a project. *He or she then plans the business analysis work with the size of the gap in mind.* Clearly recognizing and acknowledging this gap gives the BA an important insight into the scope of his or her responsibilities.

History of Business Analysis

Traditionally, everyone involved with software development came from a technical or IT background. They understood the software development process and often had programming experience. They used textual requirements along with ANSI flowcharts, data flow

FIGURE 1.2. Long Bridge for Business Analysts to Span

diagrams, database diagrams, and prototypes to document the software design. Frustration with software development was caused by the length of time required to develop a system that didn't always meet business needs. Business people demanded easy-to-use, sophisticated software and wanted it better and faster.

Many business people got tired of waiting for large, slow-moving IT departments to roll out yet another cumbersome application. They began learning to do things for themselves or hire consultants, often called BAs. These consultants would report directly to the business management and help with software design and development. As businesses experienced the benefits of having a person dedicated to finding solutions to business problems, the number of BAs increased. Individuals from the business units became BAs, with backgrounds as varied as marketing, accounting, payroll processing, and claims administration.

IT groups did not initially see the value of this new role. BAs inside business units were sophisticated users who were anxious to take advantage of new technology and were willing to look outside the enterprise for help. Some user departments purchased software packages without consulting their own IT department. Others hired outside developers to create new software. These stand-alone systems caused even more problems for IT, which was suddenly asked to support software that it had not written or approved. Small independent databases popped up everywhere, with inconsistent and often unprotected data. IT organizations realized that creating a BA role internally was critical for continuing to support the business and stay in control of software applications. In addition, as some software development projects were outsourced, the need for quality, detailed requirements became painfully obvious.

Several other factors have increased the need for and value of dedicated business analysis professionals. The explosion of customer-facing Web pages demanded an increase in the understanding of usability and human factors in design. The International Organization for Standardization® (ISO) set quality standards that must be adhered to when doing international business. Carnegie Mellon University created software development and organizational quality standards with CMMI® (Capability Maturity Model Integration). Six Sigma™ has provided a disciplined, data-driven quality approach to process improvement aimed at the near elimination of defects from every product, process, and transaction. Business process management products are dedicated to improving efficiency and consistency at an enterprise-wide level. Service-oriented architecture (SOA) encourages improvements in software design and reuse of system components (called services).

All of these movements have been driven by frustration with the quality, timeliness, and applicability of business support from technology groups. Every study of software development failures shows that incomplete, incorrect, and missing requirements are the main reason for failures. It has become clear that the software development process needs a profession of people who are dedicated to eliciting, analyzing, and presenting requirements from a business perspective and making sure that the business needs are met in the software design and development.

Where Do Business Analysts Come From?

BAs come from both IT backgrounds and business areas. In the best situations, the business analysis professional has a combination of IT and business skills.

From IT

BAs with an IT background are very analytical individuals who enjoy problem solving. They are attracted to software development because of its emphasis on solution design, logical thinking, and discipline. Systems analysis and design involves the same type of critical thinking skills as business analysis. These individuals often were strong designers and developers because of their inherent logical thinking patterns and attention to detail. They are often promoted to more analytical roles because, in addition to their strong problem-solving skills, they have strong communication skills.

Case in Point

I began my career as a developer and was successful. I found that not only did I enjoy solving problems but enjoyed finding them and learning about business processes from the business experts. I remember the first time that I was programming based on requests and specifications from a BA. I felt frustrated because I wasn't tasked with talking with the users directly. I wanted to know exactly what went on in the business and why they had requested this software functionality.

BAs with an IT background can become masters in business analysis as they build their business expertise. Often, new analysts with IT experience limit recommendations for potential solutions to software. They may not consider process changes or organizational changes as effective methods for problem solving. They may not understand the time required to implement a change in business procedures when new software is deployed. They need to look for business solutions without assuming that technology is the answer to every question. They need to learn to think like a business person, understanding the goals of the enterprise, and adjust their view of technology to one that supports the business goals rather than driving them.

From Business

Individuals from business units have also moved into business analysis. BAs who have work experience in a business typically have been acting as SMEs on IT projects, so they are familiar with project structure and requirements. These BAs bring a wealth of subject matter knowledge with them. Often, they originally joined the organization as a professional business person and excelled in their role. These individuals are promoted within the business because of their intelligence and ability to see more than just their job. They often recommend procedural or workflow changes to improve efficiency in their areas. They show strong analytical and problem-solving skills within the business area, along with strong communication skills with management and their co-workers.

Case in Point

Several years ago, I joined a project, in progress, as the project manager (and BA). The assignment was to implement an upgrade to a vendor-supplied software package that supported annuities for an insurance company. The application running in production was several versions behind and the vendor was about to discontinue support of the oldest version, so the upgrade was mandatory and had a firm due date. Because some custom development had been done to the production version of the software, the new version of the package could not be installed directly "out of the box"; it had to be reviewed and modified where necessary. This application supported thousands of annuities worth several million dollars.

Since the project plan was already done and the team was small, I should have had plenty of time to play the role of the BA. But things did not turn out as planned! The project plan turned out to be incomplete, and I also discovered that this organization did not have a quality assurance group. Suddenly, in addition to analyzing, developing, and implementing, my team had responsibility for all system and integration testing and managing the user acceptance tests. This all still may have been manageable if I had been an expert in annuity processing. But I was not. Annuities are very complex financial instruments. The owner invests either a lump sum or a series of payments, and the insurance company pays back the investment through a series of periodic payments that begin sometime in the future, along with earned interest. Some annuities are tied into life insurance policies, with payment starting or changing upon the death of the insured. There are cancellation penalties and complex interest calculations.

Insurance agents and annuity administrators spend years learning all of the calculations and payment options available with annuities. They also must understand the government regulations (i.e., the U.S. Securities and Exchange Commission) related to annuity contracts. This is not a business domain that I was going to be able to analyze and learn in a few weeks. In addition to the complexity of the product, testing had to be conducted using future dates (have you ever tried to set your system date to a date in the future?), and we had to simulate transactions over several years and several mock deaths. This was a project where an industry expert BA was critical.

Fortunately, I was able to justify the addition of a full-time BA to assist with the package customization requirements and conduct all of the testing. Even more fortunately, I was able to find an experienced BA who was an expert in life insurance and annuities! The story has a happy ending because I was able to focus my time on project management and implementation requirements while the BA handled the business stakeholder communications, elicitation and analysis of requirements, creation of test plans, and execution of the test scenarios. Without this skilled and experienced resource, the project would have failed.

BAs with a business background will benefit from increasing their technical intelligence. They need to learn as much as possible about how software is developed, what capabilities are available through technology, and the relative time and cost of developing each capability. A BA must be able to discuss options with very technical individuals and must feel confident in his or her knowledge during such conversations. BAs also need to learn about IT architecture. Often, IT components must be built in a particular order because the underlying architecture is needed before business functions. IT architecture is discussed further in Chapter 5.

Where Do Business Analysts Report?

Business analysis professionals reside in one of three departments in most organizations: IT, individual business units, or a central business analysis group often referred to as a business analysis center of excellence.

BAs who are assigned inside business units have a different perspective and a different emphasis than those from the IT area. BAs working in a business unit will be much more aware of the business conditions, competitive issues, and financial issues and will be aware of how other groups see their business unit and how these other groups work with their business. This perspective allows the BA to analyze and solve business problems at a detailed level. BAs working in the business area are often involved in writing business cases, documenting current workflows, and re-engineering processes. They also understand how critical IT support is to the business workers. When a BA is sitting in an office next to a customer service representative and hears that person's frustration because the system crashes daily, the BA is acutely aware of how much disruption this system problem is causing. By being close to the business, the analyst is better able to articulate the importance of launching a project to correct the problem. Also, understanding the competitive nature of a business unit, especially in the sales or marketing area, helps the analyst understand why new product ideas must get to market as soon as possible. There is usually a window of opportunity that if missed will decrease the long-term sales of the product.

When BAs are working inside a business unit, their line management and project sponsors usually report to the same division. This alignment allows the BA to be a true advocate for the business. There may be conflicts when the BA reports to an IT project manager or the project management office because these groups may have different priorities than the business. A challenge may also arise because the BA may not understand the software development process and may not prioritize architecture pieces as high as necessary for strong software design.

BAs working in IT will be much more aware of the technical environment, availability of new capabilities, and other current projects that may be related and will be aware of how technology is developed and maintained. This perspective allows the BA to analyze and solve business problems from a strong technology perspective. If the BA is sitting in an office next to someone at an IT help desk and hears that person voice frustration every day because callers don't understand how to use a particular application, the analyst is acutely aware of how much disruption this system problem is causing. The analyst is better able to articulate the importance of launching a project to correct the problem. Also, understanding the architectural nature of software helps to better design solutions that will interface smoothly with surrounding applications. If a BA has a deep understanding of what is possible and what IT resources are available, he or she is able to set more realistic expectations and help the customer envision more powerful solutions.

When BAs report to IT management, they often have access to resources and technologies of which the business unit may not even be aware. A challenge with this organization structure is that IT may drive the business as opposed to the business driving software development. It may be difficult for the BA to be an advocate for the business when he or she reports to and is paid by IT. This is a conflict of interest.

As the role of the BA has been refined, the work of the position has grown. The BA working in a business area often analyzes business problems *before* projects are identified, utilizing techniques such as root cause analysis. He or she may identify potential solutions and perform cost/benefit analysis, developing a business case to gain project funding. The BA working in the IT area is typically assigned *after* a project has been approved, focusing on learning the business requirements and making sure the technology solutions meet those needs. An experienced, well-rounded BA could work in either arena effectively.

A business analysis center of excellence is a business unit expressly created to support individuals performing business analysis work. The idea for this group comes from the project management office concept, which many organizations have instituted. The advantage of having a department expressly focused on business analysis work is that the best practices and guidelines are more easily standardized and available for the entire enterprise. Business analysis professionals share lessons learned on projects to improve future work. BAs have support and guidance from other BAs.

A business analysis center of excellence supports business analysis professionals by providing a list of approved analysis techniques with diagramming and naming standards. A mature center of excellence may provide analysts with software tools to support the development of requirements, requirements management, and requirements tracing.

Managers who are considering reporting lines in their organization should consider the advantages and challenges of each option. These decisions depend on the enterprise philosophy toward business analysis work and the organizational culture. Consider who is driving the development of technology solutions: marketing, sales, IT? Consider how well the value of business analysis work is understood by the organization. BAs can demonstrate their value quickly regardless of where they report as long as they are given the time and resources necessary to elicit and develop quality requirements.

WHO MAKES A GREAT BUSINESS ANALYST?

There are several important characteristics and skills that are necessary for success in business analysis work. The BA must:

◆ Be an outstanding communicator
◆ Understand general business concepts and be able to advocate for the business
◆ Have an understanding of technology
◆ Enjoy very detailed research and recording

- ◆ Be skilled at organizing and managing large amounts of information in various formats
- ◆ Be flexible, be naturally curious, and enjoy learning new business domains
- ◆ Understand the software development process
- ◆ Be able to work through complex business problems and determine the root cause of a problem
- ◆ Come prepared with a tool kit of techniques to elicit, analyze, and present excellent requirements

This profession requires a wide breadth of skills and extensive business experience. You may be considered a competent and successful BA after you have a few years of experience and learning, but the learning and increase in abilities will continue throughout your career. Compare this with the skills and ability of a musician. Many people play the piano successfully both professionally and as amateurs. Beginners can learn to play many songs and accompany groups. Intermediate and advanced players compete and win awards. Career players are invited to join symphonies and orchestras around the world. Some virtuosos have solo careers that include concert tours and recording contracts. Yet, they are all *pianists*. Ask anyone who plays whether they have *mastered* the piano and 100% of honest pianists will say: "No, I have not mastered the instrument." When asked if they could improve, most will answer: "Yes, I could improve with more lessons and more practice." Their answer will never change throughout their lives. BAs should also answer these questions in the same way. There is always more that can be learned; mastering business analysis involves work on different types of projects, dealing with different stakeholders, using different techniques, creating different deliverables, and analyzing different business areas. Skills can always be improved and honed. A BA can continue to grow within the profession throughout his or her career.

Note that number of years of experience alone is not a good indicator of business analysis expertise. If you have been doing the same tasks, in the same business area, for many years, your other analysis skills may be lacking. For example, a BA who supports maintenance changes to a particular application system may know exactly how to write functional requirements and design changes to that system. The projects all follow a similar process and the stakeholders are always the same people. This BA may be very proficient in these projects and have a very satisfied sponsor, but if moved to a different department or assigned to work on a different application, he or she might not be able to be effective because a different project might require different techniques and skills.

Many successful BAs are individuals who have worked as consultants in different organizational settings, on many different types of projects, using many different analysis techniques. Others have worked for several companies, gaining experience in different industries and working with different types of stakeholders. This may be considered a "fast track" for the business analysis professional. *If you are interested in developing into a master business analysis professional, ask to be assigned to different business units and different types of applications, using different software development methodologies and tools.* The more varied your experience, the more flexible and adaptable you become. Flexibility and adaptability are key skills for business analysis.

So how does a person learn business analysis and how does a BA become a virtuoso? To take the piano analogy a little further, you must first learn the basics and then practice, practice, practice. Pianists learn the basics like reading music, memorizing the notes created by each key, and understanding the use of the pedals, along with the fundamentals of technique (e.g., when to use the thumb vs. the index finger). They then use what they have learned on simple pieces to start to put all of the knowledge and skills together to create "music." They don't start out playing Chopin—they often start out with "Row, Row, Row Your Boat"!

Similarly, a BA must start by learning the basics:

◆ What is a requirement?
◆ What are the techniques for eliciting, analyzing, and presenting requirements?
◆ What are stakeholders and what is my responsibility toward them?
◆ How are business problems solved?
◆ What technologies are available?

The BA puts all of this knowledge together on a project (hopefully a small, simple one at first) to perform "business analysis." The basics of business analysis are: an understanding of the role of the BA, understanding requirements, and learning to think analytically and critically. There will be missed notes along the way. There will be hesitations and stalls as the BA works his or her way around the "keyboard." Have you ever listened to someone who is just learning to play the piano? It can be painful on the ears. They are encouraged to practice alone. But BAs must practice on real projects, right in front of everyone!

As with any complex work, there are always prodigies. Mozart started playing piano at the age of four and by age six was accomplished and giving performances. There are some individuals for whom analysis, problem solving, and solution design are as natural as walking. There are also individuals for whom asking questions and probing for detailed information are part of every interaction. These individuals are natural-born analysts and will quickly develop into very successful BAs once they learn the formal techniques and guidelines within which to harness their talents.

Understanding the development of a business analysis professional and his or her maturity level is very important for managers and project managers who are assigning resources. If possible, new BAs should be allowed to work with experienced BAs who can coach and mentor them through their first few projects. Quality training in analysis techniques and communication skills should be provided. BAs should have an intern period, almost like doctors, where they are supervised by an experienced BA for a year or two before they are left on their own. Support, help, and guidance for new BAs will best help them develop their skills. Experienced analysts often require little supervision. Recognize prodigies who may not produce a requirements deliverable exactly according to standards but probably have an excellent vision of a possible solution.

Case in Point

My career has spanned several industries and business areas. My first job was as a programmer for a U.S. automobile manufacturer. The career path then was to start as a programmer, move to a programmer/analyst, then a systems analyst, and finally a project manager before being considered for management. As a programmer, I worked with systems analysts who worked with the business stakeholders to understand needs and then design a solution. This was before the role of the BA was separate from that of a systems analyst. As a developer, I was also often included in discussions with users, doing everything from gathering requirements, facilitating requirements workshops, and designing user interfaces to conducting training. My first assignments were in assembly plant support. I did not know anything about building cars or trucks. My business stakeholders patiently explained the assembly process to me and gave me frequent access to the plant floor to see how parts were brought together and assembled into a working vehicle. Although today I still retain a high-level understanding of the process, I never became a business expert or industrial engineer. I was able to understand the process at a high level and ask suitable questions to develop an in-process inventory system. It was not easy, but I was able to bridge the gap between the business needs and the technology solution.

My natural interest in problem solving was supplemented by systems analysis training. I was fortunate to be working with excellent co-workers who mentored me as I learned to consider all of the ramifications of a possible solution.

Other projects included manufacturing systems, cost accounting systems, and developing a data dictionary system. These business systems are very different, and each required me to do extensive learning from the SMEs before I could help to recommend effective solutions. After my first job, I worked at a mortgage servicing company and an automobile club. Once again, at the beginning of each project, I had to learn as much as I could about the particular business area (i.e., mortgage tax pay procedures, the secondary mortgage market, emergency road service). This is the part of the job that I most enjoyed—learning new business areas. An important characteristic of excellent BAs is that they want to learn new things.

Business Analyst Suitability Questionnaire

Becoming a BA is not something that a person should decide quickly. There is a long learning curve, so you need to make a commitment to the profession. It is also not something that someone else should decide for you. Many individuals have found themselves wearing the title BA without understanding what the role involves. Others have been "promoted" into the role by managers who don't understand the skills and characteristics required.

The questions below are intended to help you determine if the BA role is appropriate for you and to determine how well suited you are to the profession. Use these questions to honestly assess yourself. These questions can be answered by anyone interested in or working in the business analysis profession. If you are feeling frustrated in your role, you may find out that you are not well suited for it. If you are well suited to the role but are having difficulty being successful, it is likely that the role is not being supported adequately by your organization. This questionnaire could also be used by career development managers to assess an individual's interest in moving into the business analysis profession. As you read each statement, decide if you agree or disagree.

Suitability Questionnaire

1. I enjoy organizing information. My personal finances are filed and easy to reference.
2. I enjoy planning my work. I like to shop and run errands with a list.
3. I enjoy, and am good at, preparing documents that are clear and easy to review.
4. I am good at drawing diagrams (e.g., maps, floor plans).
5. I am able to simplify a complex topic.

6. I have a list of tasks that I need to complete daily.
7. I enjoy learning new techniques. I am very curious.
8. I love problem solving. I enjoy puzzles and logic games.
9. I really enjoy getting into details.
10. I can step back and see the big picture.
11. I am able to motivate myself to get work done.
12. I appreciate constructive criticism and feedback so that I can improve myself.
13. I love working with people.
14. I can handle people with strong emotions.
15. I can remain calm when people around me are overstimulated.
16. I prefer not to manage/supervise people.
17. I am generally patient when others don't understand something that I do.
18. I am comfortable dealing with conflict.
19. I can honestly and politely tell people when they are straying from the main point when telling a story.
20. I am good at negotiating solutions between two other people.
21. I enjoy working on long projects.
22. I get personal fulfillment from the *act of working* more than the *delivery* of a particular product.
23. I am comfortable making presentations in front of groups.
24. I am good at conducting meetings, keeping everyone on topic and on schedule.
25. Most people enjoy working with me and help me when I ask.
26. Before I start every task, I think through how I am going to do it.
27. When I receive an e-mail message, I take a few moments to think about to whom and how I am going to respond rather than just reacting.
28. I rarely have to send follow-up e-mails to clarify my message.
29. When others review my work, they only find a few corrections.
30. When someone does not understand something that I am explaining, I can explain it in another way.
31. When I give a formal presentation, attendees understand my message.
32. I enjoy helping people learn new things.
33. I create positive relationships with people.
34. I don't mind changing my language to words that better communicate with my co-workers.

Answers

How did you do? The more statements with which you agree, the more likely you are suited to the business analysis profession. The purpose of this assessment is to honestly answer the question: "Do I want to be a BA and will I excel in this role?" If you do not enjoy the type of work that BAs perform or these are not your strongest skills, it may be better for you to find out now. Keep in mind also that there are various levels of BAs and you will probably start at the beginning level. Beginning BAs will refine and improve their skills as they gain more experience.

Things that you will probably not do as a new business analysis professional include:

◆ Manage/supervise people
◆ Direct activities
◆ Be able to immediately respond to a request
◆ Generate revenue directly for your organization
◆ See immediate results of your work

This is not a scientifically tested assessment. There are many formal assessment tools that may be useful to consider if you want to get a better understanding of how you work and how you best communicate with others. Communication skills and work preferences are so important to business analysis work that an analyst must understand his or her own styles and preferences. An analyst works with many different stakeholders and is rarely able to convince a stakeholder to change his or her style. The analyst must adapt and conform to the most effective style for each stakeholder interaction. This requires significant self-awareness, along with the ability to read and assess other people.

The Birkman Method® is one approach to learning about yourself and your preferred interactions with others. It is an assessment that results in detailed information about your everyday interpersonal style, underlying motivations and needs, and reactions to stress. It also highlights your interests and recommends the type of work for which you would be most suited (www.birkman.com).

Another useful assessment is the DISC®. DISC is a behavioral model which looks at behavioral style and preferences. Four aspects of behavior are assessed: Dominance (control, power, assertiveness), Influence (social interactions, communications), Steadiness (patience, persistence, thoughtfulness), and Conscientiousness (structure, organization). Scores describe the extent to which an individual is assertive vs. passive and open vs. guarded, in addition to the intensity of each of the four dimensions. For a complete reference, see *The Universal Language—DISC* by Bill Bonnstetter and Judy Suiter.

The Myers-Briggs Type Indicator (MBTI®) is probably the most well known and most controversial of all personality assessments. The MBTI results in a description of an individual's preferences in areas called *dichotomies*: Attitude (extroversion vs. introversion), Functions (sensing vs. intuitive and thinking vs. feeling), and Lifestyle (judging vs. perceiving). The terms used for these dichotomies have very specific meanings within the MBTI which differ from everyday usage. Volumes have been written about the meaning and applicability of the MBTI.

There are numerous other assessments and published works that strive to help improve human communications. Being aware of your personal style and preferences will allow you to more easily adjust to the styles and preferences of others. As you work with different individuals, you will become more skilled at informally assessing their styles. Carefully listening and observing others is always the best technique for improving communication skills in any profession.

Business Analyst Career Progression

If you are a new BA or working in a new organization, find a mentor—formal or informal—and utilize that person at every opportunity. Don't be afraid to ask for help and direction. No great musician got to Carnegie Hall on his or her own.

BAs who come from a business background or report to a business unit may spend their careers in the same industry or the same business area. For example, if you have years of business experience in a telecommunications company and decide to change jobs, you are likely to move to another telecommunications company because your knowledge of the industry is valuable. BAs with this industry experience and knowledge will also be excellent candidates for consulting roles. These individuals will be valuable as executive managers in their area of expertise because of their understanding of the business issues and their analytical capacity to imagine and implement solutions. If a BA is interested in moving into management, his or her experience will easily transfer to more strategic positions in the enterprise.

BAs who have IT experience or are working in the IT department may find themselves moving in slightly different career paths. To successfully understand the business requirements without having worked in the business unit requires a person who can learn quickly and imagine a situation without having actually been in the situation. These individuals have the ability to understand most business requirements at a high level and translate them into a technological solution. These individuals are often able to work in various business areas, relying more heavily on SMEs for detailed business understanding. BAs with a strong technical background and the ability to see business requirements will be excellent consultants, either internally or externally. These individuals will also be great candidates for management positions that lead to a chief information officer role. More and more chief information officers list business acumen as the most important skill necessary in their job.

Historically, people who effectively perform business analysis work in IT (often called programmer/analysts or systems analysts) have been promoted to project managers when they were interested in career progression. This is not always an appropriate transition because many of the skills and characteristics of an excellent project manager are different from those of an excellent BA (see Chapter 2 for a discussion of the roles of the project manager and BA).

There are different types of business analysis work, and people who perform business analysis work do not have exactly the same skills. A large organization may have many individuals doing different types of business analysis work. Recognizing that the organization will benefit from a variety of analyst roles often leads to a set of job descriptions, titles, and career paths supporting business analysis professionals. Formally creating professional standards for business analysis work is one of the goals of the IIBA. Experienced BAs are committed to elevating the profession, setting professional standards, and bringing recognition to the role. The more well defined the positions and job descriptions, the easier it will be for professionals to find the appropriate positions for their skill sets and their interests. See Table 1.1 for an example of a BA career path (possibly someone from a business background) and Table 1.2 for an example of a BA career progression within IT.

KEY BUSINESS ANALYSIS TERMS/CONCEPTS

Organizations use terminology very inconsistently. One of the roles of professional standards organizations like the Project Management Institute and the IIBA is to standardize definitions and the use of terms throughout their respective professions.

Language is very important to the role of the BA. BAs must learn to be very precise in their use of language and be very consistent. Words, concepts, and ideas are all used to convey requirements. Listen carefully to the way stakeholders use words so that you can communicate back to them in a language that is familiar. When a business person calls their customer a *client*, the BA should always refer to the

TABLE 1.1. Business Analyst Career Path

Title	Experience	Tasks
Junior Business Analyst (novice, BA intern)	0–2 years of experience doing analysis work; may have industry experience or IT development experience	Elicit and document requirements for small, well-defined projects, often changes to existing systems. Ideally works with BA mentor.
Business Analyst (Business Systems Analyst)	2–5 years of experience doing a variety of analysis work	Elicit, analyze, and document requirements for medium to large projects. Works with the project manager to scope new projects.
Lead or Senior Business Analyst	5–10 years of experience doing a variety of analysis work	Elicit, analyze, and document requirements for large, complex, mission-critical projects. Supervises/mentors junior BAs. Works with the business to initiate and define new projects.
Business Consultant/ Client Relationship Manager	10+ years of experience doing analysis work	Assist the business with strategic planning, business case development, and new product implementations. Helps to identify projects. Sets up and manages a business analysis center of excellence.

customer in the same way. It doesn't matter if that is not the best or most appropriate word. It doesn't matter if that is not a word with which the BA is comfortable or familiar. The word is used by the business person and as such must be used by the BA to facilitate and demonstrate understanding.

BAs must recognize that terms have different meanings to different individuals and be able to translate these words and meanings to the concepts they represent. There are a few key business analysis terms and concepts that will be used throughout this book. They are introduced here.

What Is a Requirement?

The word *requirement* is one of the most important words in business analysis work. BAs must understand the uses of this term. In the industry, the word *requirement* is used

TABLE 1.2. IT Business Analyst Career Path

Title	Experience	Tasks
Programmer/Analyst	0–2 years of experience doing analysis work; 0–2 years doing software development	Elicit and document requirements for small, well-defined projects, often changes to existing systems. Make, test, and implement the software changes.
Systems Analyst (Systems Architect)	2–5 years of experience doing a variety of analysis work	Elicit, analyze, and document requirements (or review requirements developed by other BAs) on medium to large projects. Make software design recommendations; write technical requirements and program specifications. Manage developers.
Business Systems Analyst	5–10 years of experience doing business and system analysis work	Gather, analyze, and document requirements for large, mission-critical projects. Supervises programmers and systems analysts. Works with the business to initiate and define new software projects.
Business Consultant	10+ years of experience doing analysis work	Assist the business with strategic planning, business case development, and new product implementations. Helps to identify projects. Sets up and manages a business analysis center of excellence.

inconsistently and can mean various things to different people. The IIBA chose to build on an existing definition created by the Institute of Electrical and Electronics Engineers (IEEE) many years ago:

IIBA Business Analysis Body of Knowledge® (BABOK®) definition of requirement:
A requirement is a condition or capability needed by a stakeholder to solve a problem or achieve an objective (IIBA, 2008).

Note that the IIBA definition does not say anything about the format or representation of the requirement. Analysts are free to represent it in any way that clearly communicates the need. Nor does the definition prescribe who will own or manage the requirement.

Every experienced BA has his or her own understanding of what a "requirement" looks like, but as a group, the profession does not have a shared understanding. It is almost like a piece of art. When one person sees a canvas with various colors of paint spattered on it, he or she may think of it as art while someone else may think of it as a mess.

In this book, a requirement is defined as anything that is important enough to discuss, analyze, document, and validate. A requirement can be documented and presented as:

- A sentence ("The system shall . . .")
- A structured sentence (as in a business rule)
- A structured text template
- A table or spreadsheet (list of stakeholders)
- A diagram (workflow)
- A model (entity relationship diagram with associated details)
- A prototype or simulation
- A graph
- In any other format that communicates

The format or representation does not qualify it as a requirement; it is the *intent* and the *stakeholder need* that make it a requirement. Traditionally, software developers have used the word *specification* to describe a document or diagram that specified the product to be built. This word may be used interchangeably with *requirement* when describing software design components.

Since the definition of *requirement* is so broad, it is helpful to think of requirements in terms of some broad categories or components. These *core requirements components* are the building blocks upon which very complex business areas and systems can be described. You might compare them to the letters of the alphabet. Understanding the letters and how they can be combined into words allows you to make sentences and communicate very complex ideas and concepts.

Core Requirements Components

When describing a business, there are four basic requirements components: people, information, process, and rules (these components will be covered in detail in Chapter 6). People may include individuals or departments inside or outside of the organization (called *external agents* or *actors*). This component also represents "systems" or other

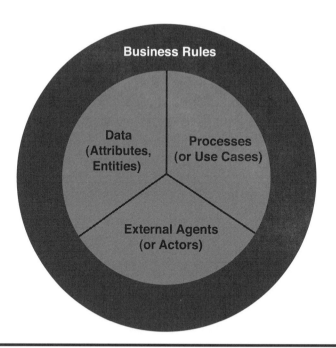

FIGURE 1.3. Requirements Components

business areas. Information is *data. Processes* are manual or automated activities or procedures that the business performs. *Rules* are business rules, guidelines, constraints, or policies under which the business operates. You can think of rules as encircling the other three components because rules guide the use of the other components (see Figure 1.3).

This is a simple way to start thinking about analyzing any business area. See Figure 1.4 for an example of the breakdown of requirements components.

By breaking requirements into their core components, BAs begin to see the business more analytically. They can identify specific parts of the business that may need improvement and develop more specific questions to get more detailed requirements.

Why Document Requirements?

To an experienced BA, this may sound like a silly question, but it needs to be answered for new BAs, managers, and the rest of a project team. New agile approaches to software development question the need for any written, formal requirements because they slow down a project and may not be seen as critical to success.

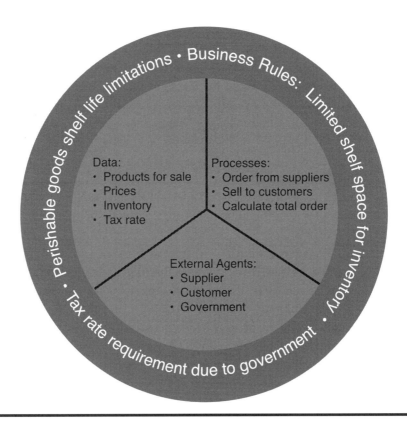

FIGURE 1.4. Requirements Components for a Grocery Store

Everyone agrees that requirements must be elicited from stakeholders and given to developers. Buy why not communicate through a conversation? Why not have the business SME talk directly to the developer and cut out the "middle man"—the BA?

Here are a few reasons why requirements should be documented:

◆ **People forget things**. Business stakeholders will forget what they tell developers. Developers will forget requirements. This leads to a lot of wasted time while team members try to remember what was discussed.

◆ **Verbal communication is fraught with errors**. Remember playing the game telephone as a child? A message that is passed from one person to another changes significantly as more people are involved. Requirements are very specific, detailed items that can easily be changed by using a different word or phrase. Verbal communication of requirements will rarely be accurate.

◆ **People sometimes answer the same question differently if asked twice**. Business stakeholders often give different answers to the same question at different times. This may be because after the first discussion a stakeholder has had time to think about the question further, or it may be that a stakeholder has simply changed his or her mind. BAs are experts at asking the same question in different ways before documenting a requirement to be sure that the SME has really answered definitively.

◆ **Writing something down forces a person to think about it more carefully than they do when they say it**. For example, an SME may say that he wants a report to show totals by month, but when he sees a report layout with 12 columns crammed together, he realizes that he actually wants the last 3 months only.

◆ **Having a second person (the BA) try to write down a user request and then have the user review it for accuracy highlights ambiguity and poorly defined requirements**. It also identifies missing requirements and undocumented assumptions.

◆ **New people joining a project need to get familiar with the requirements**. This is most effectively done by having requirements documented.

◆ **Evaluating and managing a developer assignment requires the assignment to be clear and documented**. This is actually true for all employees and is the reason why human resource departments encourage managers to articulate assignments accurately. It is difficult to hold a developer responsible for implementing a requirement when the requirement is not documented anywhere.

Why Do Requirements Need to Be Detailed?

Requirements must be discussed and agreed upon at a very detailed level. This assures that the business stakeholders have answered detailed questions about their business and clearly communicated their needs. Requirements also need to be detailed to give the solution team clear direction about the expectations.

Analyzing and developing requirements at a very detailed level is time consuming, especially for new BAs (see the skills discussed in Chapter 7 for help with this). For these reasons, many project managers and BAs don't go far enough. Managers don't understand why requirements take so long to develop, and most software developers don't like to get very detailed requirements because it stifles their creativity. All of these factors combine to explain why the industry is still so poor at defining requirements. It also explains why agile approaches are initially appealing—no documenting of requirements. Often, BAs haven't done a very good job explaining why requirements need to be detailed. Without understanding the value of detailed requirements, few organizations will invest the time.

High-Level Requirements Are Interpreted Differently

Until the BA and business stakeholders get into very detailed discussions about how the business process will be accomplished, analysis work is not complete. As the BA and stakeholder discuss initial project objectives and goals, the BA begins to build a picture in his or her mind of what a solution might look like. Meanwhile, each business stakeholder also has a picture in his or her mind. It is very likely that these vague sketches in the minds of individual team members are different. These differences will not really be exposed until detailed requirements are discussed, written down, and jointly reviewed.

Many Analysts Only Use Text to Document Requirements

Textual requirements are by their very nature ambiguous and incomplete. It is difficult to capture the complexity of a business area or technology specification with text. When requirements are not detailed enough, software developers will build the product they see in their mind. This probably will not match the picture in the mind of the BA or business stakeholder. Building the wrong product means a lot of costly rework and an unhappy customer. This is not to say that developers can't provide great creative solutions, but they need to understand the constraints around which features (or components) can be designed creatively and what areas need to follow strict business guidelines.

Discussing and documenting requirements using diagrams usually prevents wasted time and confusion about true needs and wasted business user time adjusting to a change. Any change to a business area is disruptive. The BA can help discuss the ramifications of a change with the business stakeholders before the requirement is completed to make sure the change is appropriate and necessary.

Complex Business Rules Must Be Found

Many business rules are not exposed until very-low-level detailed requirements are documented. Many business rules and business guidelines are not mentioned during requirements elicitation because they seem inconsequential (too detailed) or because the business

SMEs take for granted that everyone knows them. These business rules often drive exception processing and cause major problems if omitted. Every business rule that will be automated by software must be explicitly stated in the requirements. With business rules, the requirements should include the desired exception processing, including the exact wording of any warning or error messages. Helping the business SMEs think about how they expect to see business rules enforced often exposes other business rules and more detailed requirements.

✳ *Requirements Must Be Translated*

Requirements are usually expressed very differently by business stakeholders than the way that they are learned by developers. The BA acts as a liaison or translator, and the requirements are the tool for that translation. Ideally, the BA will be able to express the requirements in a format and style that can be understood by both the user and the technical team. This is the reason why expressing requirements in text is discouraged. Using language requires both audiences to share an understanding of terminology that must be very exact. For business people to learn IT language or IT people to learn the business language is a waste of time. The business analysis professional has the skills necessary to present requirements in visual formats that can be clearly understood by both groups. In addition, developers need requirements to be split into logical, technically related pieces. Data needs will be met in a very different technology than process needs, so these should be presented separately to IT. Some components of the requirements will be very obvious to business people (screen layouts, reports), while other components will be built into the software and not easily "seen" (i.e., business rules). These requirements should be documented and presented separately.

Case in Point

Suppose a business stakeholder requests a change to his data entry screen to add a new data element now required for government reporting. There are several important details about this requirement that should be discussed and documented before getting the developer involved. Without a BA and specific requirements (instructions), the developer will decide where to put the field on the screen (probably based on where there is open space), what the label for the field should look like, what edits are performed on the data entered in the field, and how the data is stored in the database. With these many decisions and guesses about the business need, the developer is bound to get something wrong. During reviews or testing, the business stakeholder might complain that the field is in the wrong place, the tab function doesn't follow a logical flow of the data entry, or the label doesn't make sense. In a worst-case scenario, the developer reorders all of the fields on the screen to "clean it up" or make it more aesthetically pleasing. In this case, a simple regulatory change has become a major procedural change where the software users are required to change their entire workflow. For a system with hundreds or thousands of users, the time to relearn the data entry process would have a negative impact on productivity.

When an error is found during testing, the developer must code again and risk the possibility of creating other problems. This rework is a huge waste of resources. It would only take a BA a few minutes to ask the appropriate questions and document the requirement accurately.

What Is a Project?

A project is a temporary endeavor—with specific start and completion dates—undertaken to create a unique product or service which brings about beneficial change or added value. It is critical for business analysis professionals to understand the nature of project work vs. the ongoing work of the business. Projects, which frequently involve software/technology development, are funded to accomplish a specific objective. Once the project goals have been accomplished, a project is complete. In IT departments, changes to existing software systems may be categorized as projects when their expected completion time is significant. Smaller maintenance requests may not be called projects and are managed completely by the assigned resource (usually the BA or the developer). BAs may be assigned to work on more than one project at a time. They also may be assigned to non-project work (i.e., ongoing business tasks) or pre-project work (i.e., business case development).

What Is a Product?

In the context of business analysis work, a *product* is the result of a *project*. If a project charter states that the project work involves implementing a new payroll processing system, the payroll processing system is the *product*. Most projects result in a product, but not all do. A business process improvement project may result in process redesign and increased efficiencies without the development of a new product. It is important for business analysis professionals to understand the concepts of project and product and be able to differentiate between the two. For organizations whose customer products are software, there is a clear distinction. In these organizations, people who perform business analysis work are often titled product managers. This title is also becoming common for people who manage internal products like the payroll processing system.

What Is a Solution?

A solution is something that "meets a business need, by solving problems or allowing an organization to take advantage of an opportunity" (BABOK). The word *solution* was carefully chosen by the IIBA BABOK committee to make it clear that business analysis professionals are involved with designing and implementing business solutions. The term *solution* is defined more broadly than *product* because it may include changes to a product, to existing systems, to procedures, and to organizational structures.

Case in Point

A request was made for a new field to be added to an existing screen in the customer relationship management system. The requestor wanted to be able to capture the customer's communication preference because some customers like to receive their order confirmations via e-mail and others like to receive a paper copy through a delivery service. This sounded like a very simple change to the software. But as a BA, I needed to think about the larger implications of the change.

First of all, the other users of the screen(s) were consulted to determine if there were any potential problems with this idea. Second, the employee procedure manual had to be changed to show this new field and explain its purpose. Third, decisions had to be made about whether or not this new field would be required, what it should default to, and if it could be changed. Each of these decisions had an impact on the business workers. For example, business workers outside the order department who review the status of orders or answer customer calls needed to understand the new piece of information and be able to explain it to customers. In the end, to implement this solution successfully, there were several components: (1) the software change itself (the screen and sending the confirmation), (2) data entry instruction changes, (3) communication of the purpose of the new field to all users and training in how to use it, and (4) communication of this new option to the customers. The *solution* was much bigger than software.

Traditionally, IT analysts have focused on software as the solution and often underestimated the significance of the business changes that must be made to accommodate new software. Business analysis professionals are in the unique position to understand the ramifications of a change to the entire business area. The business analysis profession is working to broaden the perspective by acknowledging that software is often a part of the solution, but it must be combined with procedural and organizational changes to effectively improve the business.

As a business analysis professional, approach each assignment with an open mind, even when someone has already recommended a solution. The act of analyzing means that you don't jump to conclusions or a solution until you completely understand the problem or opportunity and have considered many possible solutions.

What Is a Deliverable?

The word *deliverable* (root: to deliver) is used in software development to describe almost anything that is given to someone. A deliverable is given or presented to a stakeholder because it has some value to the stakeholder or the stakeholder is expected to act upon it. Examples of deliverables include a workflow diagram "delivered" to a stakeholder for review and approval, a database design "delivered" to a database administrator with the expectation that he or she will create a new database, and a new data entry screen "delivered" to software users to improve their process efficiency. To be accurate when talking about business analysis deliverables, the word *requirement* should be used as a prefix to deliverable. A requirements deliverable is then easily distinguished from a software deliverable, a training deliverable, etc.

Business analysis professionals create requirements deliverables for their stakeholders to confirm understanding of requirements, get approvals, communicate work to developers, communicate needs to vendors, communicate software testing requirements to quality assurance, etc.

Software development methodologies and processes often recommend specific requirements deliverables for their process (i.e., use cases are used with RUP). Many organizations also have company-wide standards that dictate required deliverables (i.e., business case, Requests for Proposal). BAs must be aware of the required/recommended requirements deliverables for their organizations and each particular project. In addition, the BA may decide to create other deliverables to present requirements that are not completely represented by the recommended techniques. It is important that the BA not simply follow the prescribed deliverables blindly. It is the BA's responsibility to communicate requirements accurately and completely; to fulfill this responsibility, creativity is often required.

System vs. Software

Terms are important in all BA communications. The terms *system* and *software* are often used interchangeably, sometimes causing confusion in communications. The word *system* is defined as a set of connected things or parts forming a complex whole. This word can be used to describe a computer system, an electrical system, a biological system, or a business system. Notice how the addition of a modifier makes the term much clearer. System can also mean a systematic approach to a problem or situation. *Software* is the programs and other operating information used by a computer.

Be aware that when you use the word *system* alone, your audience will envision something based on their background and experience. If you are talking with an IT person, he or she will think software. An electrical engineer will think electrical system. A business person will think business system. Use the word *system* carefully and with a specific purpose.

It Depends

One of the most common phrases that business analysis professionals use is *it depends*. Much of business analysis work is complex, abstract, and dependent on current circumstances. When a BA is asked about a recommendation for a particular approach or analysis technique, often he or she will start the answer with *it depends*. Every situation is unique, and BAs bring their problem-solving, communication, interpersonal, and teamwork skills and knowledge to tailor an approach to each new problem.

BUSINESS ANALYSIS CERTIFICATION

There are currently three types of certification programs for BAs: *certificate* programs, *certification* programs, and the IIBA certification program. Each program recognizes business analysis competency in a different way. A *certificate* program acknowledges that an individual has completed a course of study. A *certification* program proves that an individual has satisfactorily completed an approved curriculum and demonstrated the ability to perform the tasks required (a certification program also usually requires work experience). The IIBA is the industry organization that has defined the body of knowledge for the business analysis profession, BABOK. The IIBA's certification is an exam that measures knowledge of the BABOK and would be extremely difficult to pass without business analysis experience. In order to sit for the exam, you must have a minimum of five years of experience. The certification is called CBAP® (Certified Business Analysis Professional™).

So which one do you need or which one is going to benefit you the most? It depends on why you want the certification and what you are going to do with it. Proof that you have attended business analysis training and/or have knowledge of the BABOK shows that you are aware of industry terminology and techniques. It will always be considered positively by employers and will make your transition into new environments easier. From an employer's perspective, evidence that a BA possesses not only business analysis knowledge but also the ability to apply that knowledge in a day-to-day, real-world business analysis environment is invaluable. Consider your current situation and where you want to be in three or five years when making this decision. BAs may choose to earn multiple levels of recognition based on their personal needs.

Employers are looking for a certification for BAs because the profession is very young and the role is not universally understood. Many organizations use the title differently or combine the role with project management or quality assurance. Hiring managers are looking for help in discerning the tasks typically performed by BAs, and since managers often do not have personal experience performing these tasks, they need help evaluating a candidate's capability. Tasks such as requirements elicitation, business process modeling/analysis, and documenting business data requirements are key skills for a successful BA.

IIBA BABOK®

The IIBA BABOK is a compilation of the currently accepted practices of business analysis professionals written and reviewed by expert BAs. The BABOK has been released in versions (current draft version 2.0) and will continue to evolve with the profession. It is divided into knowledge areas, tasks, and techniques. Each task and technique is defined and explained briefly. The purpose of the BABOK is to provide guidance and references for business analysis professionals. It is not a learning tool.

The goal of the IIBA is that eventually the BABOK will become the *best practice* standard for the profession. This may take 5 to 10 years of reviews and revisions. The BABOK is the basis for the IIBA professional certification CBAP.

This book addresses the knowledge areas of the BABOK from a different perspective. Its goal is to help business analysis professionals learn and hone their skills, working toward mastery. The book is structured to best communicate and teach business analysis concepts. These concepts are best learned by combining topics from several knowledge areas. The recommendations are all in line with the BABOK and will assist individuals preparing for the CBAP certification.

Table 1.3 shows which chapters of this book address each of the knowledge areas. The knowledge areas were designed to best communicate the complexity of the business analysis body of knowledge. This book includes *Knowledge Area Keys* called "BABOK Connections" that map BABOK competencies to tasks or techniques that the BA can utilize to satisfy these competencies. Figure 1.5 provides an example.

TABLE 1.3. BABOK Knowledge Areas and Chapter References

BABOK Knowledge Areas V2.0	Chapter					
	2 Know Your Audience	3 Know Your Project	4 Know Your Business Environment	5 Know Your Technical Environment	6 Know Your Analysis Techniques	7 Increase Your Value
Business Analysis Planning and Monitoring	X				X	X
Enterprise Analysis		X	X		X	X
Elicitation			X		X	X
Requirements Analysis		X	X		X	X
Requirements Management and Communication	X				X	X
Solution Assessment			X	X	X	X
Underlying Competencies	X		X	X	X	X

BABOK Connection	
Knowledge Area	**Task/Technique**
Business Analysis Planning and Monitoring	Conduct Stakeholder Analysis

FIGURE 1.5. BABOK Connection Example

SUMMARY OF KEY POINTS

The first step in mastering business analysis is to acquire a very clear understanding of the work involved and the role of the BA. Business analysis work is performed by many people with various titles but always involves:

- ◆ An understanding of the communications gap between business and technology people, and the ability to accurately translate requirements
- ◆ Continuous development of knowledge about the business and the skills to develop potential technology solutions
- ◆ An understanding of the reporting structure of the organization and the importance of advocating for support of true business needs
- ◆ Being passionate about learning and being curious in eliciting requirements and helping business people articulate their needs
- ◆ An understanding of the use of the word *requirements* in the organization and throughout the industry so as to be able to justify the time needed to develop high-quality requirements
- ◆ An awareness of business, technical, and project terminology, techniques, and best practices

BIBLIOGRAPHY

Anders Ericsonn, Karl (2006). *The Cambridge Handbook of Expertise and Expert Performance.* Cambridge University Press.

Bonnstetter, Bill and Judy Suiter (2004). *The Universal Language—DISC* Target Training International.

Carnegie Mellon University, Software Engineering Institute. The Capability Maturity Model (www.sei.cmmi.edu/cmmi).

International Institute of Business Analysis (2008). *The Guide to the Business Analysis Body of Knowledge (BABOK)*. Version 2.0 Draft for Public Review.

Morello, Diane and Michael J. Belchar (2005). Research Paper: Business Analysis Placement, Competencies and Effectiveness. ID Number G00126718. Gartner.

Project Management Institute (2004). *A Guide to the Project Management Body of Knowledge*. Third Edition.

2

KNOW YOUR AUDIENCE

It may be bold to say, but understanding your stakeholders is more important than understanding a whole list of requirements and analysis techniques. If you know the motives of everyone on your project, along with their skill sets, most of the questions about how to elicit and represent requirements will be answered for you. It is critical to know your audience because the most important skill of a business analyst (BA) is effective communication. To be most effective, communication should be tailored to and for each person with whom you communicate.

The Project Management Body of Knowledge (PMBOK®) defines stakeholders as "persons and organizations . . . actively involved in the *project* or whose interests may be positively or negatively affected by the execution or completion of the project." *To a BA, a stakeholder is anyone who may contribute to or have interest in the requirements.*

The best way to understand another person's communication is to understand his or her motives, personal biases, expertise, and experiences. The more you know someone, the easier and faster ideas can be communicated. A BA must listen carefully to stakeholders. This listening is active; it involves asking well-thought-out questions, listening to responses, and then following up to clarify understanding. A BA also must be able to present the business needs clearly to the solution team and work with the team to develop the best solution design. Presenting requirements clearly and accurately also can be done more efficiently when you know the characteristics of the person with whom you are communicating.

To tailor the communication, you must really know your audience. Every book and article about requirements uses the words "it depends" and "use the best technique to communicate with your audience." These are very frustrating answers for new BAs who are trying to learn how to do their job. Even when a new BA asks an expert BA "How should I get this requirement?" the answer often is a hesitant response. The senior BA may be thinking about all of the possible options and results and is also probably thinking about the audience. If the senior BA doesn't know your stakeholders, it will be difficult to give you advice.

This chapter discusses the project members with whom the typical BA works. It discusses how and why you must learn as much about each of them as you possibly can. This is an area where the project manager and BA should work together very closely. Clearly understanding the project members is critical to the success of both the business analysis work and the project as a whole. Figure 2.1 shows the common roles with whom a BA works.

ESTABLISH TRUST WITH YOUR STAKEHOLDERS

As a BA, you have very little formal control or supervisory authority over the people with whom you will be working. Your best chance at successful requirements elicitation and solution identification will be your stakeholders' confidence and trust in you. They should trust that you will always treat them with respect and kindness. They should trust that you will always treat them fairly.

You establish trust with people by getting to know them and always behaving with integrity. Acting with integrity as a BA means doing the things that you promise to do, always dealing honestly and directly, and being consistent. You gain trust from people not by asking for things from them but by asking what you can do for them. You earn trust when you answer questions honestly even when you know that the listener won't like the answer.

Stakeholders must trust that you will not use the information they provide to you in any way that would harm them. Infor-

BABOK Connection	
Knowledge Area	**Task/Technique**
Underlying Competencies	Behavioral: Trustworthiness

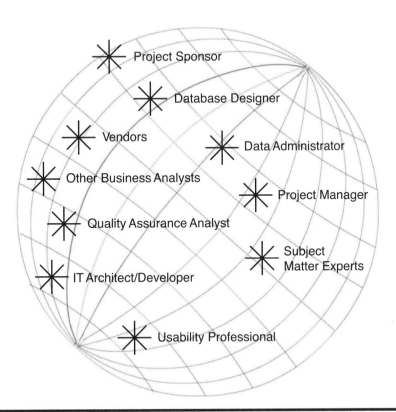

FIGURE 2.1. Business Analyst Universe of Roles

mation is very powerful. People who control large amounts of information have a responsibility to treat it with respect. You are going to be gathering and compiling large amounts of information. You will be learning about what other people's jobs are, how they perform their jobs, what problems they have, etc. How you use the information and how you represent your sources will tell your stakeholders about your integrity and your professionalism. Some information must be kept confidential for political or legal reasons. In this respect, your job is a bit like that of a journalist. Protect your sources and they will be willing to provide you with information again in the future. When you receive information "off the record," keep it to yourself. If you misuse your sources, you may have a tough time restoring trust on future projects.

WITH WHOM DOES THE BUSINESS ANALYST WORK?

Each stakeholder plays a role in each project. Although each organization and each project is different, there are several common roles with which the BA will be working on a regular basis. The most common roles are:

BABOK Connection	
Knowledge Area	**Task/Technique**
Business Analysis Planning and Monitoring	Conduct Stakeholder Analysis

- ◆ Executive or project sponsor
- ◆ Project manager
- ◆ Other business analysis professionals
- ◆ Subject matter experts and users
- ◆ Quality assurance analyst
- ◆ Usability professional
- ◆ IT architect
- ◆ IT developer
- ◆ Data administrator/architect/analyst
- ◆ Database designer/administrator
- ◆ Vendor

Executive or Project Sponsor

The sponsor is effectively the "boss" of the project. The sponsor has secured funding for the project and has specific objectives for the funds. The sponsor determines the success of the project based on how well it meets his or her objectives. Although you may not report to the executive sponsor in your organizational structure, he or she will make a judgment about how well you did your job and can be instrumental in your career success. The most important thing for you to learn about the sponsor is why he or she wants this project done and what his or her success criteria will be. The answers to these questions are part of the project initiation or project scope phase of a project. At the beginning of a project, you may be working with a project manager (PM) or you may be working alone. Either way, your main goal is to gain a thorough and complete understanding of *why the organization has decided to spend money on this project and why the sponsor is spending his or her budget.* This will be discussed further in Chapter 3.

In a capitalistic society, most organizations are trying to increase profits, decrease costs, or improve service. In corporations, profit usually drives decisions. In government agencies and non-profits, costs are usually paramount. Therefore, ultimately, every project is undertaken with a financial goal. This will be discussed in Chapter 3. The sponsor knows the organization's goal for the project and is the person who will ultimately decide whether or not the project succeeds. All of your communications with the sponsor should be from the sponsor's perspective and should always be focused on that ultimate goal.

The biggest mistake that can be made with a sponsor is to spend his or her limited time listening to excuses and problems. The sponsor wants to know what can be done to get things back on track and what he or she can do to influence the correction. Knowing what the sponsor is looking for gives you a great advantage. Having a solid relationship with the PM and the sponsor makes it likely that you will be able to get the resources you need to complete your work. This is where your reputation for honesty and integrity really gets you great results.

Sponsors often want *executive summaries.* Executives are too busy to read long detailed reports and want the BA to "cut to the chase" and give them the highlights. This can be difficult for BAs because of their attention to details. This is where you need to use conceptual thinking. The most important question to answer in the executive summary is:

Is the project still going to provide the profits or cost savings goals that we intended?

When you and the PM talk with the sponsor or provide any written status reports, always answer that question. If the answer is "No, the project is not going in the direction intended," then you must tell the sponsor what is needed to get the project back on track. Most of the time, sponsors don't want the details of why things are not going as planned.

Case in Point: Giving the Sponsor Bad News

A few years ago, I consulted with an organization as a PM/BA to manage the implementation of a vendor-supplied software package. The IT director explained to me that the package had already been selected, the contract had already been negotiated and signed, and they needed me to coordinate and oversee the implementation of and training for the new software. It sounded pretty straightforward to me. As any good PM does, I immediately set about building my work breakdown structure, identifying and learning about the tasks that would be necessary for a successful and smooth implementation.

Since I had worked on package implementations before, there were many tasks that I could assume would be necessary. But a good analyst never assumes anything, so I began introducing myself to stakeholders and asking if my assumptions were correct. One of the first people with whom I spoke was the network administrator, Jeff. I wanted him to help me determine how big an impact this new software would have on the network and estimate how long it would take to install and set up individual access.

His first sentence was a huge clue to me that this was not going to be as easy as I hoped: "What new software?" Apparently the selection committee had not included the network administrator when choosing this package. He quickly asked me a few technical questions about the package and its network abilities and requirements. In less than 10 minutes, he concluded that this particular software package would not run on the company's network. Period—end of discussion—not compatible.

I would be lying if I didn't admit that one of my first thoughts was "Well, there goes my consulting contract!" I asked Jeff a few more questions about how we might make this package work and if he could think of any options. Setting up a brand new network for the users and working with the software on stand-alone machines were the only options that we could come up with. Neither could be supported by the current IT staff.

I had to report to the director and the business people that the package selected was not the right choice for the company. Being the bearer of bad news sometimes falls to the PM/BA. In this case, I was telling them that the person who had headed up the selection committee had not done his job well and that we had no plan for implementing the software which had just been purchased. The managers and business subject matter experts were very disappointed and upset. The selection committee had spent several months making this recommendation and the software functionality was desperately needed. Now we would have to start all over with package evaluations. No one wanted to tell the sponsor. I offered to meet with him. (Being an outside consultant, my only risk was losing my contract.)

I am often amazed at the reverence with which we treat our corporate executives. They are human beings just like the rest of us. They have good days and bad like everyone else. They just tend to look at things from a higher perspective and often make decisions faster than other employees. Once we had decided that I would tell the sponsor, Ben, everyone came into my office telling me everything that they knew about him. "Ben is a great guy; he just gets angry sometimes." "Ben is very quiet; he may not say anything to you." "When are you going to see Ben? Are you nervous?"

The climax of the story is really anti-climatic. Ben was a very nice, soft-spoken man who enjoyed golf and had two children. His office was nicely furnished with a few golf pictures. Since I play golf, I felt comfortable asking him where and how often he played. I really believe that in most interactions with people, a brief conversation about something other than work relaxes the situation and puts things in perspective. It allows people to let their defenses down and be open to the conversation.

Ben invited me to sit down, which usually indicates that the stakeholder is ready to get into the business conversation. I told him about the software/network problem. I gave him a brief, clear statement of the problem. He sat silently, thoughtfully for a few minutes, and I waited patiently for the news to be processed. His next question, as expected, was "Is there anything we can do?" I told him about the possibility of a separate network or stand-alone machines but admitted that they were not really good ideas. He shook his head in agreement and simply said, "Well, we've got to break the contract, get our money back, and find another package." And then I was excused. This was an excellent sponsor—he accepted the reality of the situation and was able to quickly go to the next logical step. My contract was extended to include selection of another package, contract negotiations support, and implementation.

When communicating with sponsors, brevity is the key. Be brief and to the point. Stay at a high level, supplying details only when necessary to make a point. Be concise, clear, and respectful of their time. They want to know what the bottom line is.

If you feel intimidated by your sponsor, you may not be able to ask good questions and get the information that you need to be successful. Take opportunities to talk with executives whenever you can. You will discover that they are people just like the rest of us. Put yourself in the sponsor's position and tailor the communications appropriately.

Project Manager

Project management is well recognized as a critical skill needed for business and software development projects. Although PMs have long been appreciated in fields like building construction and engineering, it has only been in the last 15 to 20 years or so that IT organizations have truly realized that their projects need managers who are dedicated to managing them. Most organizations have also learned that a great PM doesn't necessarily have to be a great technician. The growth in popularity of the Project Management Institute's PMP® certification in IT departments demonstrates this realization. Most large organizations also have a project management office where PMs are supported and project management methodologies are administered. The growth and recognition of the role of the PM are the same growth and recognition which are expected for the role of the BA in the next 10 years.

A PM is responsible for managing a project and making sure that it meets its objectives. The PMBOK defines project management as "... the application of knowledge, skills, tools and techniques to project activities to meet project requirements."

Project management and business analysis are two distinct professions with two intersecting skill sets. Project management work includes identifying project requirements, establishing measurable objectives, and managing the resources, time, scope, and quality of a project. There is overlap with the work that has been defined as business analysis work. In many organizations, PMs have actually been expected to do all of the project management work in addition to all of the business analysis work. Most PMs in this situation are overwhelmed and sometimes projects are not successful. Statistics prove that poor requirements are the main cause of failed software development projects and reflect the fact that requirement elicitation and analysis are not assigned to a dedicated, expert resource (Standish Group, 2006).

How do a PM and a BA work together to make a project a success? Fundamentally, the PM manages project *resources* (people, money) and the BA manages the *requirements*. The BA reports to the PM on his or her progress on the tasks in the work breakdown structure related to requirements. Usually at the beginning of a project, the PM and BA work very closely together, often working on the same tasks. Later, as the project gets going, they each focus on their particular responsibilities and talk together frequently to share their progress. Excellent PMs and BAs will work hand in hand to make the most of each other's strengths.

It is the healthy tension between the PM and BA, the PM pushing to move forward and the BA cautiously wanting to gather just one more detail before going forward, that makes the combination so successful together. They are interdependent because their goals are in conflict.

Why Does a Project Need a Project Manager and a Business Analyst?

There are many projects where one person is assigned to act as both the PM and the BA. This is common and probably appropriate on small projects or when an organization is short-staffed. Unfortunately, it is also common in organizations where there is a lack of understanding of the BA role and where the expectation is that business analysis is just another task a PM performs.

Leading organizations have come to understand that having both a PM and a BA professional is critical to a project's success. These two roles, working together from the beginning of a project, set the stage for success by planning accurately and clearly defining the expected outcomes. Both roles are required because each is responsible for a different set of tasks and each possesses a set of skills that complement the other. Each role provides specialized capabilities that can

BABOK Connection	
Knowledge Area	**Task/Technique**
Business Analysis Planning and Monitoring	Plan the Business Analysis Approach

make the difference between a project that succeeds and one that struggles or fails.

PMs and BAs each have unique skills and knowledge areas that, when used together, produce a high-quality product. They both want the project to be successful and want to satisfy their customer—the sponsor. They both understand the ultimate goal of the project: to meet the project objectives. They each work on their own tasks within the project to achieve these objectives. There are some areas of project work where the PM and BA work together or back each other up. There are many other areas where the two individuals diverge and do very different types of tasks.

Project Manager and Business Analyst Skills Comparison

Common skills: One of the reasons why many organizations assign one person to act as both the PM and the BA is that people who operate well in these two roles have many skills in common. Both the PM and the BA must have very strong communication skills. This is probably the most important skill needed to operate effectively in either role. Individuals in both roles also must have an understanding of how projects are accomplished and an awareness of the methodologies and approaches to designing and developing software solutions. Because both roles are often responsible for bringing together groups of people, negotiating, and gaining consensus on how a particular solution will be implemented, they require an individual who has strong interpersonal and client management skills. These skills are actually useful in many careers.

Unique skills: There are also unique skills for PMs and BAs that allow them to perform the unique tasks for which they are responsible. PMs need to be able to see the "big picture" for a project. They must be able to see how all of the resources working together will accomplish the ultimate goal. Although this "big-picture" view is useful for a BA, it is more important that the BA is a very detail-oriented person. He or she must be very skilled at listening, analyzing, and documenting exact details about business processes, data, and business rules. The PM *builds* the work breakdown structure for the project, whereas the BA *performs* some of the tasks within the work breakdown structure.

Similarities and Differences between the Two Roles

The PM is responsible for ensuring that the product is delivered to the customer *on time* and *within budget.* The BA is responsible for ensuring that the product is *built according to the requirements.* This difference in focus is the reason why having both roles on the team is critical. The product will be built correctly, according to requirements, on time, *and* within budget!

Role of Project Manager

◆ Usually the first person assigned to a project
◆ Responsible for planning the project and ensuring the team follows the plan
◆ Manages changes, handles problems, and keeps the project moving
◆ Manages people, money, risk, and project scope
◆ Chief communicator of good or bad news to the sponsor and management
◆ Helps clear obstacles

Role of Business Analyst

◆ Usually assigned to a project after it has started
◆ Responsible for bridging the gap between the business and IT
◆ Learn the business needs and environment in detail
◆ Essentially the architect of effective business systems

Dynamic Duos

When assigning PMs and BAs to a project, executive management should be aware of the importance of this dynamic duo. Their success depends on their respective experience, knowledge, and skill sets. The results will vary depending on the individuals selected.

If a strong PM is assigned to work with a weak (inexperienced, unskilled, or insecure) BA, the requirements gathering and analysis tasks may be rushed and important requirements may be missed. The PM will be pushing for the project to make progress, and the BA will not be strong enough to convince the PM that complete, accurate requirements are critical to project success. This may result in rework late in the project when the missing requirements are identified. Rework may result in schedule and budget overruns.

In the opposite situation, if a weak PM is assigned to work with a strong BA, too much time may be spent in requirements gathering and the project will fall behind schedule. BAs want to get every single detail 100% correct before moving forward, and if the PM lets the BA try to accomplish this virtually impossible task, the schedule will be jeopardized. Also, if the PM does not strictly enforce the change control procedure, the BA may allow business people to add more and more requirements, resulting in "scope creep" and project delays.

Obviously, the worse-case situation is a project with a weak PM and a weak BA. No matter how involved the subject matter experts are, and how good the technical team is, a project is likely to fail without strong leadership and clear requirements.

Therefore, the best-case situation is a project with a strong PM and a strong BA. Assuming the rest of the project team is competent, this project will be well run and the end product will be of the highest quality. There is a great balance between thorough requirements gathering and project progress. The project will be on schedule and meet the expectations of the sponsor.

The PM is much more of a *director* than the BA is. The PM directs the project team, making assignments, giving specific directions, and making sure that the team members are working on the appropriate tasks. He or she works to remove barriers to progress for team members. The PM requires strong *management* skills. BAs are more focused on listening and analyzing. They must listen carefully to subject matter experts and *discover* requirements, not create or invent them. The BA is actually looking for problems or issues that may not have been identified during project scoping and that may impact the success of the project. The BA alerts the PM to these potential problems and works with the PM to address them. The BA requires strong *investigative* skills. The PM is focused on helping people on the team get work done, while the BA is focused on helping people describe how and why they do work. The BA also must communicate these business needs to the technical team and listen for suggested solutions.

During the course of a project, the PM manages the change control process. Any changes to a project will impact the original plan, so the PM assesses this impact, works with the executive sponsor to decide whether a change will be accepted, and then revises the plan to accommodate any changes. BAs only manage changes to the business and functional requirements and usually only assist the PM with the formal change control process for these changes.

Tips for Those Performing Both Roles

For the individual playing this dual role, the challenge is to be aware of the conflicting focus and to try to act in one role at a time. You may find you are having disagreements with yourself, and it may be helpful to have a fellow PM or BA listen to your internal debate to try to help you make decisions. Be aware that you probably have a preference for one role or the other, and you may find yourself neglecting the tasks of the role that you enjoy the least. If you prefer doing PM work, you may miss requirements. If you prefer doing BA work, you may allow the schedule to slip or forget to direct your team members. This situation is further complicated if you are also assigned to other project responsibilities (e.g., you are also the technical architect) or assigned to work on other projects. Your project schedule, budget, and product quality may be affected. Be sure to plan for the time needed to do both jobs adequately.

If you frequently find yourself in this situation in your organization, use your excellent communication skills to heighten management's awareness regarding these conflicting roles. Make management and your team aware of your conflicting responsibilities and the challenges associated with them. Seek help in managing the schedule and help in gathering and documenting the requirements. If possible, try to minimize your involvement in other concurrent projects.

Other Business Analysis Professionals

For large projects, more than one BA may be needed. When multiple BAs are working on the same project, they need to plan the business analysis work and then divide the work appropriately. When one of the BAs is designated as the senior BA, he or she usually will decide which tasks will be assigned to each BA. BAs must work closely together during project initiation and requirements elicitation since they may be working on closely related business areas.

There are many different strategies for dividing business analysis work. Some teams delegate one BA as the data analyst, one as the process analyst, and one to gather business rules. This division allows each analyst to focus on a particular type of requirement and then cross-check their work by linking or tracing their requirements components to the others. Another delegation strategy is by high-level business process. Each BA is assigned to a high-level business process and is responsible for analyzing all of the requirements components needed for that process. Regardless of the delegation approach used, BAs should consolidate their requirements and make sure that all relationships between requirements components have been documented.

Subject Matter Experts and Users

A subject matter expert (SME) is a person who has a particular expertise needed on a project. The expertise may be on the business side (a person who understands the business needs), on the technical side (a person who can provide design ideas), or outside the organization (an external customer). The acronym SME has become popular because it can be used to describe anyone on a project who has expertise.

The role name *user* is also used frequently. This word refers to a person who "uses" the software under discussion. Many people prefer the role name *SME* to *user* because it sounds more positive and because it is more accurate during analysis/requirements elicitation. Be aware that although many SMEs may also be "users" of the software, many are not. A department manager may be an SME because he or she understands the business goals of the department but is not a user because he or she doesn't actually enter any data into the software system. Alternatively, a user is not necessarily an SME. A data entry person who simply enters data on a computer screen without any knowledge of the reason for the data entry is not an expert.

As mentioned earlier, business analysis professionals must be able to use varied language when talking and writing to best communicate to the intended audience. Titles and role names of stakeholders are used inconsistently. Be sure to clarify terminology and titles when listening. Some people use the word *customer* to mean a person external to the organization who purchases products. Some IT people use the word *customer* to mean anyone inside the organization who uses IT services. A simple mistake like the confusion around this term can cause requirements elicitation to take longer than anticipated.

Business domain SMEs know about the business area being analyzed. Ideally, they are *experts* on the business. They are workers and managers in the business area and they are people outside of the business who have some interaction with the particular area of the business being studied. These are the people who BAs sometimes refer to as their *customer*; these are the people for whom the BA is trying to solve a business problem and create a solution that will make the business more efficient and effective.

During the requirements elicitation phase, it is important to talk with *experts* on the business. An SME can really be anyone who has some information about the business that you are analyzing. These are the people who provide you with the critical understanding of the business: why things are done, how they are performed, and what the results are. Without these SMEs, there is no business analysis. Some of the SMEs may report to the sponsor, but some will not. On small projects, the sponsor may be the head of a department using application software that interfaces with other departments. SMEs are business people from various organizational units who have varying amounts of interest in your project. Your biggest challenge is to convince these people that they should spend time with you and tell you everything that you want to know about their business. Successfully convincing them that you are on their side and working to help them is the best secret to being a successful BA.

Users of the solution must be identified and supported during the design and implementation phases of a project. They should be involved in screen and workflow design. They also should be involved in user acceptance testing (see Chapter 5). In addition, BAs usually are responsible for training users in the software and procedural changes that will be necessary upon solution implementation.

All SMEs are not created equal. Expect many challenges with personality types, working styles, and motivations. Understanding and winning over these experts will not be easy. It will require you to get to know these individuals, do research before meeting with them, and use every bit of charm that you can possibly command to convince them that they should tell you their deepest, darkest secrets. These are not personal secrets, but honest revelations about how they do their jobs, what their most important issues are, and why broken processes are not working.

Getting to Know Your Subject Matter Experts

Ideally, you will be given the names and titles of your SMEs before any project meetings or facilitated sessions are scheduled. Take a look at the organizational chart. This will give you a chance to do some research before you meet with each one. Your research may include looking for the SMEs' names on previous project requirements packages, sign-offs, or testing documents. You should be able to determine to which software applications they currently have access. You may be able to find out how long they have been with the company and how long they have been in their current position. Anything that you can learn about these people will be beneficial. Think of it like doing research before going on a job interview. You will want to make a good impression on these people the first time that you meet, so anything you know up front will help.

Although you don't have to find out which high school or college an SME attended, it would not be a bad idea. You would not want to start off a relationship by saying "I'm happy today because my team beat the Bulls this weekend!" if an SME is a huge Bulls fan.

You don't have to wait until you are assigned to work on a project to get to know potential future stakeholders. The successful business analysis professional is always building relationships with people in various areas of the business.

It is helpful to learn as much as you can about each SME so that you are better able to build a relationship and build trust. It is also important to try to discover each SME's work style so that you can match as closely as possible their most comfortable method of interacting and getting work done. If someone likes to get to work early in the morning, you might ask if an early interview time is convenient. These seemingly small gestures will improve the speed at which you can elicit requirements and, more importantly, give your SMEs—your customers—a confident sense that you are on their side.

How do you do this "research"? Think of yourself as a private investigator. You are trying to learn as much as you can without anyone suspecting what you are doing.

- Walk by the SME's cubicle or office to observe his or her workspace.
- Does it appear well organized or cluttered? This may give you an idea about how this person works.
- Are there a lot of people around socializing with the SME or does he or she seem to be a loner? This will give you an idea about how willing the person will be to talk with you.
- Are there any certificates or awards hanging on the walls of the office? This may indicate experience, training, and pride in work accomplishments.
- How old does the SME appear to be?
- What nationality is he or she? Can you detect an accent?
- Are there posters or pictures that indicate outside interests? Family photos? Finding a common interest outside of work can be a great icebreaker and a way for you to develop a friendship with an SME.

If you know other BAs or PMs who have worked with this person in the past, talk with them. Carefully, discretely, subtly ask questions about how the SME participated on the last project. Did he or she show up for meetings on time? Was he or she prepared with information that was requested at previous meetings? Did he or she contact the BA with questions or follow-up information or wait for the BA to initiate all contact? How knowledgeable was this individual about his or her business? How comfortable was he or she with change?

If you know someone else in the business area who works with the SME, talk with that person. Again, carefully just mention who you will be working with on your next project and that you are looking forward to getting to know him or her. Watch for facial expressions and body language. Does your contact give any hint of a positive or negative reaction? If so, ask a follow-up question, like "What has your experience with this person been?"

Obviously, if you have worked with this SME before, you already know the answers to many of these questions. Even so, try to keep an open mind and learn even more about the person. If you did not have a positive experience on the last project, think about what you might do differently this time. The more you know about your customers, the better you will be able to service them. There are some common challenges related to SMEs, as discussed in the following sections.

A Manager Who Does Not Understand His or Her Employees' Work

Unfortunately, this situation occurs frequently. In some organizations, managers are routinely moved from department to department, often functioning in business areas in which they have no real knowledge or experience. This causes difficulty for the BA because interviewing the manager does not result in accurate business models or requirements. The BA initially may not be aware that the requirements are inaccurate. A solution may be delivered and be inadequate to support basic key business functions.

The first assessment that a BA must make in each business area that he or she analyzes is who knows what. The BA needs to know who in the department is considered the "expert." Who are the consistent, experienced workers? What are the views of these experts on the current management? How does management view the workers? Does the manager like his or her job and employees? Do the workers like the manager? Respect the manager?

You will never see the answers to any of these questions in a requirements package. These are important questions that the BA must answer in order to gather accurate requirements, but they will never be explicitly stated as a project task. When you are planning and estimating your project work, be sure to include time for this analysis. (You will want to give this a politically correct name like "getting to know the stakeholders").

These questions are also not the type of questions that you will ask directly (i.e., "How do you like your boss? Does the manager have any idea what really goes on in this department?"). Rather, you must be a detective and cleverly learn the answers to these questions indirectly. Your first meetings with your stakeholders will give you a lot of information, especially if you are able to read the non-verbal clues given by the group. Do all of the workers defer to the manager when a question is asked? If so, it may be that they have learned not to express an opinion without first knowing where the boss stands. Does the manager hesitate to answer when you ask a specific question about work in the business area? Does the manager defer to one of his or her employees? Which one? How do the other employees react to this? Is this employee a favorite?

In most cases, a manager who is not as knowledgeable as his or her workers will tell you this directly and recommend that you rely on one or two experienced people in the group for your requirements elicitation. This is the ideal situation and gives you permission to ask others in the group for the business details. Managers who are open and honest about their knowledge typically develop employees who are open and honest.

Even if a manager does not volunteer this information, it will become very clear to you quickly if he or she is not knowledgeable about the business. Ask the same question in a couple of different ways during the meeting and see if you get the same answer. Ask about exceptions. Ask closed-ended questions that require the manager to answer yes or no. Watch for hesitations, uncomfortable body language, and a lot of imprecise, vague answers.

If you determine that the manager is not a business area expert, discuss this with the PM as soon as possible. You may be able to get around the problem, but this is the type of obstacle that can put a project behind schedule, so the PM must be involved. The two of you can decide how to proceed and back each other up when necessary. You can work to get more time with others in the department. You can give the manager an out by offering to save his or her time by asking detailed questions to employees because you know the manager is busy. If the manager insists on being your only source of requirements, let the PM handle this issue with the executive sponsor. Remember that you are working to really understand the business needs of all of the stakeholders. If one person is preventing this task from being accomplished, the project will be negatively impacted, and your responsibility is to report the problem and help find a resolution.

When the Expert Is Not Really an Expert

Although called subject matter *experts,* BAs don't always have experts with whom to work. Sometimes the manager of a business area assigns a person to the project team who does not have significant work experience in the business area (or who is not very useful to the business area). This is common because, from the perspective of the business area manager, he or she can't afford to have the best people away from work attending Joint Application Design™ (JAD) sessions or testing software. The newer or less valuable people are much easier to send to the project meetings. So, what does a BA do when the expert is not really an expert?

When assessing your requirements team, determine if you have been assigned an SME who is not an expert. Be careful not to jump to any conclusions. Just because someone is new to the area doesn't mean that they don't have some valuable knowledge. You should give the person a chance by interviewing him or her just like you would any other SME. Evaluate whether or not you are gathering relevant, accurate requirements. If the SME is frequently answering your questions with "I don't know," you obviously have the wrong person for the job. Many people, however, don't like to admit they don't know something, especially when being referred to as an expert. They may guess at answers rather than admitting they don't know or may answer with a confident demeanor and be completely wrong. Confirm the SME's understanding (or lack thereof) by using other analysis techniques like observation, reviewing existing system documentation, and looking for holes in the requirements. Ask the same question in a different way. Have two sources to confirm each requirement.

This is where your skills in diplomacy will be tested. You need to be careful not to accuse the SME of misleading you, but in effect, this may be what he or she is doing. You must determine if you have a creditable person. Let the SME and the PM know that you need to talk with multiple people about the requirements to confirm your understanding of the process. You want to make sure that everyone in the business sees it the same way.

If you feel that the SME is not knowledgeable or is misleading you, have a private conversation with the PM and indicate your concerns about the SME's knowledge level. This gives the PM an early warning of possible problems. The PM may be able to work through business management to get you a more knowledgeable SME. In the meantime, try to talk with other people in the department. Formulate brief questions, especially on the requirements that you feel are the most critical. You will quickly determine whether or not the SME was steering you in the right direction. Keep the PM informed of what you find out.

This is one of the most difficult problems with which a BA must deal. Most people dislike conflict and don't want to have to report a problem with another team member. However, you must always keep your project objectives in mind. If a particular SME is going to negatively impact project success, it is your responsibility to wave the red flag—as gently as possible. A solution that is based on inaccurate requirements will not be the correct solution. Ignoring a problem early on in a project is the surest way to help the project fail. Address a problem when you can most easily correct it. Don't point fingers. Explain what you need by being objective and stating the facts. Hopefully, the PM and sponsor will allocate other resources and get you a true expert. If not, do the best you can with the people who are available. Be sure to double- and triple-check the requirements by asking the same questions to multiple people. Better to find problems now than allow inaccurate requirements to be implemented.

When the Expert Is Truly an Expert

This should be the ideal situation for a BA. You have been assigned an SME who knows everything there is to know about the business. So, what is the problem? Well, the SME may know the business so well that he or she fails to tell you simple, critical facts and assumes that you already know them. When experts talk about something within their area of expertise, they use terminology specific to the area and make assumptions about the listener's general knowledge of the area. Think about the last time your doctor explained a test or diagnosis to you. You probably had to ask follow-up questions or maybe you left feeling like you didn't really understand the situation. You need to ask a lot of questions and validate your understanding of every requirement. The SME knows the business so well that it seems very simple to him or her. The tendency is to oversimplify complex processes, forget to mention common exceptions, and minimize the size of the business area by explaining it so quickly. The SME may also get impatient with you and your lack of knowledge. On the other hand, some SMEs enjoy sharing their wealth of knowledge, even getting outside the scope of the project. They may provide irrelevant history or so much information that it is difficult to pull out just the pieces that you need.

Your approach to eliciting requirements from a true expert is preparation and repetition. You have access to all of the information that you could ever want, but you need to pace yourself in terms of how fast you can take it all in. It is important for you to understand your most effective approach to, and pace of, learning new things. If you are a visual learner, you will ask for diagrams and pictures of how things work. If you learn best with repetition, then explain to the SME that you will want to go over the same requirements a couple of times on different days to make sure that you truly understood them.

You may want to schedule a greater number of short interviews so that the expert can quickly give you a lot of information and you can go back to your desk to process it before your next meeting. You also have to constantly remind the SME that he or she is the expert and that you are just learning. You may have to ask the same question several times before you really understand the answer. Ask the SME to be patient with you and work to make the best use of his or her time. This may be a situation where you would benefit from talking with a less experienced person first who can help you get an initial foundation of understanding before talking details with the expert. The expert probably doesn't remember how difficult it was to learn the basics because he or she learned them so long ago.

The Expert Who Is Reluctant to Talk

Some SMEs don't feel like experts. They are hesitant to tell you anything because they are afraid that what they tell you may not be correct. This fear may be based on experiences where mistakes were punished by unsupportive management. The key to working with this type of SME is establishing trust and developing a relationship where the SME feels safe talking to you.

One approach to working with an SME who is reluctant to talk is to present your understanding of the business and ask for corrections or confirmation. Since you don't know much about the business, your initial presentation will be naïve, incomplete, and probably incorrect in places. As the SME points out the missing pieces and corrects your errors, that individual is building confidence in his or her knowledge. The SME will begin to realize that he or she does know a lot more about the business than you do and that you are really interested in learning what he or she knows. This should make it easier for the person to share information and he or she will be more willing to explain complex topics.

Another approach is to hold interviews with two to three SMEs at a time. The reluctant SME may be more comfortable if other experts are there to help with the answers to your questions.

The Expert Who Is Angry about Previous Project Failures

Unfortunately, many software development projects have failed. A large established organization may have tens if not hundreds of project failures in its history. In most of these projects, there was at least one SME who was interviewed and involved with the project. You may meet people who were involved in several of these projects. They may be angry because they haven't seen many successes. Try to put yourself in an angry SME's shoes. The SME was assigned to a new project and initially was enthusiastic about it, spending time with a BA or developer to carefully explain his or her business processes. The SME patiently answered questions, made suggestions, and reviewed requirements documents and design documents. The project may have even made its way to the testing phase. And then, for one reason or another, the project was canceled or the software developed didn't look at all like the SME expected it to. All that work and time, wasted. Then, a new project is started and the SME does it all over again. You couldn't blame an SME who dreads a new project with a new BA knocking on the door asking for a description of his or her business. "Describe my business! I've already done that several times! Didn't you people write anything down? Don't you all talk to each other? Why bother? You never listen anyway. If by some small chance the software actually gets developed, it never does what I want it to do! Why should I bother?"

Good question. You can't blame a business person for being angry. IT departments have not done a good job of developing software that actually benefits the end user.

How do you start up a dialogue and relationship with this angry SME? First of all, search for any notes/documents/plans from previous projects so that you don't have to start from scratch. If you can find some of the previous work, the SME will at least feel like someone listened to him or her on the last project. Another important part of your initial conversation with this SME requires you to show empathy and regret for all of those previous failures. Even though they were not your fault, from the SME's perspective you represent the group of people who failed, and he or she wants to hear that your group is sorry about the wasted time and the frustration. This is a critical step in getting past this anger. It doesn't cost you anything to apologize. All you have to say is: "I know that you have worked on similar projects in the past that have failed. I am very sorry that your time was wasted. We have learned from those failures and are hoping that you will help us again, using our new approach. As the BA, I am your advocate, and my job is to make sure that your business needs are met on this project. I will be working with the solution team to make sure that they understand what you need and that they design and build it correctly." Apologizing and taking responsibility for the source of the SME's anger and frustration will disarm the person. The SME may be able to let go of his or her anger simply because you have listened to him or her. Once you get past this, your interactions with the SME will be much easier.

The Expert Who Hates His or Her Job

Occasionally, an SME may be someone who is very unhappy in their current role. You will detect this unhappiness from the person's body language, tone of voice, and attitude, or he or she may tell you directly. An SME who hates his or his job will not propose solutions to problems, will not be enthusiastic about the project, and will not be easily engaged in the process. Offer to meet the SME in his or her office or in a conference room in his or her area for your first meeting. Allowing someone to be in their environment will put them more at ease. Start out your conversion on a positive note by telling the individual that you are looking forward to working together. Introduce yourself very briefly and watch for body language. Is the SME interested in who you are or anxious to get on with the meeting?

Another approach is to meet the SME somewhere away from the work environment. Going out for coffee or lunch will allow the SME to relax and get to know you with a more positive attitude.

As with many negative emotions, it is often helpful to allow the SME to talk with you about his or her frustrations. Listening empathetically and showing interest may lessen the intensity of the negative feelings and allow the SME to focus on your questions. You do have to be careful not to let the negativity go on throughout the interview because it may prevent you from eliciting true requirements. It may be helpful for you to acknowledge the problems and then move the conversation on to a more positive or at least neutral footing. For example, you might say: "I can see why you would be frustrated with this situation. Hopefully, our new system can make your job a little less tedious [or whatever the complaint is]." You may also want to explain why the SME was selected for this project. He or she may have specific expertise or a lot of experience that will increase the likelihood of project success. You may be able to say that the SME was "hand-picked" to participate because of his or her knowledge and value. Put a positive spin on the SME's participation in the project based on what you know about the situation.

Lastly, make sure that the SME understands the project. Explain your understanding of why the project has been initiated and the project objectives. Tell the SME what the project will do for him or her. There is a saying in training: "What's in it for me?" If you can convince the SME that his or her job will be more tolerable if the project is a success, you may have an ally. Set expectations about what you will be looking for in your requirements gathering activities.

SMEs provide the materials (information) upon which to build a solution. It is critical that a BA work closely with all of the SMEs on a project to ensure accurate requirements.

Quality Assurance Analyst

A quality assurance (QA) analyst (whatever their title) is a gift that many BAs never receive. People who are experienced, knowledgeable QA professionals add enormous value to any project or process in which they are involved. QA professionals have been trained to focus on building quality into products from the beginning, not just looking for errors at the end. In addition, the QA group will be responsible for validating the requirements against the resulting software at the end of a project. They will be planning how the resulting product will be tested right from the beginning of the project.

Involve the people in the QA department in your projects as early as you can. Invite them to your project scope/initiation meetings. Include them in as many of your requirements reviews as they can attend. Give them drafts of your requirements deliverables anytime they are willing to look at them. QA people are trained to look for inconsistencies, incorrect requirements, and descriptions that are too vague. Because the QA group will be responsible for testing at the end of the project, they will be reviewing each requirement for testability. This is one of the most valuable gifts that they will give to the project. If a test cannot be designed for a particular requirement, then the requirement is not specific enough. The classic example of "software should be easy to use" reminds us how easy it is to write a requirement that is not testable.

You will probably act as a liaison between the QA analyst and the SMEs. The QA analyst is going to ask questions that are extremely detailed, and an SME may not understand why the detail is necessary. Also, in many methodologies, the QA analyst is a required sign-off for the requirements. This means that you have to write a requirements document that satisfies not only the SMEs but also the QA analyst.

The skills required to be an excellent BA are very similar to those required for QA work. Both professions focus on accurate details and have a continuous improvement mentality. Many individuals work in both areas or transfer from one to the other. QA analysts are very interested in contributing to the quality of a product by anticipating (noticing) potential problems. The BA should get to know the QA analyst, just like all of the other stakeholders. Try to determine the analyst's motives, interests, strengths, and weaknesses. As with any stakeholder, the better you understand the QA analyst, the more you will be able to help him or her be more productive on the project. Play into that person's strengths, especially if they are your weak areas. Many BAs like to start a brand new document, draft it, organize it, etc. They don't enjoy revising and rewriting as much. A strong QA analyst will enjoy reviewing, rewording, and revising and would therefore be a great partner for a BA. Together they would produce a really excellent requirements deliverable.

A well-established QA organization is the Quality Assurance Institute (www. qaiworldwide.org).

When "QA" Is a Bad Word in Your Organization

The words "quality assurance" have been used in many different ways. Unfortunately, some organizations have given this title to people who do not have the appropriate training or experience. Those on the QA team may not be given very clear direction about what they should be doing or may be assigned to too many projects at one time. They may be given the responsibility to sign off on project deliverables but given no authority to manage the process. This situation has caused some negative feelings about the QA function. Some IT people think a QA person is constantly looking for fault in other people's work and reporting all of these defects to management. This perception creates a negative attitude toward the QA department, and project teams begin to avoid all contact. They conveniently "forget" to invite QA to project start-up meeting and reviews. The more the QA person is made to feel unwelcome on project teams, the angrier they can become and they develop a negative attitude. This negativity just feeds on itself, and this is one of the reasons why the QA department has been eliminated in many organizations.

If your organization treats the QA person like a leper, don't join the crowd. Anyone who reviews your work can give you helpful suggestions if you are open to them. Make the QA person your friend and he or she will help you. Invite him or her to every meeting, review, walkthrough, etc. Provide him or her with a copy of every relevant deliverable. Work very hard to convince the QA person that you are different and that you do value his or her opinion.

Usability Professional

There are various titles and roles that focus on software usability, including human factors, usability engineering (which is a subset of human factors), user experience design, and user-centered design. Usability professionals (UPs) are a specialized type of business analysis professional. Individuals in these roles are experts in designing products that are easy to use. They work with users, performing task analysis and eliciting requirements to assist in the development of prototypes. The very structured, proven techniques of usability testing are then applied to the prototype and design changes made based on the results of testing.

UPs have become extremely valuable to organizations for a couple of reasons: (1) the creation of e-commerce and external customer use of Web sites have made usability a competitive advantage and (2) the realization through metrics-based analysis (i.e., Six Sigma, Lean) that a usable application significantly improves productivity and data integrity.

When a UP is assigned to a project, the business analysis professional should meet with that individual to determine their respective responsibilities. UPs are skilled in business analysis, with a concentration in usability. Like all BAs, they are skilled in requirements elicitation, stakeholder analysis, and communication. In addition, they are skilled at screen design, prototyping, simulation, and usability testing. These skills allow them to focus on the human-computer interaction and work with developers to create a highly usable product. UPs will also be excellent resources for requirements reviews.

To learn more about usability engineering, a great resource is Jakob Nielsen's book by the same name: *Usability Engineering.* To learn more about the usability profession, visit www.usabilityprofessionals.org. This is an area into which some business analysis professionals may move as they specialize.

When a project does not have access to a UP, the BA is expected to play this role. It is important that every BA be aware of the main precepts of usability and most importantly be able to look at each project and determine if usability engineering is a critical skill that is required for the success of the project (see Chapter 5). Alerting the sponsor and PM to this need as soon as it is recognized may facilitate the acquisition of the needed resource or may give the BA time to learn more about usability as it would relate to the current project.

IT Architect

IT architects design IT solutions. They understand how to structure software to accomplish specific objectives. They understand the organization's technology strategy and current environment. They are aware of upcoming technical initiatives that may impact business projects. They ensure that

BABOK Connection	
Knowledge Area	**Task/Technique**
Business Analysis Planning and Monitoring	Expert Judgment

new applications will integrate with the existing infrastructure. IT architects should be involved with every project at its inception. They will review the high-level business objectives and requirements to determine how technology can best solve the business problem and assess the feasibility of solution alternatives. The PM, BA, and IT architect form the critical project planning trio.

Case in Point

One of our students related an experience which shows the critical role played by the IT architect. She had elicited business requirements from her business stakeholders using a structured process template that included metrics for the current process and desired metrics for the solution. She asked her stakeholders for their ideal performance requirements for a new Web application. Once her high-level business model was complete, she reviewed it with the IT architect to assess the feasibility of the solution. He immediately noticed the performance requirements and told her that a Web application could never deliver on those constraints. She was able to go back to the business stakeholders and help them rethink the project objectives, saving the project team hundreds of wasted hours.

IT Developer

IT developers build IT solutions. They are the ultimate consumer of requirements and will be the people who make your solution vision a reality. To work effectively with IT developers, familiarize yourself with IT terminology and concepts (see Chapter 5). BAs who have an IT background will easily be able to converse and work with IT professionals. The one thing that you will notice is how quickly your technical skills become obsolete once you step out of that world. Things change very quickly in the development area. Don't feel bad; your basic understanding of software and development will always be relevant.

IT professionals are people who are very interested in making/building things. They are similar to engineers, artists, and builders. They enjoy coming up with ideas for new products, and they enjoy seeing those products come to fruition. Some developers are more interested in building new products, while others enjoy fixing/improving old products. Some would rather design, while others would rather code. A few rare individuals enjoy doing both. As a BA, it will be helpful to you if you get to know your IT people individually and understand their individual interests. The better you understand these technical stakeholders, the easier it will be for you to explain the business needs and work with them to design effective solutions.

Some developers will want to understand the business reasons for the products that they are building. These individuals may eventually choose to become BAs themselves. If you find yourself working with a developer who is frustrated working in a technical requirements vacuum, include that person in SME meetings if possible. You can really look at this developer as a BA-in-training and you can mentor him or her on communicating with the SMEs. Don't feel threatened by this direct communication between the

SME and development team. The role of the BA was invented because some developers don't communicate well with business people, but don't assume that all IT people are poor communicators. As with all human beings, get to know people individually and work with each in the way that they will be most comfortable.

Case in Point

When I was a programmer/systems analyst in my first job, we didn't have any BAs, so I was responsible for gathering requirements and developing the software, working directly with the SMEs. In a later position, my project team included BAs who interfaced with the SMEs for the programmers. I quickly discovered that I didn't like working with a go-between. I wanted to know what the business people were doing, why they wanted the software, and I wanted to see them use it at the end. My frustration in working through a BA is what led me to become one!

Do the developers have special training/certifications? Were they trained internally or before they joined the enterprise? Have they been working in this organization for a number of years or are they relatively new? Turnover in the IT industry can be very high. BAs must become very adept at building relationships with IT people wherever and whoever they are. To successfully work with the technical architects and developers, a BA must be able to communicate with them in the context of their environment.

When you are getting to know the developers, there are several things which will be useful for you to learn:

- ◆ Is the developer an organized worker? Does he or she keep a to-do list or rely on memory? Does he or she approach tasks in a sequential order or more randomly?
- ◆ Is the developer creative? When given a requirement, does the developer build as is requested or loosely use the requirements to build something that is clever, graphically aesthetic, or overly complex?
- ◆ Does the developer readily turn over his or her work, or does he or she postpone showing it to anyone while testing it, making sure that it is completely done? (In other words, does the developer test his or her own work? Is the developer a competent tester or only test cases that he or she knows will work?)

◆ Is the developer interested in understanding the business needs and user preferences? Does he or she ask detailed questions about business rules and then listen carefully and develop code that supports those rules?

◆ Is the developer familiar with the analysis techniques and presentation formats included in your requirements documents?

Understanding how a developer works best will help you decide appropriate requirements deliverables and communication approaches. One of the attractive aspects of the agile approaches to software development (see Chapter 5) is the myth of no requirements. Because many developers don't like to read or follow written requirements, they are drawn to the idea that they won't have to deal with documents. In reality, an agile project has just as many requirements as any other project. The requirements may be given to the developer verbally, but they still must be implemented. They are given to developers in small chunks, which works well for developers who are not used to working off of a to-do list. Providing one requirement at time with a tight deadline keeps the developer focused and discourages creativity.

The Developer Who Is Very Creative

Developers who are very creative are wonderful people. They are the people who have created Google™, Yahoo™, and many exciting games and gadgets. They see the world from a very different perspective and are constantly looking at old things in new ways. These individuals are critical resources in organizations where leading-edge technology is a critical success factor. The challenge for BAs working with these extremely creative individuals is their feelings about requirements. Creative IT people often appear to be ignoring the requirements, which can be very frustrating for the BA. In actuality, they see the requirements as guidelines. Giving them a detailed set of requirements is like putting them in jail. You are limiting their creativity and preventing them from doing the thing that they are really good at and enjoy best. Make sure that they understand the true business need and then allow them to use their creativity in the functional design. Be sure to keep them within the scope of the project.

The Developer Who Codes Exactly to Specs

At the other extreme are developers who write program code that supports the written requirements or specifications *exactly*. They will not add any additional functionality, even when it seems obvious that something was simply missed in the specs. These individuals will not make suggestions for better approaches or ask questions about possibilities outside of the requirements. Often, developers working for contract and/or outsourcing companies are instructed to code exactly to specs.

This can be a challenging situation for BAs since the requirements are supposed to be complete and accurate and should provide everything that the developer needs to know. Realistically, no requirements specification is perfect, so having a developer who thinks logically about the code he or she is writing and asks questions when he or she sees potential holes is ideal. The best way to handle a developer who codes blindly to specification is to have structured walkthroughs on each requirement deliverable and talk about the needs with the developer. Try to get the developer to ask questions and find the missing pieces right away so that you can amend the requirements before he or she starts work. Ultimately, the business needs must be supported by the code, so if changes are required after coding because of errors in the specifications, they may have to go through the project change control process.

The Developer's Industry Knowledge

Most developers specialize in a particular set of technical skills which are independent of a particular business industry. It is not uncommon to meet a developer who has worked in a manufacturing organization, followed by a telecommunications company, and then a financial services or health care business. Developing software for business functions that are not well understood is possible when developers work with BAs and system architects who understand the business domain. Some developers are not really interested in what the organization sells or services as much as they are interested in using the latest technical tools and approaches. The less a developer knows about (or is interested in) the business domain, the more dependent he or she is on complete, accurate requirements. The business terminology will not be known, so specific design components like screen labels and error messages must be explicitly stated and followed.

Alternately, some developers have experience/knowledge in a particular industry or business domain. For example, there are developers who specialize in commercial off-the-shelf applications like SAP© or PeopleSoft™. These developers may be very familiar with a set of terms unique to the application or business domain. They will provide less of a communication challenge because they know the language of the business. Just be sure that the developer knows the language of your particular business. Your organization may use terminology differently from other businesses in the same industry. In the training industry, there is inconsistency in the use of fundamental terms like class, course, and seminar. If a developer with industry experience joins your organization, make sure that he or she doesn't assume terminology is used exactly the same way. Again, detailed requirements avoid ambiguity.

Data Administrator/Architect/Analyst

Data administrators (DAs) and data architects utilize many of the same analysis skills as BAs. Some of them may have the title *data analyst.*

A DA is responsible for managing corporate data definitions. He or she maintains a data dictionary, data warehouse, and/or other repository of descriptions of the pieces of information that are important to the organization. Not all organizations have DAs. This role emerged in the 1990s as organizations realized that data was a corporate asset. Numerous databases and files had been created with redundant, often inconsistent data. The DA helps project teams reuse existing corporate data and use it consistently. Having one central view of business data helps an organization provide accurate answers to questions posed by its customers and its executive management. Another name given to this management of data at the enterprise level is master data management.

If your organization has a data administration team and a corporate data repository, it is critical that you become familiar and comfortable with them. This is a great resource for you on every project and will allow you to gather and analyze requirements much quicker. As discussed in Chapter 1, business requirements are made up of data, process, and business rules. When data has already been defined and documented for your organization, then possibly a third of your requirements definition is done before you start. Since many business rules are data related, the business rules are included in an entity relationship diagram, which is a common diagram used to represent data (see Chapter 6). This already available, quality, consistent view of data requirements allows all projects to be completed faster and the resulting solutions to be more easily integrated and interconnected.

DAs are strong analysts and usually have a technology background. They may have experience as a database administrator (see the next section), as a developer, or in another technical role. DAs are motivated by high-quality reuse of data and are often very protective of "their data." You should get to know the DA, just like all of the others on your team, and develop a relationship based on trust. You must learn to trust that the DA knows quite a bit about your project even before you get started. Understanding the data of an organization gives the DA a strong understanding of the organization itself.

At the beginning of a project, meet with the DA/data analyst and ask for background about this particular business area. Learn from him or her about the data that has already been identified and documented. Learn which pieces of information are currently stored in a database, in which databases and systems they exist, and who maintains them. You are eliciting requirements from someone who has already done the difficult work of picking the SME's brain and can give you the requirements in their purest form. Take advantage of this jump-start on your project by learning everything that you can before you meet with the SME. You will be able to formulate more intelligent and detailed questions for your first interviews and will be able to allow the SME to talk almost exclusively about process (which SMEs love to do). Your work will be to make sure that the processes they discuss can be supported by data that already exists. The DA will also tell you about data that has been identified but has not been thoroughly documented and organized. These are areas where you will need to spend more time focusing on data. The DA will be a great resource to assist you as you develop these requirements.

As much as possible, have the DA review all of your requirements, not just data. He or she may see process and business rule inconsistencies with existing data. Because the DA is a strong analyst, you have another peer to help you find weaknesses in your requirements as you go along. The DA also will be a great resource when you move into design, working with the database administrator and technical team to determine where new data elements should be stored.

Some DAs have developed negative attitudes and you may hear that someone is "difficult to work with." This is often because the data administration function is underfunded and underappreciated. Many organizations that created a data administration group in the 1990s were very excited about the data repository when the stock market was booming and business indicators were up. But when an economic downturn was predicted and companies began tightening their belts, the DA group was an easy area to cut. Many data repositories were left incomplete and only partially maintained. This led to a situation where not all corporate data had been defined and described, so new projects couldn't always use the common information. With fewer people in the data administration group and incomplete data definitions, it was easy for BAs and project teams to skip the DA reviews and just create their own data requirements. This often caused more redundant, inconsistent data sources. The DAs that were left felt that their authority was undermined and their importance to the organization diminished. This leads to unhappy, disgruntled people.

Database Designer/Administrator

A database designer is responsible for determining where data should be physically stored, how it will be accessed, how it will be protected, who will have access to it, and where it will be used. These are critical decisions for an organization that have long-term effects on the efficiency and quality of information systems. Database designers and database administrators also maintain these data stores for the life of their use. They maintain backup procedures and disaster recovery procedures; they correct problems with the data values when errors are introduced.

When a project involves creation or storage of new information, the database administrator must be involved. Even if you are going to use existing data in a new way, it is a good idea to discuss this new usage with the database team. Creation of and access to data can have huge performance impacts for software users, and providing inaccurate data from a software application is the quickest way to sabotage trust in your work. Make friends with the database administrator, and check with him or her even when you think you don't need to. As with all stakeholders, when you establish a good relationship, always act ethically, and keep the database administrator informed, you will have a valuable ally when you need one.

Vendor

A vendor is a company from which services or products are purchased. There is typically a contract relationship between the purchasing organization and the vendor organization. There are many types of vendors with which a BA may work on a project. A company that sells and supports application development software is the most common one. Examples include SAP, PeopleSoft, and Siebel™. Other vendors may be hardware vendors, consulting services companies, and outsourcing vendors.

Figure 2.2 shows the typical life cycle of a vendor relationship. As a BA, you may be involved from the beginning of this relationship or may be brought in at any point. Chapter 3 will discuss software package implementation projects and Requests for Proposal (RFPs) in more detail.

There are a few key points in this life cycle where a BA can add great value: at the beginning (sales, demos), during creation of an RFP, and in reviewing the responses to an RFP. A skilled BA will help the organization select the best solution available and will expose the gaps that will occur with any package solution.

Sales people and marketing people are very good at their jobs—and no more so than in software companies. They have outstanding descriptions of the wonders of their software and describe how it will make your company more successful and your workload lighter. The demonstrations are slick and polished and make the software appear easy to customize and easy to use.

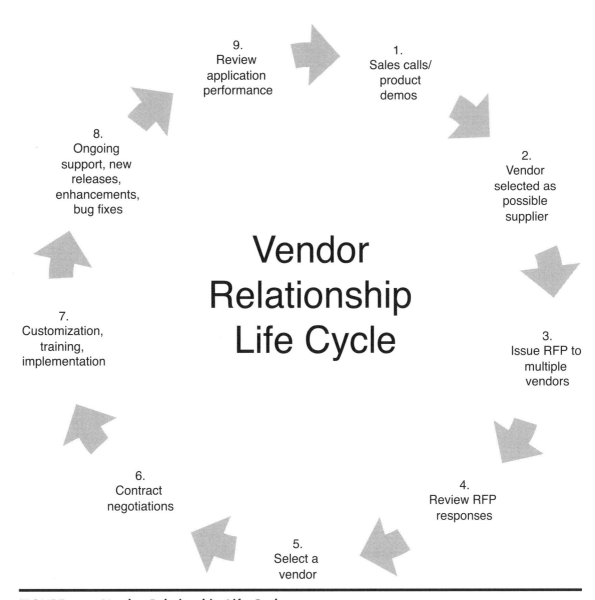

FIGURE 2.2. Vendor Relationship Life Cycle

All of these wonderful claims play right into the frustrations of users and their management. Everyone wants to believe that if the company just buys this software package, all of the problems will be solved! But BAs know that there are no magic wands.

In truth, buying and implementing software does not guarantee a better chance of success than developing an application internally. There are different issues and challenges, but they are no less critical than the issues that arise during development. The experienced BA is aware that just because software is purchased *doesn't necessarily mean* that:

◆ It will be up and running faster
◆ It will cost less money than developing an application internally
◆ It will support the business better than a home-grown application

These three fundamental assumptions are the driving forces in decisions to buy software rather than write it. These three fundamental assumptions are often wrong, and the person who can best evaluate them is the BA. Evaluate these assumptions by eliciting and understanding the business requirements, brainstorm for possible solutions, and work with the solution team to estimate cost/time. Go back to the project objectives and assess how well they would be met. Only when you have thoroughly analyzed the business and the solution options will you be able to assess the viability of a package and estimate its true value.

In terms of relationships with representatives of the vendor, treat them with the same respect as other stakeholders. Be aware, however, that it is not in their best interest to be entirely truthful with you. They will emphasize the positives, minimize the negatives (often called "features" by the vendor), and gloss over any unanswered questions that you have asked. This difficulty in really understanding what you are buying is handled well with a formal RFP process. The RFP requires the vendor to document, in writing, what it will provide. Careful development of RFPs and careful review of vendor responses is the best approach to rendering a fair and unbiased verdict on the purchase decision.

Stakeholder Analysis

The relationship that you will build with each stakeholder on a project is unique. Some people will be easier to communicate with than others. You will like some stakeholders better than others. It will be beneficial for you to think through what you know (or have heard) about each person to plan your communication techniques and your project tasks.

In thinking about an individual stakeholder, there are probably hundreds of things that you could consider. Human beings are so complex and never really completely understand each other. In the context of a work environment, only a limited view of each individual is available. Having acknowledged that complexity, there are several concrete characteristics of each individual which you should consider and plan for:

◆ Do you already have a relationship with the stakeholder?
◆ Is it a good working relationship?
◆ Do you think the stakeholder trusts you?
◆ What is the stakeholder's relationship to the project? (Will the project have a significant effect or a minor effect on the stakeholder's work?)
◆ What is the stakeholder's attitude toward the project? Is he or she excited about it or dreading it?
◆ How knowledgeable is the stakeholder about the business area?
◆ How many years has the stakeholder been with the organization?
◆ At what level in the organization (management?) is the stakeholder?
◆ How does the stakeholder communicate? Does he or she explain concepts clearly? Is he or she detail oriented?
◆ How does the stakeholder learn?

Obviously, you will not know the answers to all of these questions for every stakeholder on a project. The more you know about a particular stakeholder, the better able you will be to tailor your communications to him or her. For stakeholders with whom you haven't worked before, you will be adjusting your communications as you get to know them. This is a good example of an area where a BA must be flexible. You will try a particular communication technique, and if it doesn't work, you will try something else.

BALANCING STAKEHOLDER NEEDS

When there is more than one stakeholder on a project (and there almost always is!), stakeholder needs must be balanced. This is an important and challenging part of the work of the BA. The BA's role is to represent the business stakeholders to the technical team and make sure that the business needs are met. But what if the business people don't agree on what their needs are? This requires the BA to be a strong facilitator, consensus builder, and even a negotiator at times.

To balance stakeholder needs in the way that benefits the enterprise as a whole the most, the BA must first understand the goals and strategy of the enterprise. This will be discussed in Chapter 3. Second, the BA must understand which stakeholder/group is funding a particular project and the specific goals the project is trying to address. Hopefully, the project goals are in line with and support the enterprise-wide goals. If not, it will be difficult for the project to be successful. The PM and sponsor need to address this problem.

Even when the project and enterprise goals are aligned, different stakeholder needs may arise. Enterprise and project goals can be accomplished in various ways, and different stakeholders will have different ideas to accomplish them. The BA's role is to listen very carefully and work to understand each of the different stakeholder issues. The first step in resolving a conflict is to clearly understand both sides. This will often be difficult because you may personally agree with one side and have a difficult time being open minded about the other. Work hard to maintain your neutrality—a BA is Switzerland! If the differing groups have difficulty discussing the issue together because they are emotional or impatient, talk with them individually. Work to really understand their perspectives and their motives. Don't try to change their minds or convince them of another way until you can completely see their side; use the win-win approach (Covey, 1989).

Occasionally, when you truly listen and understand each side of a conflict, you will see common ground. This is the important area on which to begin your consensus building. Help both sides see their shared knowledge, goals, and desires. Show them that the areas of disagreement are small by comparison and can be resolved. Consensus does not mean that everyone agrees; it means that everyone can support the solution.

When the two sides have large areas of disagreement, be open and honest in acknowledging the issues. Let everyone know that reaching consensus may be impossible. Ultimately, the project sponsor will be the decision maker, and all stakeholders should understand this reality.

Case in Point

I worked on a project to convert an old IMS® (IBM's first Information Management System) database system to a relational database management system. This project was initiated by IT because developers who could support IMS systems were hard to find and a relational database system offered more opportunities for direct user queries and a more flexible platform for future development. Our project team was assigned to rebuild current business functions on the new platform. Our goal was to make as few changes as possible to the user interface portion of the system, but some changes were unavoidable. When we interviewed business stakeholders about the changes, they did not understand why we were making changes that did not give them any additional functionality or features. They did not understand why the company would spend money on a project that didn't do anything for them. Since the sponsor was IT, IT had the final say on the changes but wanted the business area to be satisfied with the results. We were constantly explaining the advantages of a relational database management system to business people who really couldn't see any short-term or long-term benefits.

Understanding the Political Environment

Recently, a BA asked if there is any training on how BAs should navigate the politics in their organizations. She was facing a situation where the IT group disagreed with a business unit request, but she was a paid consultant, hired by IT!

Although dealing with office politics is necessary in many professions, BAs face some unique challenges, often driven by where they officially "report" in the organization. Many BAs "report to" or "reside in" IT. This means that they are paid out of the IT budget and evaluated by IT management. Promotions and assignments to plum projects are controlled by IT. As a BA, you are tasked with representing the business to the IT group. Business analysis professionals are supposed to be *advocates* for the business. But what happens when the business disagrees with an IT decision or direction? Guess who is stuck in the middle: the BA. All of the talk about being a bridge or a liaison can be destroyed by an organizational structure that puts the BA's career progression at odds with the best interest of the business. Of course, there are also instances when a BA "reports" to a business unit. Ideally, BAs would be an independent group and could truly act as liaisons. Analogous to the project management office, a business analyst office or center of excellence may eventually help with these conflicts. A recent Gartner report on business analysis placement also defines a *hybrid model* where there are BAs in IT and in the business units (Morello and Belchar, 2005).

In the meantime, a BA must represent all of his or her stakeholders as fully as possible and work to resolve conflicts through communication and consensus building. Business analysis professionals have to walk a fine line between representing business stakeholders and not alienating management. This is possible because BAs are excellent communicators and listeners. Sometimes simply listening and asking questions help disparate groups to reach a common vision.

There are some good references on how a person can gain creditability and assert influence without having any official authority. Read *Influence without Authority* by Allan R. Cohen and David L. Bradford (1991) for advice on this important skill.

WORKING WITH DISPERSED TEAMS

Many organizations assign project team members who are geographically dispersed. There are many reasons why stakeholders might work in different locations: company offices in multiple cities or countries, IT functions outsourced to companies in other cities or countries, or purchasing software from vendors in other locations. A useful resource is Dr. Lojeski's book entitled *Uniting the Virtual Workforce: Transforming Leadership and Innovation in the Globally Integrated Enterprise* (Lojeski, 2008).

Working with stakeholders in different locations poses unique challenges for the BA, whose main work involves communication. Face-to-face communication is usually the most effective because the BA can *listen* to not only the spoken word but also the tone of voice and body language, which convey as much as 55% of the message. Personal relationships are much easier to build in person, which can more quickly translate to trust. Misunderstandings are more easily identified and resolved using direct communication.

A BA who must communicate with stakeholders using remote communication techniques must be aware of the limitations of each technique. The BA must plan to use the most effective technique available and plan extra time to ensure accurate and complete requirements are elicited, analyzed, and confirmed.

Planning communications with dispersed teams requires the BA to consider the physical distance, time zone and work hour differences, nationality/cultural differences, language issues, and the communication options available at each location.

BABOK Connection	
Knowledge Area	**Task/Technique**
Requirements Management and Communication	Communicate Requirements

Physical Distance

Even separation of a few miles adds a challenge to communication. Depending on the travel time required and the project travel budget, the BA should meet with each stakeholder in person when possible. These meetings must be well planned and ideally should occur earlier rather than later in the project. The PM and BA should invite key stakeholders to the project initiation/scoping session to kick off the project with direct communication. This is even more important when key stakeholders have never met each other in person. Starting out a project with a team-building activity like scoping establishes relationships that can be maintained over long distances.

Ideally, the BA should travel to the stakeholders' work site to observe the environment and meet other business workers. This demonstrates that the BA is truly interested in the business unit for which he or she is advocating.

Time Zone Differences

When stakeholders work in different time zones, scheduling phone calls and conference calls is challenging. Project team members may be asked to work different hours than those to which they are normally accustomed. The PM and BA need to balance the needs of the project with the needs of the team members. Different requirements elicitation techniques may be used even though they are not the ideal. For example, if the developers are in India and the business stakeholders are in California, a teleconference will require someone to work in the middle of the night. Instead of talking with everyone together, the BA may instead meet with each group separately and relay the communications back and forth. Remember to plan extra time for this work (and for your sleep!). A BA who relays messages is often required to go "back and forth" between the two groups several times before all questions are answered and resolved.

When you schedule group meetings, try to alternate meeting times to equally inconvenience all stakeholders. Although the development team may be contractors, they are still your stakeholders, and being an excellent BA means assisting with communications and supporting all stakeholders.

Nationality/Cultural Differences

When you are assigned to a team with members in a different country or from a different cultural background, do some research to learn about communication differences. As businesses become more global, there is universal recognition that working with people from other cultures presents unique challenges. There are many resources to help a BA get familiar with basic cultural differences. Visit Web sites or take a class to learn the basics about the country where your stakeholder resides. Find out when national or religious holidays occur, because they may affect stakeholder availability. Find out about working hour norms (e.g., if people put in overtime after work or on weekends or if working on a Sunday is completely unacceptable).

If you are able to travel to your stakeholders' country, read travel books to learn as much as you can about the history and current issues of the country. Be prepared to meet people with the customary local greeting (i.e., a handshake or bow). The more you know about the customs and habits of your stakeholders, the faster you will build relationships and establish lines of communication. Offer to explain your customs and history as well. Working with people from other cultures is a great opportunity to learn, so allow your natural curiosity to facilitate project success while also enriching your personal experience.

Language Differences

Most global organizations standardize on one language for their internal business communications. If the BA and a stakeholder do not speak/know a common language, a translator must be employed to manage all communications. This is rare, but when necessary adds both cost and time to the business analysis process.

More often, the project team members will share a language but some team members will be more fluent than others. Those for whom English is a second language, for example, often have a smaller vocabulary than native speakers. They may also have an accent, which makes understanding them more difficult.

As early as possible, talk with each stakeholder to listen for vocabulary usage and accent. If you determine that one or more stakeholders are less fluent, plan more time for elicitation sessions and follow-up communications. If possible, exchange written communications (e.g., e-mail messages) as soon as possible to assess writing skills. Often, people who have learned a second language in school are better able to communicate in writing because pronunciations are not involved. Choose your communication techniques based on your assessment of each stakeholder. Having an agreed-upon set of terms that are used consistently (see Chapter 6 for a discussion of the glossary) will also help to make project team communications effective when there are language differences.

Using Team Collaboration Tools

A BA working with team members who are located in another geographic area will benefit greatly from using collaboration tools. Working with people at remote locations is very challenging. The more adept you can become at managing information across distances, the more successful you will be. There are many very sophisticated online collaboration tools. As with requirements tools, the tool is less important than your ability to use it to increase your team's productivity.

Planning the use of collaboration tools is critical. Don't just start a meeting, log into a tool, and try to start documenting requirements. Plan ahead, as you would do for all meetings and information gathering sessions. You should be able to answer the following questions before you begin a working session:

- ◆ What is the reason for the meeting?
- ◆ How many people will be involved?
- ◆ What are we trying to accomplish?
- ◆ What is the deliverable?
- ◆ How will it best be created, during the meeting or afterward?
- ◆ What type of collaboration tool is appropriate?

Using a Shared Presentation

When you have information to present to a group, for review or approval, a shared view of the information can be very helpful. You should prepare your presentation materials just as you would for a formal, in-person presentation. This formality is required because your listeners are remotely located and you may not have the advantage of watching their body language to read their understanding. With many tools, you can present material and ask the participants specific questions. Your questions should be well thought out in advance, easy to answer, and should assist you with the remaining material. With a large group, you will need to ask closed-ended questions so that you (or the tool) can quickly tabulate responses. You may want to have some backup presentation materials to support an area where many participants have questions. Questions during the presentation also help participants stay focused and involved. When you are working remotely, you cannot be aware of all of the distractions with which the participants may be dealing. When you ask a question, if all participants do not answer, be specific: "John, do you have a question about this requirement before you can answer?"

Having an assistant facilitator in each location is an effective way to manage virtual meetings and presentations. The remote facilitator will make sure all attendees are present, introduce each participant, work with the main facilitator to manage participation, and make sure that participants adhere to standard meeting etiquette (e.g., one person speaks at a time).

Sharing a Document

When working with a small group, a tool that allows you to share a document may be appropriate. This technology allows multiple users to edit the same document while all participants see the changes instantly. Both diagrams and text representations may be developed or refined in this manner. This would be very useful for paired BAs who are working on the same requirements document.

The more people you have involved, the more difficult document sharing will become. If you need to have a session with a large number of participants, you should allow them to view the working document but not physically contribute. Too many people adding to a document at once will really make the meeting confusing and result in a low-quality product.

SUMMARY OF KEY POINTS

The most important skill of a BA is effective communication. To be effective, communication must be tailored to and for the audience. Understanding all of the people in your project is the first step in being an effective analyst.

- People who are involved with a project are commonly referred to as "stakeholders."
- To tailor communications, BAs must really know their audience. They should get to know each project stakeholder and develop a relationship of trust and open communication.
- Knowing the motives of everyone on a project, along with their skill sets, allows the BA to determine how to best elicit and present requirements.
- The PM and BA should work together very closely. Ideally, two different individuals who are appropriately trained fill these roles on most projects.
- Technical and solution team members are also stakeholders with whom communication is very important. BAs need to communicate in the technical language used by these stakeholders.
- Stakeholders also include individuals outside the organization, like vendors, suppliers, and contractors. Communication with these stakeholders is usually more formal and structured.
- BAs design communications to balance all stakeholder needs and manage the challenges of dispersed team members.

◆ BAs should not let attitudes and history prevent them from developing a relationship and making the best use of the people available to them. Every stakeholder is a valuable resource; some just may require a little more TLC. Treat them well, involve them in the project as early as possible, and win them over to your side, and you will have excellent teammates.

BIBLIOGRAPHY

Cohen, Allan R. and David L. Bradford (1991). *Influence without Authority*. Wiley.

Covey, Stephen R. (1989). *The 7 Habits of Highly Effective People*. Free Press.

Lojeski, Karen Sobel (2008). *Uniting the Virtual Workforce: Transforming Leadership and Innovation in the Globally Integrated Enterprise*. John Wiley & Sons.

Morello, Diane and Michael J. Belchar (2005). Research Paper: Business Analysis Placement, Competencies and Effectiveness. ID Number G00126718. Gartner.

Nielsen, Jakob (1993). *Usability Engineering*. Morgan Kaufmann.

Standish Group (2006). *2006 Chaos Report* (www.standishgroup.com).

3

KNOW YOUR PROJECT

Most of the work assigned to business analysis professionals is within the confines of a project. A project is a temporary endeavor initiated to achieve very specific goals. It is critical for the business analyst (BA) to thoroughly understand the project to which he or she is assigned. The BA must be aware of the parameters set for the project, the individuals involved with the project, and most importantly, the purpose of the project. Without clearly knowing the goals of the project, an analyst will not be able to focus elicitation and analysis in the right direction. Knowing why the project was initiated is the first step in business analysis planning.

To help understand the goals of each project, a BA should be aware of the organization's strategic vision and long-term goals. The enterprise strategic plan is the organization's road map to long-term success. Each individual project supports a piece of the strategic plan. The BA's work during project initiation is to understand the alignment with corporate goals and plan analysis activities to best support those goals.

WHY HAS THE ORGANIZATION DECIDED TO FUND THIS PROJECT?

It is critical for the BA to understand why the organization has decided to fund his or her project. The business analysis professional must be sure that analysis work is always aimed toward accomplishing the business objectives and is aligned with the organization's mission. Project work always costs money, even if a project involves only internal resources (such as employees). Employees are very expensive resources and need to be used wisely. Everyone on a project, especially the project manager (PM) and the BA, should be constantly evaluating the expenditures against the expected benefits. If they have been assigned to project A, then project B is not being done. Every organization faces these trade-offs.

For many projects, the benefits to the organization are very obvious. You offer customers the opportunity to purchase products over the Internet because you expect to increase sales. You streamline a complex business process to decrease costs. But some

BABOK Connection	
Knowledge Area	**Task/Technique**
Enterprise Analysis	Define the Business Need

project benefits are not so easy to see. The successful BA must know the underlying rationale for funding a project (from the viewpoint of the project sponsor) before he or she can begin analyzing and understanding the requirements.

Business Case Development

Most organizations decide to fund a project because they anticipate a return on the investment. A business case describes this anticipated return. For a BA to know a project, he or she must understand the business case. It may have been developed by the business sponsor, stakeholders, or PM. Sometimes the BA will be asked to develop the business case as the first task of a project or before a project has been approved. Understanding the importance of developing business cases is a key business analysis skill.

Have you ever tried to convince your spouse that you should get a new car? How do you decide to hire someone to cut your grass rather than do it yourself? Why did you decide to buy a new pair of shoes or install cable TV? When you are working to persuade someone (even yourself) to take action, you are building a *case*. You think through all of the positive results that will occur if the project is approved. You prepare to counter any objections that your decision maker has. You evaluate the potential benefits and weigh those against the anticipated costs/effort, and when the benefits outweigh the costs, the action is approved. Companies have to make these decisions all the time. They are presented with ideas and opportunities and need to evaluate the relative merit.

A business case is an explanation of why the organization has decided to go forward with a project. The word *case* comes from the legal profession and means an argument for or against something: "We are building a case for . . ." Business cases, which depict the value of an endeavor, have become more common as organizations realize that projects may be expensive and sometimes do not deliver the expected results. A business case documents the justification for a project for executive decision makers and provides a mechanism to evaluate the success of the project at its completion.

Related activities are called feasibility studies and cost/benefit analysis. A feasibility study determines the practicability and workability of a potential solution before a project is approved. It answers the question: "Can it be done?" Cost/benefit analysis focuses on a financial analysis of the potential solution, using economic calcula-

BABOK Connection	
Knowledge Area	**Task/Technique**
Enterprise Analysis	Develop Business Case
	Economic Models and Benefit Analysis

tions to project the potential return on investment and payback period. It answers the question: "What are the costs vs. benefits of doing it?" Some costs and benefits are not easily measured. Benefits like goodwill and positive public relations are referred to as *intangible*. Costs that are easily measured are referred to as *tangible*. Many business cases include a feasibility study and cost/benefit analysis.

BAs are often asked to write and present a business case for a project or potential project. This is a very important skill for a senior BA who is interested in moving into consulting, strategic planning, or corporate management. Building a business case can be challenging because it requires significant research, analysis, and strong communication skills. But the task seems harder than it really is. BAs are good at research and analytic thinking. Building a business case involves bringing together research, logical reasoning, and financial estimates. In addition, business case development requires creativity and big-picture thinking.

Business case development and cost/benefit analysis are important skills for business analysis professionals to develop early in their careers. Although a formal business case document is not created for every project, someone in the organization should always consider a project's worth before funding is approved.

Think about convincing your spouse (or yourself) that your family needs a new car. Take a few minutes to think about the costs vs. benefits. Try to break down your thoughts—analyze your decision-making process. You can start by looking at the pros and cons of the decision, as shown in Figure 3.1.

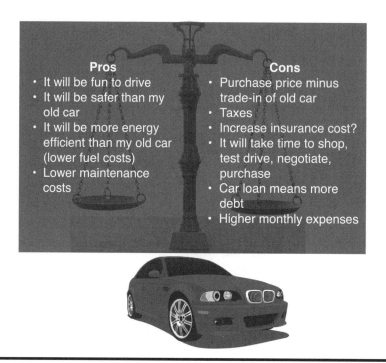

FIGURE 3.1. Pros and Cons of Buying a New Car

Be sure to list everything, regardless of whether or not it can be measured or costed. Cost/benefit analysis often includes items that are *intangible* or difficult to measure, like "fun to drive."

Next look at each pro and con to determine if there is some way to quantify it. The more quantifiable the analysis, the more objective it will be. If you can show your spouse that a new car will require a smaller monthly cash outflow, then you would probably have a pretty good business case.

Research costs to represent the most accurate picture possible. When you must estimate, document the assumptions upon which you based the estimate. See Table 3.1 for the *one-time* costs and Table 3.2 for the monthly or *recurring* costs of the buying a new car example. It is very important to separate one-time costs from recurring costs for payback period calculations (the length of time required for the organization to recover its investment). BAs should enlist help from a finance professional when necessary. There is not a standard format for representing costs and benefits. The analyst must design a business case that clearly communicates the facts and expected results of the project.

TABLE 3.1. Example of One-Time Charges

Purchase price of car	$25,000.00	Written quote from dealer
Taxes, destination charges	$4,200.00	Written quote from dealer
Tags, license	$300.00	From Secretary of State Web site
Loan closing costs	$2,000.00	Written quote from bank
Total purchase cost	$31,500.00	

For cost and benefits that cannot be quantified, describe each intangible and how it would benefit or hurt the organization:

◆ **Fun to drive**: I will look forward to running errands and going to work and will be in a more positive mood. This will make our whole family feel more upbeat and optimistic.

◆ **Safety**: Less chance of a breakdown when away from home that might put the driver and passengers in jeopardy. Better safety features in the car mean that in the unfortunate event of an accident, there may be fewer injuries and less trauma, which may also result in fewer medical costs.

When building a business case, work hard to justify the recommendation that you feel is the best. Often, your intuition and experience point you toward the right conclusion, but management wants hard proof, not a gut feeling.

TABLE 3.2. Example of Recurring Charges

Item	Old Car	New Car	Notes
Fuel	$200 per month	$175 per month	Based on last year's mileage, estimated 25 mpg, $4 per gallon of gas
Loan payment	0	$350 per month for 60 months	
Maintenance	$150 (average of expenses for last 2 years)	0	Maintenance included in purchase price for 4-year warranty period
Net	$350 per month	$525 per month	

Case in Point

I worked for a loan serving company that frequently purchased loans from other financial institutions. Our strength was in servicing: accepting payments, managing loan changes, and handling delinquencies and payoffs. When we bought a group of loans (often referred to as a pool), they were delivered in two parts: (1) boxes of loan documents and history and (2) one or more electronic files which contained all of the data describing each loan (borrower name, address, original loan amount, current balance, next payment due date, etc.). Rarely did this file format match ours because our loan serving system had been developed in-house. An IT loan acquisition team was assigned to each pool. The team's job was to perform gap analysis on the data. We mapped the data and wrote a data conversion program to load the data into our systems. During one particular acquisition, I heard one of the developers say "All of this work for 50 loans!" The team was struggling because the data conversion was very complex. It occurred to me that we had never performed a cost/benefit analysis on one of these acquisitions. I wonder how many hours would have been needed to simply enter the 50 loans into our system through the data entry screens. My guess is that we would have saved a significant amount of resources on these smaller pools if we would have converted them manually. But we were in the habit of converting these loans in the same way.

There are several common reasons why an organization decides to fund a project:

◆ Because of a problem
◆ To eliminate costs (jobs)
◆ Outside regulation
◆ An opportunity
◆ For marketing or advertising
◆ To align business processes

Project Initiated Because of a Problem

Most projects are initiated because there is a problem that needs to be solved. It is important during project scoping to make sure that you really understand the problem that is to be addressed. This sounds very simple and sometimes it is. Sometimes the problem as stated by the project sponsor is exactly the problem that needs to be addressed. But sometimes the stated problem to be solved is not really the problem. There may be a deeper problem. In other cases, you are being asked to solve the wrong problem. The excellent BA will work to understand the true business problem before trying to solve it.

A technique used when trying to discover the source or reason for a problem is called root cause analysis. Root cause analysis involves identifying the known symptoms and looking for the cause of each symptom. Another technique, the five whys, is often used to organize and facilitate root cause analysis (see examples of the five whys in Chapter 7).

Case in Point

I was assigned to a project as the BA studying a specific cash management function. The project objective was to automate a manual transaction and decision with an online data entry screen and set of business rules. The underlying assumed reason for the project was to decrease costs by saving employee time. One subject matter expert, Frank, performed this work. He was an older man who had been doing this same work for many years. He primarily worked alone, and I had no reason to think that he was making mistakes or bad decisions. As I learned about his work, I began to wonder how much time automation would really save. He had a very efficient process. He also did not understand why the company was spending money to build this software. But we built it and implemented it. It wasn't until a couple of months later when I heard an offhand comment from a corporate director that I learned the real reason for the project. Management was concerned that Frank was the only person who knew how to do this work and he was nearing retirement. Management wanted the process automated so that it was not dependent on one person's knowledge. The concern was that Frank would never be willing to share his procedures or decision rationale. The true reason this project was funded was to avoid the risk of losing corporate knowledge as a result of a personnel change.

Project Initiated to Eliminate Costs (Jobs)

Often, the project objective is to save money by cutting costs. Unfortunately, one way to cut costs is to decrease head count; in other words, reduce the number of people working in the business. This is not uncommon and is a situation that you should be prepared to handle. It will present you with some of your most difficult communication challenges.

There are many IT innovations that have decreased the number of business workers in many industries. The ATM has significantly decreased the number of tellers needed at a bank. Word processors and laptop computers have decreased the number of secretarial and administrative positions needed. Online Web sites ask customers to enter their name and address data, which has decreased the number of data entry personnel needed. E-mail and other alternative delivery options have severely cut the volume of the postal service. Many retail stores have installed automated check-out machines so that customers can pay for their purchases without an employee.

When you are assigned to gather requirements for a project with the objective of cutting personnel, try to get as much information from the management team as you can before you start talking with the subject matter experts. Questions should be posed to the PM, executive sponsor, corporate management, human resources management, and any other executive-level people who will be involved in the workforce reduction. You must ask some difficult questions and press for answers. The more you understand about the corporate vision, the better you will be able to deal with the consequences in the business area. Questions that need to be asked include:

- ◆ Exactly how many employees are to be eliminated?
- ◆ Will the employees be transferred to other positions within the company?
- ◆ What types/titles of employees are to be eliminated?
- ◆ Have the specific individuals impacted been identified yet?
- ◆ What criteria were used to select these individuals?
- ◆ Have they been notified yet?
- ◆ If the employees are not being transferred to other positions, will they be given any outplacement services? Severance packages?
- ◆ When will employees be notified?

It is possible that the answers to these questions have not yet been determined or have not even been thought about or discussed. If they have not been considered, then you have already provided a very valuable service to your organization and to the impacted individuals because you are encouraging the company to think ahead about what will happen to these individuals. Often, a project lasts for several months or more, so the organization has time to try to place these individuals in another area within the company.

It is also possible that decisions about personnel changes cannot be determined yet because a business solution/change has not yet been defined. In these cases, it is important for you to be aware that whatever solution design you recommend will have a direct impact on people in the business area. It may be difficult for you to be objective if you see a solution design that will automate someone out of a job. You must remember that you are working for the organization's long-term success. Ignoring a good solution that will increase organizational effectiveness just to save someone's job will make the organization less competitive and may decrease its long-term viability. It may be an extreme thought, but if you save one or two jobs now, you may contribute to the failure of the entire organization in the long run—resulting in a much larger loss of jobs. You must keep an objective perspective.

Typically, workforce reduction goals are outside the responsibility of the BA. This information is often kept confidential until close to the time that the employees will be notified. It is often counterproductive to tell people too far in advance that their jobs are being eliminated. This causes the strongest employees to begin job searches, and they may leave while they are still needed. It also decreases morale and employee productivity as the end date approaches. In addition, the information that these employees provide to you as you are trying to understand the business requirements may be suspect.

Your first goal is to have as much information as possible before meeting with the subject matter experts (SMEs). When you interview the SMEs, be as honest as you can based on management's direction. If you are unsure about job eliminations and an SME asks you directly, do not lie or try to cover up the possibility of workforce reduction. Acknowledge that one of the project goals is to cut costs and that you are assigned to help improve the business area's efficiency and effectiveness. Be positive about the project by emphasizing the resulting improvements for the corporation and the long-term health and success of the organization. If you know that some employee transfers will be considered, encourage SMEs to learn as much as possible about the organization and other job openings. Offer to introduce them to people you know in other business units. When SMEs express fear about being fired, encourage them by suggesting that other companies are often looking for qualified workers. Talk about your past job changes and how much happier you were after finding a new job (if it is true). Empathize and be positive. These are the keys to working with people who are worried about their jobs. Also, you can mention that the more helpful an SME is on the current project, the more visibility he or she may have. This increased visibility may open up opportunities for management to gain a new appreciation for the SME's contributions. Maybe the individual is even interested in becoming a BA like you! Try to remain neutral and be sensitive to the people with whom you are working.

Luckily, BAs are rarely asked if employees should be fired and even more rarely asked which employees should go first, so you shouldn't have to make these difficult decisions. If you are asked, you may want to talk with the human resources representative before responding. Always be honest, but don't answer a question if you feel uncomfortable.

Project Initiated by Outside Regulation

Many projects are initiated due to outside regulations. A regulation may be imposed by a government agency, industry watchdog organization, or standards organization. New regulations may be created, existing regulations updated, or an organization may be changing (i.e., growing) such that it will soon be affected by regulation. Many government regulations are only enforced for large companies, so if your company grows, it may suddenly be required to follow a rule that did not apply in the past.

Many companies don't think about the true cost of regulation. They may consistently prioritize regulation projects as mandatory without performing any cost/benefit analysis. A value provided by the business analysis professional is to ask the *why* question, even about these projects. Ignoring regulations is not recommended, but each organization impacted by regulation should make a choice about whether or not to comply. Non-compliance usually results in negative consequences like penalties, bad press, or elimination from some markets. An organization should develop a business case, including a cost/benefit analysis, weighing the cost of the regulation against the "benefits," which may simply be avoidance of negative consequences.

For example, if an organization estimates that it will cost $1 million to enforce compliance to a new regulation and the annual penalty for failing to comply is $100,000, the organization may consciously decide not to comply. Of course, if there is also a risk of negative publicity for the organization, the true penalty may be greater. In this case, an organization usually performs a risk assessment (probability and potential consequences) to help make the decision. In some cases, there is also a moral component to the decision to comply. If the regulation is a safety issue, a company may risk harming its customers, employees, suppliers, or community. The potential cost of this harm is very difficult to estimate. A company whose disregard for safety is exposed often goes out of business.

Another alternative may be for the organization to make changes in its structure or size to get out of the regulation applicability. When the U.S. government enacted Sarbanes-Oxley financial reporting regulations for publicly held companies, some companies decided to buy back all of their shares and reorganize privately to avoid the costly regulation. Blindly deciding to comply with every rule/guideline is not always a good strategic plan. Each relevant issue should be examined and analyzed for its true cost/value.

How does a BA participate in this analysis? Cost/benefit analysis and risk assessment are critical. Business analysis professionals know how to ask in-depth questions to get to the root of an issue. The BA assigned to a regulatory project should ask questions to be sure that the organization has made a wise decision to fund the project.

Making a change to comply with regulation costs money and rarely results in increased revenue. Keep the project costs low by defining a tight scope and only doing work necessary to comply with the regulation. Resist the urge to add other objectives to the project. It is very common for SMEs (and BAs) to say "While we are changing this screen, let's also fix another problem that we have identified." Adding even small tasks that are not part of the original project scope can add significant costs.

Project Initiated by an Opportunity

Many projects are initiated to support a new business opportunity. The definition of *opportunity* is "a set of circumstances that make it possible to do something." For example, a new product design may be appealing to potential customers who have not purchased existing products. A simple phone with large buttons appeals to an older population more than standard phones which are very small with a lot of features. When an opportunity is identified, the organization decides if the opportunity is worth pursuing and how it will be implemented.

Opportunities may be identified by an existing customer who asks for a customized product. They may be created by an employee in customer service who hears similar requests from many customers. Opportunities are also often identified by review of competitive offerings. Leveraging and improving on the ideas of others is a common and successful strategy. Of course, be sure that the organization is not violating copyright, trademark, patent, or any other legal ownership. The organization's legal department will help with these issues.

Some opportunities are very large, like offering a brand new product. Many opportunities are smaller, incremental changes to existing products or processes which will improve customer service, increase quality or efficiency, or decrease costs. The small opportunities often can have a huge impact in an organization. Suppose a supermarket chain identifies a change in its distribution process that would save two cents on every dairy product sold. The savings could quickly reach millions of dollars.

When opportunities are identified, a business case should be built. Most executive-level managers are looking for the benefits to outweigh the costs before they will give approval to go forward and fund a project. Positive cash flow or return on investment is typically required because pursuing an opportunity is purely optional to an organization. Whereas a regulatory change or problem resolution may be considered mandatory, an opportunity is a choice.

The business analysis professional must be aware of the projected benefits of a project. If he or she learns something during requirements analysis that changes the scope or cost of the project, it must be communicated. It is a huge waste of corporate resources to pursue an opportunity that will never pay back its costs unless there is a significant intangible benefit. The PM and sponsor may need to reconsider the project based on the new information. It is better to abandon a bad project than to continue spending money on it when you know that the results will not pay back the costs.

Projects for Marketing or Advertising

Projects requested by marketing or advertising departments differ from other projects in that they are usually focused on selling more products and/or services, similar to opportunities. These projects are driven by an expected increase in revenue. Marketing and advertising projects include queries for direct marketing campaigns, enhancements to screens to capture additional data, new product support, customer relationship management systems, and specialized reporting. Many tend to be short projects that are needed immediately. Because they are often small projects, the BA frequently plays the role of PM and quality assurance analyst in addition to being responsible for the requirements.

These projects often make use of existing data, exploring it for sales opportunities (referred to as *data mining*). The marketing group may want to target existing customers for repeat purchases or other product offerings. Marketing requests are typically queries with complex criteria. For example: "We want a list of students who have attended class A, have not attended class B, live close to one of our public class locations, and have requested a catalog in the past year." Analysts need to first ask the *why* question and then probe for even more criteria because marketing stakeholders frequently assume criteria without realizing it. The more an analyst knows about the data available, the better the questions that will be asked to completely detail the request. For example, the analyst might ask: "What about students who have tested out of class B?" Answer: "Well, of course we don't want to market to them!" When you hear a stakeholder say "of course," you are discovering an underlying assumption that the stakeholder has made that should be captured in the requirements because the SME expects that the developer will adhere to it.

For complex query requests, the analyst should not only ask questions to flesh out all of the criteria but should also review the results of the query before providing them to the marketing stakeholder. Initial query results often expose problems or challenges with the request that the analyst may be able to catch. Providing inaccurate data to the requester diminishes credibility and frustrates the requester. Carefully capturing the query criteria and reviewing the results will ensure the request is completed quickly and accurately.

Case in Point

A query request from the marketing department required several complex SQL joins (see Chapter 5 for the definition of SQL and join). Marketing asked for a list of customers who had purchased product A within the last two years, but had never purchased product B. My developer ran the query and sent the list of selected customers directly to the requester. The requester called me almost immediately and said, "There are too many names on this list!" After discussing how she knew that the list was too long, we determined a criterion that had not been included in the original request. "Of course I only want customers who are in the United States!" indicated to me that the requester had made an assumption that the developer had not.

Projects to Align Business Processes

Commercial off-the-shelf (COTS) software packages are used by many organizations to support business activities which are well defined and standardized. Rarely will you find a company developing its own accounts payable or receivable system. It would be a waste of corporate resources to "recreate the wheel" for these types of applications. These applications are well understood and performed fairly consistently by organizations in many industries. Other examples of well-defined business activities are human resource management and payroll systems, general ledger and bookkeeping systems, customer relationship management, sales force automation, and contact management. Since these applications are fairly consistent from organization to organization, many vendor packages are available to support this work.

When a project has been initiated to select and implement a COTS solution, your first questions should be: "Is this a well-defined business activity that we perform consistently with industry standards?" "Is there something unique about the way that we perform this work that will make it difficult to find an appropriate solution?" Be sure to think about whether or not this business area represents a competitive advantage to your organization because of the way that it is performed or structured. For areas that are unique and represent a competitive advantage, a COTS solution may not be appropriate.

Most organizations find that COTS solutions require some customization, development of interfaces with other systems, and significant maintenance resources.

COTS solution selection is analysis work that is similar to the analysis work performed on a software development project, but it differs in that the focus is on *finding* a solution that most closely fits the organization needs rather than *designing* an application that supports the business exactly. No COTS solution will fit perfectly into your organization. You are searching for the "best fit." There are three common techniques or requests used to aid in the selection process: Request for Information, Request for Quotation, and Request for Proposal. These requests are prepared by the organization interested in purchasing or licensing a COTS system. They are sent to vendors that offer systems in the application area needed. Each request is a formal petition asking vendors to respond.

These formal requests are used to make sure that all vendors are given an equal opportunity in the bidding process. This procurement process of sending a formal request and receiving formal replies was first used by U.S. government agencies and private companies that were concerned about employees showing favoritism to a particular vendor and wanted to have a well-documented explanation and justification for the selection process. It is not uncommon for vendors that are not selected to question the fairness of the selection, raising questions about discrimination. To avoid these accusations and possible legal action, most large organizations follow a structured process and have rules that strive to make the process as objective as possible (e.g., employees are not allowed to accept gifts from vendors over a small dollar amount, employees are not allowed to talk with vendors during the proposal process, and all vendor inquires and answers are written and published to other vendors).

A Request for Information (RFI) is a brief document that outlines the business problem or opportunity that a company is trying to solve and asks vendors to provide initial, general information about product offerings. Vendors typically respond by sending brochures, catalogs, and product descriptions. The RFI may be sent to many vendors, giving as many as possible a chance to participate in the bidding process. Often, some vendors will choose not to reply because their products do not meet the need or they do not think that they can support the customer on an ongoing basis.

The second type of request is a Request for Quotation (RFQ). This is a brief document asking vendors to provide a formal price quotation. This request is rarely used for COTS purchases and was created for bids on products that are standard from one vendor to another (i.e., equipment, supplies).

The third and most frequently used type of request is the Request of Proposal (RFP). This is usually a longer document that describes, in detail, the needs of the company. It asks vendors to specifically describe how their product will match the needs of the organization. An RFP is effectively a requirements package (see Chapter 7) that describes the needs of the business area. Creating an RFP and reviewing vendor responses for COTS systems are primarily business analysis work. An RFP may also contain requirements related to the contract (written by the legal department) or the procurement process (written by procurement), but typically a BA or PM is responsible for writing and assembling an RFP. An RFP includes a request for pricing of the system along with support costs. Support costs may include items like customization of features, training for software users, consulting on implementation/rollout plans, development of interfaces to other applications, ongoing maintenance changes, etc. An RFQ and its replies are used to formally compare the costs of various solution options and are used when contracts are developed between a vendor and a company.

STRATEGIC PLANNING

Projects are initiated for very specific reasons, and those reasons can be traced back to an organization's strategic plan. Strategic planning is an important activity for every enterprise. It is the development of a cohesive, long-term plan for the organization. Strategic planning may be performed for an entire organization or at a department/division level. In some large organizations, there are entire departments dedicated to strategic planning and measuring the organization's adherence to the plan.

Most junior to mid-level BAs will not be involved in strategic planning, but it is an important activity for all BAs to understand. You need to be able to read and understand the plan because it sets the direction for the organization. BAs should always be making sure that project work is moving the organization toward its strategic goals.

Senior-level BAs often participate in strategic planning. If this is an area that interests you, working your way up through the BA ranks in your organization is one way to get involved in strategic plan development or be part of a strategic planning team.

Ideally, all employees understand why the organization has a strategic plan, what the plan entails, and then must make sure that their work aligns with the plan. This is one of the ways that BAs distinguish themselves. Executives look for individuals at all levels of the organization who are able to look at the big picture and understand how day-to-day work supports the big picture.

Figure 3.2 provides an overview of the relationship between strategic planning and individual projects. In large organizations, strategic planning leads to the identification of

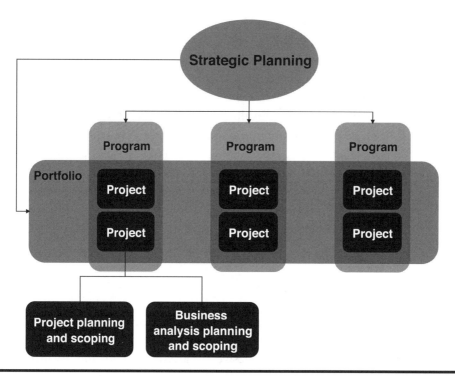

FIGURE 3.2. Example of a Strategic Planning Structure

programs within which most projects operate. Many organizations also use the concept of a portfolio of projects that are managed similar to the management of a portfolio of assets.

Portfolio and Program Management

A *portfolio* refers to a collection of projects and programs that an organization has identified and prioritized to support the strategic plans. A *program* is an ongoing strategic business initiative that supports multiple related projects. Programs and portfolios are two different ways to group projects together logically.

Portfolio management and program management are important terms that every business analysis professional should learn. These disciplines have grown out of the project management profession and represent higher level management of projects. Small to medium-size companies may not have formal portfolio and program management groups, but the ideas are still important. Projects in a program may be in various stages: some may just be ideas, some have been approved and funded, and some have been started and are in the process of being completed.

The goal of portfolio management is to review all of the projects on a regular basis to confirm that the organization is making the best use of its limited resources. Projects are prioritized, and higher priority projects are assigned more resources based on their needs.

It is important for the business analysis professional to know where his or her project falls in the portfolio priority list. If your project is a very-high-priority project, you will often be successful when requesting additional resources. Very-high-priority projects (with high expected benefits) may justify the purchase of requirements tools or new development tools.

If your project is a low priority relative to the rest of the portfolio, be aware that your resources may be decreased at any time. When a high-priority project needs more help, you or others on your team may be reassigned even though your current project is not done.

How Does Your Project Relate to Others?

It is important for the PM and BA to be aware of other projects that may be related to their project. Learn about projects that are already complete and impacted any of the same stakeholders or business processes. Learn about projects that are currently under way. Projects should share as much "corporate knowledge" as possible. Sharing information always results in a better quality product and often speeds project completion. This is one of the primary benefits of a corporate business analysis center of excellence or community of practice. BAs share corporate knowledge, including an understanding of the detailed business processes that are performed, descriptions of the information needed by each business process (data), business rules, guidelines, policies and constraints of the business, information systems (software), hardware and equipment, and detailed procedures and workflows (see Chapter 6 for information on reusing core requirements components). Spending a little time at the beginning of a project researching available corporate knowledge will pay off in time savings and, more importantly, solutions that are consistent and in sync with the rest of the organization.

Enterprise Architecture

One of the activities that may take place during strategic planning is development of an enterprise architecture. The enterprise architecture may contain more specific descriptions of the current environment and future plans. Examples of these architectures include:

◆ Business architecture
◆ Information architecture
◆ Application architecture
◆ Technical architecture
◆ Security architecture

Don't let all of these words and phrases confuse you. They are just ways for the organization to articulate the plan. Many planners use diagrams and sections to break up the plan into logical components that make it easier to review and understand.

The business architecture is the one with which BAs are most likely to be involved. A business architecture is a plan for where the business is going, or what the business should *look like* in the future. The word "architecture" has been borrowed from another profession where accuracy and planning are key components. To create a "business architecture," senior executives are asked to describe how they see the organization in the future. There are several ways that they can choose to describe these goals.

An organization sets goals at a very high level. No matter how large the organization, its leaders have some very specific plans and a direction in which they are moving the organization. This is also referred to as the *mission* of the organization. Ideally, all of the work done inside the organization is done with these goals in mind. Everyone understands the goals and is moving in the same direction. This requires that the organization leaders not only decide on the goals but also clearly communicate the goals and direction to everyone in the organization.

BABOK Connection	
Knowledge Area	**Task/Technique**
Enterprise Analysis	Enterprise Architecture

Business Architecture

A business architecture describes the current structure of an organization and outlines a plan for where the business is headed. The business architecture may be broken down into components such as goals, locations, products, etc.

Goals

What are the goals of the organization and/or its management? If a company is privately held, what are the goals of the owners? Identify goals for 0 to 5 years, 6 to 10 years, and longer term. This is one of the most critical components of the business architecture and strategic planning. Identifying and documenting these high-level goals and communicating them to the organization gives everyone in the organization specific information about the direction in which they should be headed. For example: XYZ Corporation will be the number one provider of telecommunication services around the world by the year 2020. Goals are usually documented in a bulleted list.

The Organizational Chart

What are the departments/divisions/business units of the organization? How are they related to each other? How do the senior executives imagine the organizational chart will change in the coming years? In other words, how many resources does management plan to add or remove? How will departments be structured? Will reporting lines be different than they are today? An organizational chart is usually represented by a decomposition diagram (see Chapter 6).

Locations

How many physical locations are supported? How many are anticipated in the future? Will the current locations still be used? If new locations are to be added, where are they? How will they be acquired and set up? Locations can be cities, countries, and/or buildings. Locations are often represented on a map or geographic diagram.

SWOT (Strengths, Weaknesses, Opportunities, Threats)

SWOT analysis asks participants to list the company's strengths, weaknesses, opportunities, and threats. Strengths and weaknesses are identified for the organization itself. Opportunities and threats are identified for the outside environment in which the organi-

BABOK Connection	
Knowledge Area	**Task/Technique**
Enterprise Analysis	SWOT Analysis
	Opportunity Analysis

zation operates. These components help to clarify where the company should look for growth opportunities (e.g., areas where the organization has a strength and there is an external opportunity). For example, if a company strength is providing consulting services

	Strengths	**Weaknesses**
Opportunities	Pursue opportunities that are a good fit with strengths	Overcome weaknesses to pursue opportunities
Threats	Use strengths to mitigate threats	Establish a defensive plan to prevent vulnerability

FIGURE 3.3. SWOT Diagram

in the insurance industry and there is an opportunity to work in the banking area, the senior executives may decide to offer banking consulting services. SWOT analysis is done using a four-grid matrix. Figure 3.3 shows an example of a SWOT diagram.

Products

This is a list of the current products and services offered by an organization. The list may include a description of each product, past sales volume, profit margins, etc. It is very useful to examine each product to determine if it is profitable or causing financial losses or if it is causing customer service problems or negatively impacting shipments of other products. Understanding which products are the true winners for an organization is critical. When working on projects to support and enhance these key products, team members know the importance of their work. Some products are "loss leaders." They are offered to get people into the store because of their low price and act as enticements to encourage customers to buy other products. Spending a lot of time and money enhancing these products may not be a good use of limited resources.

Information Architecture

Information or data is a very valuable asset of every organization. Over time, an organization collects billions of pieces of information about customers, vendors/suppliers, products/services, expenses, etc. The value of the information is directly related to how quickly a particular piece of data can be retrieved when needed. An information architecture is a plan for where the organization will store information so that it is safe, secure, and easily accessible. As you work on a project, you should always be aware of the data used by the project and where it belongs in the enterprise information architecture plan. The plan may not be fully implemented, but each project should work toward its fulfillment.

Application Architecture

This is a plan for an organization's application systems. It includes plans for maintaining legacy applications and strategies for replacement, plans for new applications and their interfaces, awareness of how new technologies may impact existing and future applications, and plans to support the expected business growth. The application architecture plan must be flexible enough to be able to evolve with the business. BAs should consult with the application architecture team at the beginning of large projects to make sure that all work is done in alignment with the plan.

Technology Architecture

The technology architecture supports the application architecture by outlining the strategic direction for brands and types of hardware, software, operating systems, networks, programming language, database management system, etc. that will be used. By having a long-term plan, IT departments are better able to obtain beneficial purchasing and licensing agreements with vendors and plan for periodic upgrades of equipment. This "IT road map" often includes an inventory of an organization's current equipment and software. This information is often useful during brainstorming for possible solutions. It is important to be aware of the available equipment when designing a solution.

Case in Point

An IT development team at an insurance company built a new client-server application for the company's independent agents to replace an old mainframe system. The new software utilized GUI (graphical user interface) components like drop-down lists, radio buttons, and auto-fill data entry fields (where a user types the first letter in an entry field and the software lists options that begin with that letter, which the user can select to save keystrokes). The team was very proud of the new application and eagerly awaited rave reviews from the agents. Unfortunately, as the rollout of the software to the agents got started, the team realized that few of the agents had PCs that could utilize the new software. Agents were unwilling to replace their old equipment because of the expense, so the application had to be rewritten to work with the older equipment. A simple review of the current technology inventory would have saved thousands of hours of development time.

Security Architecture

The security architecture outlines the plan for ensuring security of corporate assets like databases and business rules. It also plans for the protection of application systems by specifying backup, restore, and recovery plans. The security architecture typically includes common elements like individual PC protection, network security, user access levels, and employee computer usage policies. BAs should include the security officer in their list of stakeholders for most projects. Security officers should be consulted early in new projects so that security can be built into a project rather than retrofitted later.

Communicating Strategic Plans

Unfortunately, in very large organizations (and sometimes even medium-size ones), corporate goals and direction are difficult to communicate well. Corporate executives may have spent days or weeks working through a strategic planning session to develop these goals and then try to communicate them to thousands of employees throughout the world in just a half-hour employee meeting. Most employees have never really thought about what their organization's high-level goals might be, so when they hear them, they don't really make an impression. An individual employee in a large organization may wonder: "How can I have an impact when I am just one of thousands and such a small piece of this huge puzzle?" This mentality is one of the true challenges of managing a large organization: communicating corporate strategy successfully.

An excellent BA works to see the organization from the perspective of the corporate executives. Work to learn as much as you can about the strategic plan and direction of the company. Truly listen at those company meetings and ask questions. And then think about how your projects, no matter how small, will support the strategic goals of the company. You impact the bottom line goals of the organization. Every employee does. The more aware you are of these goals, the more focused your work will be and the more on target your requirements elicitation will be. You will also help your stakeholders keep the correct perspective when they have conflicts about how to handle specific problem areas.

Project Identification

Once strategic direction is determined, tactical or shorter term goals are determined. These shorter term goals will support the long-term, strategic plans. Projects to accomplish these tactical goals are identified and prioritized. As those on the planning

BABOK Connection	
Knowledge Area	**Task/Technique**
Enterprise Analysis	Define the Business Need

team complete the strategic plan and business architecture, they begin to see where the major problems are with the organization and where the biggest opportunities lie. These areas are where projects are often identified and outlined. BAs can assist in this project identification by examining the business architecture and strategic plan. They can help stakeholders by suggesting manageable-size projects.

PROJECT INITIATION

Ideally, a PM and BA are assigned to each project at its inception. The two highly skilled professionals work together to assess the project request, talk with the sponsor to understand the objectives, and bring the team to consensus about the scope of work to be done.

Realistically, there may be one person playing the role of the PM and BA or one of the roles may be assigned to the project before the other. Business analysis professionals must be very flexible and be able to come onto a project at any point. If you

BABOK Connection	
Knowledge Area	**Task/Technique**
Enterprise Analysis	Define Solution Scope

have a PM, work with him or her to scope the project. If you do not have a PM, be sure to initiate the project as a PM would, in addition to scoping the analysis work.

Naming the Project

Although most organizations put little effort into naming projects, a project name is actually very important. Think about projects that you have worked on. What did their names really mean? Did the name clearly describe the work that was done or was it the acronym for the software system being installed? Typically, projects are named by IT because IT initiates or owns them. When the IT department has already decided on the

TABLE 3.3. Examples of Project Names

Poor Project Name	Better Project Name
SAP Financials Implementation	Standardize Accounting Practices
CMRS (Corporate Meeting Room System)	Manage Meeting Room Usage
CCS (Call Center System)	Call Center Process Improvement

solution (and that solution is software), it names the project for the software. IT people love acronyms and clever naming schemes for projects.

BAs should help to adjust this thinking by influencing project naming when possible. The owner of a project is actually the sponsor and the business unit(s) for which the work is being done. The name should reflect the business's understanding of the project. In addition, since the goal is to analyze and understand the problem/opportunity and business before recommending a solution, the project name should reflect that goal. Name the project with a clear business name that describes the problem to be solved, the opportunity to be capitalized on, or the area to be analyzed. The name should have meaning to the business stakeholders and allow others in the company to also understand its purpose. Table 3.3 lists some examples of project names.

Initiation

When a project is initiated, it is important for the team to truly understand and agree upon its definition. In addition to its name, a project starts with a one- to two-sentence statement of purpose or description. A description of the project request may be supplied by the requester. The BA should work with the PM to more finely detail their understanding of the project. There are many approaches to defining and documenting project initiation and scope. When using an iterative development approach, where requirements and analysis work is revisited as the solution is developed (see Chapter 6 for more details), this work should be done before the decisions about specific iterations are made.

The components of a complete project initiation analysis are:

◆ Approach or methodology
◆ Statement of purpose

◆ Objectives
◆ Problems/opportunities
◆ Stakeholders (all SMEs and team members)
◆ Business risks
◆ Items out of scope
◆ Assumptions
◆ Scope of the business area (external interactions and high-level processes)

Project initiation work and the resulting documentation will vary depending on the importance and size of a project. A small enhancement project may only require a few minutes of thought and a few sentences. But even on a small and—what appears to be simple—project, the few minutes spent at the beginning will be well worth the time. The goal of project initiation work is to make sure that the project makes good business sense and that everyone on the team has the same expectations about what will be accomplished. The components of project initiation do not have to be learned or agreed upon in any particular order.

Approach or Methodology

This is simply an acknowledgment/description of how the project work will be done. It is a paragraph or two describing the overall approach that will be taken by the team. When an organization has a standard software development methodology with analysis guidelines, a project management methodology, or structured analysis road map, this section describes which path of the methodology will be followed and notes any variations that are anticipated. It may also include a description of requirements management software that will be used. The purpose of this analysis is to confirm with all project stakeholders the approach to getting the project done. The project initiation documentation may also include the *next steps* for the project.

Statement of Purpose

This is a short description of the project focused on explaining why the project has been initiated/approved/funded. It is the "elevator speech" that can be given quickly when someone asks you what you are working on. It should be written in business language and be at a fairly high level so that everyone in the organization understands the project goal.

Don't discount the importance of formally writing this description. It may be more difficult to write than anticipated, so several revisions may be necessary. The act of writing something down, reading it, and revising it forces analysis. Think about each word being used. Does it truly convey the meaning intended? Is it accurate? The project statement of purpose should not describe how the project objectives will be met, but it should clearly describe what will be accomplished. It may also include a sentence on the current environment or situation and should describe the main problem or opportunity being addressed. This is the one component of project initiation that must be formally documented. Even if no other document is produced, a project must have a clearly stated reason for its existence.

This description may be referred to as the problem description, vision statement, or project request. The larger and more complex the project, the longer the statement of purpose.

Most requirements work benefits from a glossary to define terms used during the project. Examples are provided in Chapter 6. As soon as a project is started, terms and phrases should be defined and agreed upon. Inconsistent use of terminology, especially at the beginning of a project, often leads to unclear scope definition and inadequate planning.

Objectives

An objective is a specific goal or outcome of a project. There are many great resources and tools to help PMs and BAs develop outstanding project objectives. Spending time clarifying these objectives with the business stakeholders is a valuable task. Objectives should be SMART—Specific, Measurable, Agreed upon, Realistic, and Time-framed.

Having written, clear, accurate objectives is important because they define the success criteria of a project. They also give the project team clear direction for project work. Project objectives, once approved by the sponsor, should be shared with everyone on the project team and reviewed frequently throughout the life of the project. This is a great resource for the BA if he or she starts to experience "analysis paralysis" (see Chapter 7) or gets overwhelmed by the work of eliciting, organizing, and analyzing requirements. Take a few moments to reread the project initiation documentation and focus on the objectives. Remind yourself why the project was started and what goals are to be accomplished. Taking a step back from the details (seeing the forest, not the trees) is an excellent way for a BA to regain perspective and to refocus his or her efforts on the most important requirements work.

TABLE 3.4. Examples of Problems and Opportunities

Problem	Opportunity
	Our competitors have Web sites to sell their office supplies online. We need to compete in this area.
We get many calls about store locations, product prices and availability, and order status.	
Our delivery department is not being utilized to full capacity.	Deliveries of both Web orders and phone orders could be combined.

Problems/Opportunities

As discussed earlier in this chapter, projects are typically initiated in response to a business problem or opportunity. At the beginning of a project, the business stakeholders often state a number of things that they want from the project (opportunities) or problems that they have. In many organizations, these are referred to as the high-level business requirements, but these items are not necessary requirements yet. They are raw and unrefined. They have not been analyzed or approved. These problems and/or opportunities should be clearly stated and included with the project initiation material. This is a place to give more details than in the statement of purpose about why the project work is important and how it will benefit the organization.

Table 3.4 lists some sample problems and opportunities. Note that every problem does not necessarily lead to an opportunity and every opportunity is not identified as a result of a problem.

Stakeholders

As discussed in Chapter 2, identifying and understanding project stakeholders is a fundamental task of the PM and BA. The list of stakeholders should be included in the project initiation documentation. An important component of scoping the project is knowing who will be involved and how many individuals will be participating.

Business Risks

There are two types of risks to be considered for a project: project risks and business risks. Project risks are potential problems/events that may impede the success of a project. These are typically identified by the PM and include things like a resource not being available when needed. Business risks are potential problems/events that may impede the success of the business with respect to the project. These risks should be identified by the BA working with the SMEs. It is important to understand these risks because they help to prioritize requirements, test cases, and implementation plans. When a business has a risk like "if the new software calculates taxes incorrectly, government penalties will be incurred," the BA knows that clearly eliciting and analyzing the tax calculations and rules are important. The risk also highlights the importance of thoroughly testing this calculation before implementation.

It is worthwhile to think about risks and formally document them on medium- to high-impact projects. Each risk should be clearly stated, along with the potential loss/result and a risk strategy. Contingency plans are also included. A great resource on risk is *Risk Management* (Mulcahy, 2003). See Table 3.5 for an example of a business risk assessment table.

TABLE 3.5. Sample Business Risk Assessment

Business Risk	Probability	Risk Response/ Contingency Strategy	Impact
Students who want to attend a class will not be able to register due to full enrollments.	High	Mitigate: By automating our registration process, we will have time to schedule more classes.	High
Students who are registered fail to show up for class.	Medium	Mitigate: Send a reminder e-mail a few days before class.	Medium
Instructors who are scheduled to teach fail to show up for a class.	Low	Avoid: Accurate, up-to-date schedules will always be available and training administration personnel will talk with each instructor before each class.	High

There are four main risk strategies:

◆ **Avoid**: Change the project to eliminate the threat
◆ **Transfer**: Shift the risk to another project or group
◆ **Mitigate**: Reduce the probability or impact of the risk
◆ **Accept**: Allow the risk to exist as is and develop a contingency plan

Items Out of Scope

This list provides a place to notify all stakeholders of specific items, requirements, features, objectives, etc. that *will not* be addressed by the project. It is important to get clarification on what is out of scope. This section is necessary when there are specific items that seem to be very closely related to the project scope and could easily be assumed to be included. Explicitly stating that particular items will not be addressed clearly sets expectations about these items and also tells stakeholders that the items/requests were heard and not ignored. Items are identified for this list during initial project discussions with the project sponsor and key SMEs. The PM and BA work together with the business area to develop a project scope that can be accomplished in a relatively short amount of time. Business people are not always aware of how long a particular requirement will take to develop and implement. They need to understand the organizational cost of each request, along with the expected time required to complete it. When armed with this information, they can make good business decisions about what to include in the project/iteration vs. what to leave out.

Assumptions

Another optional section of the project initiation is *assumptions,* or facts that are assumed to be true and will remain true for the duration of the project. A false or missing assumption can steer the project team in the wrong direction. People always make a lot of assumptions, and the PM and BA,

BABOK Connection	
Knowledge Area	**Task/Technique**
Requirements Analysis	Determine Assumptions and Constraints

with experience, will be able to discern which assumptions should be explicitly stated. For example, most American business people assume electricity will be available in their offices 24/7, but this assumption will rarely be documented and included in a requirements package. However, it may be an important assumption for a project in another country. An assumption such as "customers will continue to purchase product A in current quantities" might be included with project initiation documentation for a Web ordering project. Some organizations include *constraints* with assumptions. Constraints limit the solution, whereas assumptions are underlying circumstances within which the solution will operate.

Scope of the Business Area

The most important part of the project initiation work for the BA is a description or diagram showing the scope of the business area to be studied (also referred to as the *area of study*):

◆ Scoping the analysis area using a context-level data flow diagram
◆ Area of study
◆ High-level business processes
◆ Scoping the analysis area using a use case diagram

Scoping the Analysis Area Using a Context-Level Data Flow Diagram

It is important that a BA understands how to determine and document the scope of the area to analyze. Scoping helps set boundaries around the *area of study* and keeps the team focused. Since BAs are naturally curious and enjoy learning new things, having a well-defined analysis boundary is critical.

There are several well-established, useful techniques for scoping. One of the most effective is the development of a context-level data flow diagram. See Figure 3.4 for an example of a context-level data flow diagram.

This seemingly simple diagram requires the business stakeholders to answer several key questions and clearly articulate what part of the business is to be studied. BAs should be very familiar with this technique and be able to use it at a moment's notice. Even a project that appears small may have hidden complexities that will be revealed by using this analysis technique.

The power of the diagram is in its simplicity. Anyone reviewing the diagram can quickly learn and understand several important pieces of information about the project:

◆ Organizational units that will interface with the project (external agents)
◆ Existing enterprise applications that may require an interface to the project (external agents or interactions)
◆ Personnel, customers, vendors, etc. that will be involved with the project (external agents)

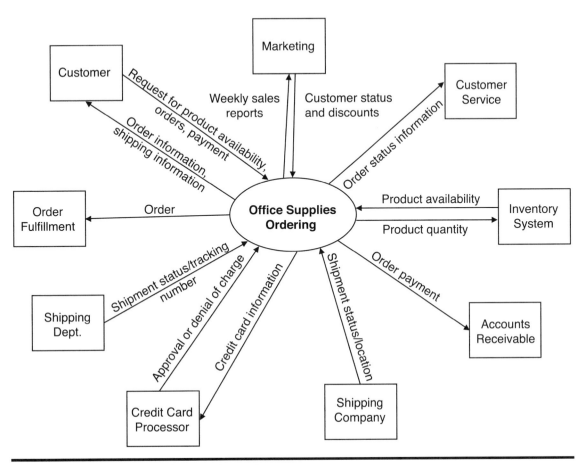

FIGURE 3.4. Context-Level Data Flow Diagram

◆ The name of the project or area of study (the circle)
◆ Information that flows into and out of the project (arrows)

Area of Study

Ideally, instead of thinking of the center circle in a context-level data flow diagram as *the project*, the BA should think of it as his or her *area of study*. This is a very valuable concept and something that many experienced analysts do naturally. True business analysis work starts with an understanding of the business. Ideally, that understanding is completed before a project is even started. How does an organization really decide to initiate a project before understanding the business needs and core processes? The context-level data flow diagram can serve to give the BA boundaries around which to analyze and understand. Obviously, no one has the time to learn everything in an organization, so some limits need to be put around the analysis work. A clear scope helps the analyst stay focused and not get overwhelmed with business modeling (see Chapter 6). The context-level data flow diagram provides the analyst with a clearly defined area of study and should not prescribe any particular solution or answer. It should guide the analyst and business SMEs in their learning about the business needs.

BAs will find this scoping technique much more challenging than it looks. It requires asking excellent questions and requires the business stakeholders to make decisions about what will (and will not) be included in the project. In most cases, the specifics of the project scope will not have been considered in this way by the sponsor or SMEs. The true value in using this technique lies in the development of the diagram, not the diagram itself. By asking questions about who is affected by the project and what information they provide and receive from the business area, the team thinks about the scope of upcoming work in more detail. Traditional project scoping performed by the PM does not usually include discussions about information flows and external agents. This is necessary to define the scope of the analysis work specifically.

This book will not explain the technique itself because there are several good resources that provide the details. See *Software Requirements* by Karl Wiegers (2003) for a complete explanation of this technique.

There are a few guidelines to consider when using this technique. Although the technique was invented for software design, a BA may use it at the business level to scope the *area of analysis* or *area of study*. This means that the project name (in the center circle) should be a description of the business area, not a software package name. This also means that external agents should be external to the business area, not just software interfaces.

Use care when discussing employees or business workers. If they become external agents, their job is assumed to be outside your area of study. This limits your ability to recommend changes to their processes and workflow. (See Chapter 6 for a discussion of external vs. internal agents.)

High-Level Business Processes

The context-level data flow diagram is an outstanding technique and provides numerous benefits to the team. It does miss one important component that should be added: high-level business processes. A *process* is an activity performed by a business that transforms information (data). (A more detailed discussion of processes is included in Chapter 4.) Processes may be named and described at various levels of detail. During scoping, high-level processes should be named and listed with the context-level data flow diagram. Only identify the top five to seven processes that are included in the area of study, and name each in such a way that it completely describes the work done in this area of the business.

Scoping the Analysis Area Using a Use Case Diagram

Another scoping technique is the use case diagram. Again, this diagram was invented to support software development, but a BA can use it at the business level. This technique is similar to context-level data flow diagramming in that it defines a business area and outside parties (called *actors* instead of external agents). When using this technique for scoping, a few high-level use cases are identified. Putting too much complexity into the scope diagram defeats the purpose of having quick agreement on the area of study (see Chapter 6 for more on use case diagramming). Figure 3.5 shows an example of a use case diagram used to scope an analysis project.

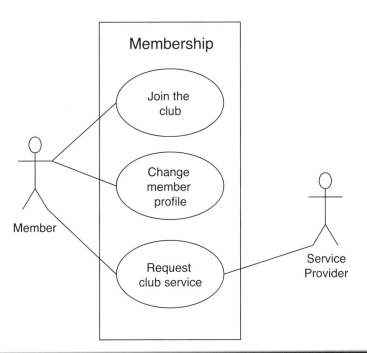

FIGURE 3.5. Use Case Diagram

The scope of the analysis area must be documented in some form, even if just on a flip chart. This is necessary because during analysis and requirements elicitation, the BA, PM, and business stakeholders will often start discussing requirements that are outside the project scope. Business people will talk about their work that is both inside and outside of scope because they don't think of their work in the context of any one particular project. The BA uses the scope diagram to remind himself or herself and the SME to stay on topic. This will keep everyone on the team focused on the agreed-upon scope. The documented scope should be formally reviewed and approved before the BA begins detailed requirements work. This is a very useful deliverable for business analysis planning (see Chapter 7).

Project Initiation Summary

Revisit Scope Frequently

Hang your scope diagram (context-level data flow diagram or use case diagram) on a wall in your office. Carry of a copy of it in your project notebook when you go to interviews and meetings with stakeholders. Periodically ask yourself and everyone on the team: "Are we getting outside of the scope of this project?" Keeping the project on track and within scope is something that PMs are very good at. BAs also need to learn this discipline. It is more difficult for analysts because they are naturally curious and want to make sure that every single requirement has been captured, but eliciting, analyzing, and documenting requirements that are outside of the true project scope are a waste of time. Don't get bogged down. If this is one of your weaknesses, force yourself to step away from project details at least once each day to ask yourself: "Am I spending time on the right things?"

Scope Creep

Although the meaning of this phrase is fairly obvious, it is important to think seriously about scope creep. It is natural to feel the urge to expand the size of a project. As much as PMs work to avoid additions to project scope, changes will occur. Think about projects that you have worked on in the past. At the end of the project, how closely did the result match the expectation at the beginning? If the answer is "barely," then the project initiation and scoping activities need to be improved on future projects.

There are a lot of valid reasons why scope creep occurs. As a matter of fact, you should acknowledge that there will almost always be some scope changes when planning project work. There will always be new information that becomes available during analysis that will cause you to vary from the plan. How will you handle the new information and how much do you allow the plan to change? This is the real question. Just because new information comes to light doesn't mean that it must be acted upon. It should be carefully considered and its impact forecast into the project. How would the project change if this new knowledge was incorporated? What will the impact be if the knowledge is ignored or not included? Does this new information give reason to believe that there will be even more new information exposed as the project moves forward? Was a major area/component of the business understanding missed?

Legitimate causes of scope creep are:

◆ The business changes while a project is under way (e.g., a new customer requests a custom product or demand increases or decreases suddenly)
◆ Outside regulatory change
◆ Analysis uncovers a part of the business that will be impacted but was not included in planning
◆ A new business stakeholder comes into the business area

One of the most important uses of a diagram to represent project scope is the visual reminder that it provides for the team. The scope diagram should be prominently displayed during requirements elicitation sessions and referred to often. When the group starts to get out of the project boundaries, reviewing the scope diagram will bring everyone back to focus. If a change to scope is requested and approved (via a change control process), update the scope documentation to reflect the change.

SUMMARY OF KEY POINTS

It is critical for the successful BA to understand and be able to explain why his or her project is important and why stakeholders should be excited about the ultimate goal of the project. Knowing the ultimate objectives of a project will drive the direction of the analysis work. As BAs learn about the reasons for project initiation, they may be asked to develop a business case, cost/benefit analysis, or feasibility study. A BA should also understand how his or her project aligns with the organization's strategic plans. BAs may not be involved in creating strategic plans or business architecture, but they must be aware of them and make sure that all of their work aligns.

Much of the work performed by a BA is within the context of a *project*. Some is not. Regardless of whether or not you are working on a project:

- ◆ You should know why the project is being done. The most important word here is *why*.
- ◆ You should always know what you and your team are doing to help the organization achieve its long-term goals.
- ◆ When you are faced with a situation where someone is recommending a choice that would not be aligned with the high-level strategic plan, you should be able to explain why this idea does not align and how it would negatively impact the organization as a whole. This is a great opportunity for a strong BA to shine.
- ◆ There are many reasons why a project is initiated, including a government mandate, response to competitive pressure, or a clearly cost-justifiable change. Most software development projects are being funded in the hope that productivity will increase and improved competitive advantage will be the payback. It is critical for you to understand why the project is being funded.
- ◆ Project initiation involves working with the project sponsor and PM to define the boundaries of the project and plan for its completion.

BIBLIOGRAPHY

Gartner Research (2005). Research Paper: Business Analysis Placement, Competencies and Effectiveness. Paper ID G00126718.

Mulcahy, Rita (2003). *Risk Management: Tricks of the Trade for Project Managers.* RMC Publications.

Robertson, Suzanne and James Robertson (1999). *Mastering the Requirements Process.* Addison-Wesley.

Wiegers, Karl (2003). *Software Requirements: Practical Techniques for Gathering and Managing Requirements throughout the Product Development Cycle.* Second Edition. Microsoft Press.

4

KNOW YOUR BUSINESS ENVIRONMENT

The title *business* analyst (BA) is so named to emphasize the importance of the *business* in analytical work. Understanding the business of an organization requires that the business analysis professional understand the products and services offered by the organization. Why does your corporation exist? To perform detailed analysis, you need an overall understanding of the business and the context within which you are working. You must understand how all of your project work ties back to the high-level corporate goals.

From the moment that you start work at a new company, take every opportunity to learn about the organization from the top down. Use time between projects to brush up on new products and services. Encourage your BA community of practice to highlight different organizational divisions and share information about various business areas. A BA is never without work; if you find yourself with spare time, use it to learn something new.

To learn about your business, start with the company vision and mission statements. A vision statement is an enduring reason for being and energizes stakeholders to pursue common goals. A mission statement describes the operational, ethical, and finan-

BABOK Connection	
Knowledge Area	**Task/Technique**
Underlying Competencies	Business Knowledge

cial guidelines of the organization. Most organizations with revenues over $1 million have a vision and/or mission statement. These statements have been developed by company owners or key shareholder representatives and tell an enormous amount about the business as a whole. In a well-run organization, every project should tie back to the corporate vision; otherwise the organization would not fund the project. Understanding the vision and mission is foundational for excellent business analysis. Everyone in the organization should always be working toward the organizational vision and mission, making sure that all work is in line with those goals (see the section on strategic planning in Chapter 3).

Case in Point

Google's mission is to "organize the world's information and make it universally accessible and useful" (www.google.com). Chevron: "At the heart of The Chevron Way is our Vision to be the global energy company most admired for its people, partnership and performance" (www.chevron.com). Starbucks: "Establish Starbucks as the premier purveyor of the finest coffee in the world while maintaining our uncompromising principles as we grow" (www.starbucks.com). These statements clearly set the tone and direction of each organization.

The BA should also understand the industry in which his or her business is operating. Your understanding of the competition, competitive pressures, and market forces will put you in a better position to make recommendations for long-term solutions to business problems. You should know where the industry is headed, what technologies are being used by other organizations in the industry, and what vendor packages are available that support your industry and business.

Part of knowing your business environment is being aware of the job roles of the stakeholders working in the business area. Do these workers have specialized training or certification to do their work? Have they been trained by the current organization or did they learn their skills in another organization? Understanding the background and experience of the business stakeholders improves your communication.

Finally, you must be aware of each business unit's importance to the organization as a whole. Is a department a mission critical area or is it a support area? Is it a profit center or overhead? Understanding the priority that the enterprise places on each particular business unit involved with a project helps you to choose how to spend your time and drives what types of recommendations to make. Review the corporate organizational chart and learn the reporting structures of the organization.

HOW DOES A BUSINESS ANALYST LEARN ABOUT THE ENTERPRISE?

Every organization and industry has unique complexities. Business analysis professionals work to learn as much about their industry and their specific organization as possible. Some industries require specialized knowledge (e.g., engineering, investment banking) and some BAs specialize in a particular business area (e.g., accounting, human resources). BAs can learn about their businesses by:

◆ Reviewing marketing materials
◆ Reviewing financial reports
◆ Reviewing the corporate strategic plan

Read the Company's Marketing Materials

There is no better way to get a foundational understanding of a company's products than reading what marketing materials say about them. Marketing materials have been designed by expert communicators who have a specific goal in mind. The goal of a particular brochure may be to create brand awareness or to reinforce the corporate image. Another marketing piece may be aimed at selling a particular product. Marketing materials show how the company positions itself to potential customers and against competitors. Study your organization's Web site and visit it frequently to review new content. The more the BA knows about the marketing message that has been developed for outside customers, the better he or she will be able to communicate with business stakeholders about products and customers. This knowledge is most critical for BAs assigned to represent business areas like sales, marketing, product development, and customer service. This is similar to the preparation work that you would do before interviewing for a job at a company.

This suggestion also applies to BAs who are working as external consultants. Before you walk in the door of your next client, visit the company's Web site and read everything that you can about its products and services. There is nothing more annoying to

BABOK Connection	
Knowledge Area	**Task/Technique**
Enterprise Analysis	Define the Business Need

business executives than an outsider who is hired to come in and help and doesn't even know the product or service around which the company is built.

Read the Company's Financial Reports

Publicly held corporations and non-profit organizations are required to provide financial statements to the public. These reports contain a wealth of knowledge, not only for accountants but for anyone working with or inside the organization. A BA should know how to review the basic financial reports and know their purpose. These basic financial reports include the profit/loss or income statement, the balance sheet, and cash flow analysis. If you don't have any accounting or financial knowledge, sign up for a class at a local university or read an introductory book. There are numerous courses on "finance for the non-financial manager."

Look at how well the company is performing in terms of profit, market share, shareholder value, and amount of debt. Knowing a company's financial situation tells you an enormous amount about how the business stakeholders will feel and behave. When a company is doing well, you will typically find an upbeat and optimistic attitude in most business areas. Employees feel secure in their jobs, they are being rewarded for the work, and their ideas are welcomed by management. Most stakeholders for projects will be glad to spend time with you because new projects are perceived as building the future of the company and they want to be a part of that work.

When a company is struggling financially, frequently you will walk into a situation where people are wary of why you are there. Employees may be fearful about layoffs or may have suffered pay cuts or received only small raises for a number of years. New projects initiated by management are assumed to be cost-cutting measures, which means that you are there to eliminate jobs. The BA who walks into this situation is wise to enter quietly and begin building trust, one stakeholder at a time.

There is other information that you can learn by reviewing the financials and also reading between the lines. Look at the overall size of the company compared to the size of your project. If the company has annual revenues of $40 million and you are working on a project budgeted at $100,000, your project is a small part of the organization's work. Alternately, if your project budget is $1 million, it will have a significant financial impact on the company as a whole. Knowing how your project compares to the organization's size tells you about its importance (priority) and will give you the facts you need to convince stakeholders that their time spent on the project is important.

Is your project specifically mentioned in the financial statement published to shareholders? If so, they will expect to see progress reported in the next annual statement. If the project involves some improvement in customer service, they will begin to look for signs of improvement. Announced projects are highly visible and have high business impact (refer to Chapter 7 for more on business impact).

Review the Corporate Strategic Plan

Read all of the documents that you can find about the company's strategic vision, mission, and plan (refer to Chapter 3). Often, the high-level plans are mentioned in the financial report. They may be available on an employee intranet system. What is the

BABOK Connection	
Knowledge Area	**Task/Technique**
Requirements Analysis	Organizational Modeling

company mission? How is that implemented? Your project, no matter how small, should be traceable back to a high-level strategic goal of the organization. Investigate; ask questions, read, and try to find out how your work fits into the big picture.

SEEING THINGS FROM THE BUSINESS PERSPECTIVE

Experienced BAs put themselves in the business stakeholder's position and try to see things the way the business sees them. This is especially important for projects with an IT or software component. Business people often have a very different perspective than IT people, and until you can put yourself in their shoes, you will never be able to really connect with them.

One of the fundamental concepts with which many business people are not intimately familiar is that of a "project." For many business areas, most work is done on a continual or ongoing basis. The same tasks are performed every day.

Case in Point

Each day, customer service representatives come to their desks, wait for their phones to ring, and then answer the questions that are posed. Most of the questions are ones that they have answered before. Some of the answers or problem resolutions may require a database search of a knowledge base or logging into a customer service system. A call log is updated. As each call is completed, the customer service representative has finished one task and is ready for another. When a rep is on a call, he or she is completely focused on that task. There is no multitasking in this role. At the end of the customer service representative's day, after the last call is completed, he or she leaves work with a virtually empty desk. The customer service rep does not have to plan what will be done the next day because every day is basically the same. There really are no projects going on in this business area.

Suppose that Bill, a BA, arrives to discuss the development of a new customer service call logging system. Bill wants to schedule interviews with all of the customer service representatives to discuss their needs. When would be a convenient time? The customer service reps acknowledge that the call volume is low on Friday afternoon, but the rest of the week it is pretty steady. If Bill wants to meet with a representative, it means that customers calling in will have a longer wait. Making customers wait goes directly against the department's goal of high-quality customer service.

This is only the first hurdle that Bill will encounter. Every time he has a question for someone in the customer service group, he negatively impacts their customer service goals. This makes the department less enthusiastic to see Bill as time goes on. In addition, if Bill's project goes on for weeks or months, many customer service representatives may wonder what he is doing. Why isn't he done yet? What is taking him so long?

Of course, this problem is easily solved when the head of the customer service department wholly endorses the project and lets everyone know that time spent with Bill will help the group reach a key departmental goal. This is one of the key success factors for all projects: management commitment.

Now take this scenario a step further. When Bill talks about implementing a new customer service support system, he will probably get a positive response since the old system has been determined to be inefficient or difficult to use. When the customer service representatives hear that a new system will be faster and easier to use, they will be very excited and anxious to start using it. This is when Bill has to break the news that the new system probably will not be installed for six months. He explains that he must thoroughly understand what they need and then make sure that the solution built matches those needs. Six months! Imagine what a customer calling in would say if a representative promised to answer his or her question in six months! That level of customer response is completely unacceptable to these business stakeholders. Some customer service representatives may feel that if it is going to take that long, why bother?

This reaction points out a fundamental difference between project work and operational work. Many business people respond to their customer needs immediately. Think about some of the business areas in your organization. Sales people take an order as soon as a customer wants to buy. The sales cycle may take a few weeks or even months, but during that cycle the sales person is constantly reacting to every customer need. The sale may include answering questions, preparing proposals, and delivering pricing and product information. The sales person is ready for the customer to request anything and then immediately replies. Think about the accounts payable or accounts receivable department.

When invoices arrive, the accounts payable clerk immediately logs them in, checks the due date, and makes sure they are paid on time. In the human resources department, a new employee is added to the system on the day he or she starts, if not before. All of these business people work on tasks as each task is received. They have been taught to respond to their customers as quickly and efficiently as possible. This approach to getting work done is very different from the way most IT projects are handled.

Prioritizing Requests

In IT, small projects or problems are addressed quickly. The help desk professionals in IT work exactly like the customer service representatives, handling calls as they come in. But when it comes to medium or large software development projects, work is done in a very different manner. Each request becomes a *project*. This difference, when not understood by the business stakeholders, will be a huge source of frustration. One of the first tasks in learning the business is to determine if the business stakeholders have ever been involved with a project and what their experience has been.

When a business person requests a change from the IT department, the request is rarely answered or completed immediately. Best practices in IT management dictate that all IT requests are reviewed and prioritized. Often a preliminary estimate is prepared. If the request is large, it may be presented to a governance board for approval. Typically a business case is developed. When the request is approved, it is prioritized against other outstanding requests and is scheduled when resources are available.

This diligent consideration of every request takes time. Requestors may not be adequately informed about how their request is being evaluated. Many business people feel like IT requests disappear into a "black hole." *Business analysis professionals must understand the differences in working styles between their business stakeholders and IT.* Learn the IT prioritization rules and practices and be able to explain them to the business stakeholders. Offer to assist the IT prioritization committee with cost justification for important requests. Be the advocate for the business to get requests quickly approved and scheduled. Most IT departments have more requests than they can answer, so properly prioritizing work is critical in providing the highest value to the business. This backlog is one of the reasons why agile approaches to developing software are becoming popular (see Chapter 5). IT recognizes that it has to answer business requests faster.

Ideally, BAs would have work experience in both the business and IT environments. Acting as a bridge between business people and technology people, BAs need to understand how both sides work. If you only have experience in one of these two environments, talk with your manager and consider working as an intern in the other group for six months or so.

Case in Point

Most of my work experience had been in IT departments when I started my first company. My work experience had all been project work. I was suddenly acting in the role of a sales professional. For me, working in an environment where I had to be immediately reactive to customer requests was very difficult. When I initially moved into this role, I did not return phone calls immediately. I prioritized and scheduled them around my other work. After losing several sales due to slow responsiveness, I learned that being responsive and reactionary is a very different mind-set from project work. I don't think that either situation is better than the other or that workers in one environment work harder than the other; they are just different.

BAs must be aware of these differences and prepared to discuss them with stakeholders. IT people get frustrated when the users are not available for testing. Users get frustrated waiting for software fixes that they reported months ago. A BA's job is to understand the source of these frustrations and communicate the reasons for the different working styles. There are very good reasons why a company has different departments and different working rules for each. Truly understanding these differences helps BAs to more effectively serve all stakeholders.

HOW A BUSINESS ANALYST LEARNS THE BUSINESS: ELICITATION TECHNIQUES

There are many techniques that business analysis professionals use to learn about the business, including:

- ◆ Review existing documentation
- ◆ Observation
- ◆ Interviews
- ◆ Surveys and questionnaires
- ◆ Facilitated sessions
- ◆ Focus groups

◆ Competitive analysis
◆ Interface analysis

BAs should learn and practice as many of these techniques as possible. Experience will help in determining which technique is the most appropriate for each situation. BAs should think about making the best use of their stakeholders' time. Choose techniques that are the most efficient and most effective based on your understanding of the individual stakeholders.

Review Existing Documentation

This is the best technique for BAs to use first. Reviewing existing material helps the analyst by introducing the terminology used by the business. It also helps the analyst formulate questions to ask stakeholders. Read system or software documentation, employee procedure manuals, policy handbooks, etc. Read anything you can find that might give you some insight into the business and most importantly the workers. Look at forms, screen layouts, and reports. A BA should not waste stakeholder time asking questions when answers to those questions are readily available in existing documentation.

When reviewing documentation, be aware that not everything you read will be 100% accurate and up to date. Plan to verify facts with stakeholders. Even when the documentation is incomplete or out of date, you will gain important information from reviewing it.

BABOK Connection	
Knowledge Area	**Task/Technique**
Elicitation	Document Analysis

Case in Point

When I started one of my jobs as an analyst, I was told that my first project was a rewrite of an old, purchased software package. As with any new job, the first few days were slow; I learned login procedures, filled out employee payroll forms, and learned the names of my co-workers. I browsed the bookshelves in the IT area and found an old, dusty binder titled with the name of the software system that we were planning to replace. I took the manual to my desk and reviewed it. It was the original user manual that the vendor had delivered with the software package many years ago. The pages were yellow and it was clear that no one had used this manual in a long time, but I didn't have any specific assignments yet so I read it—cover to cover. I learned much about the business itself; it was a mortgage origination system. I was exposed to terminology and learned the meanings from the usage and context. I learned about the core data elements from the screen layouts. I learned workflow from the procedure descriptions. Without intending to, I was learning the as is environment. I was aware that the manual was old and probably out of date, so I didn't rely on its specific information. I just used it to become familiar with the business area.

Later that week, I was invited to attend a project kickoff meeting where the project manager expected me to listen and learn about the project and meet the key stakeholders. They began to discuss the possible outcomes of the project and some of the problems with the old system. Since I had familiarized myself with some of the business terminology, I understood most of the discussion. I was able to participate and ask a couple of useful questions because I had just finished reading the manual. When I first spoke up, my project manager gave me a strange look, wondering what I could possibly have to say that would be of use in my first week on the job. But when I made a relevant comment and asked a specific question about the old system, the business stakeholders looked pleased. One of them later complimented the project manager on what a good hiring decision she had made by bringing me on board. I was able to start participating and bringing value to the project within one week of employment!

Observation

One of the most enlightening ways for a BA to learn about a business area is to work in or observe the work as it is being performed. This is easier for some types of businesses than others, but it is always worthwhile for BAs to see where their stakeholders work and understand a typical day in that role.

The first thing that a BA sees when observing work is the office setup or work environment of the stakeholders. Valuable information can be gleaned from simply being in the work setting. Does each employee have an office? This implies that the work requires individual or quiet time; it implies a certain status in the organization. It also tells you that if you want to meet one on one with someone, there is a space in which to do that. If employees have their own spaces, they may not interact with each other frequently. This implies that talking to one person about your project will not necessarily mean that anyone else will know about it.

Do employees sit in cubicles or in large shared spaces? Typically, these environments are noisier than offices. There are more visual and audio distractions. Employees don't have much privacy. Can they hear each other's phone conversations? Is it a fast-paced, active area or is it quiet and sedate? Do workers interact with each other frequently or not much? When workers interact frequently and can hear each other's conversations, word of the project will spread quickly—both good and bad news. Be aware that when you ask a question of one employee, others will know about it. They will anticipate you asking the question of them and may be more prepared. All of this information will help you to better understand how best to solve their business problems.

For workers in warehouses, factories, mail rooms, distribution centers, or other environments outside a traditional office, observation will be an extremely important source of information. Often, these employees are doing the primary work of the business that all other employees are supporting. Understanding the core business is so important that every employee of a company should have time to really see how products are produced and distributed. If you work for a shipping company, spend time observing the movement of packages (sorting, moving, and delivering) to get in touch with the core business. If you work for a manufacturer, observe the assembly line or production process. An understanding of the core business work helps you think about how users could be better supported by IT solutions and prevents you from suggesting changes that will negatively impact the work environment.

Case in Point

When inventory control systems (computer terminals) were first introduced in manufacturing plants, the workers had to type in part numbers, quantities, etc. Data entry is time consuming and error prone. Employees had to walk from the assembly line to a computer workstation to key in information and then go back to work. This slowed their productivity. Collecting data was important to management to measure corporate productivity and efficiency, but capturing the data, by its very nature, slowed productivity. This learning resulted in systems that are designed specifically for manufacturing environments. Scanners, interfaces to assembly lines and manufacturing equipment, and robotics all were developed to address the specific work environment where they were needed.

Observation may reveal that there are variations in how a process is performed. This is another reason why observation is an important elicitation technique. There may be as many as three different descriptions for a single process and a single worker: (1) the way the process should be performed (usually documented in a procedure manual), (2) the way an employee describes his or her process, and (3) the way an employee actually performs the process (seen through observation). When a worker performs his or her process, you may notice that he or she makes assumptions or performs steps that are not in the procedure manual. The worker may forget to tell you about these steps when describing the process because they have become second nature and the individual is not even aware that he or she is doing them. Beware of the possibility that employees may behave differently because they know that you are watching. Workers may follow an established procedure only because they want you to think that they follow it. Encourage employees to perform their work as they normally do.

Observation requires great patience on the part of the BA and the worker being observed. The BA should limit questions during the observation because interruptions may prevent a typical procedure from being followed. If you think of questions or comments during an observation, write them down and save them for a follow-up interview. If employees feel that their work is not very interesting, remind them that you are trying to learn as much about the business as possible, that their work is very interesting to you, and that they should try to work as they normally would.

When planning for observation, consider timing and business activities. Be sure to observe workers at all levels of the organization, performing all of the activities relevant to your project. Be aware of daily,

BABOK Connection	
Knowledge Area	**Task/Technique**
Elicitation	Observation

weekly, monthly, annual, and seasonal fluctuations in work volume and requirements. It may not be possible to observe the year-end process when your project is due in April. Plan more time for interviews around the activities that you are not able to observe.

Case in Point

I worked for an organization that provided emergency road service to customers having car trouble. When I was assigned to help rewrite the payment processing system for this business area, my IT director insisted that I "ride along" on a few of the emergency calls to observe the work being performed. I couldn't understand why I needed to watch cars being towed to be able to develop a payment processing system. It was winter in the Midwest and sitting in a tow truck in the cold for several hours held no appeal for me. My director arranged my "ride along" for one day in February. I don't have the space here to tell all of the stories from that day, but I can tell you that it was an education I will never forget.

Before the ride along, I drafted a new payment form that required the tow truck driver to fill in the VIN (vehicle identification number). This is a unique 17-character code, a combination of letters and numbers that gives a lot of information about the vehicle (e.g., model year, country of manufacture, engine type). I was convinced that this valuable data could be used for future analysis, like which models of cars were most frequently breaking down. A brilliant idea from a young, ambitious BA—right? Wrong!

One day sitting in the passenger seat of a tow truck dispelled that notion entirely. As we began to travel to help the customers who called, I saw that requiring tow truck drivers to find and correctly record a long series of digits in these conditions was unreasonable. One vehicle in distress was buried under 15 inches of ice. Chipping away at the ice on the windshield to find the VIN would have taken an hour! Another call took us to a high-crime area which was very desolate. We didn't want to spend any more time there than was necessary to jump-start the vehicle. I really didn't care about the VIN of that car! I asked one driver if he would mind supplying the VIN on his payment tickets, and he just looked at me and laughed. I also learned that on a busy day, some of these drivers work 16 hours straight digging cars out of snowdrifts and hauling them miles to the chosen repair facility. Taking time to fill in a lot of details on a payment form would slow the service to our customers.

In addition to challenges in getting the VIN, the drivers had to fill out these payment forms while wearing heavy gloves, during rainstorms and snowstorms, at night, etc. They just wanted to fill in the bare minimum of information necessary to get their payment and then move on. Our final design incorporated lists of items that could simply be circled and boxes to be checked. My ride along showed me that understanding the business environment was the key to developing a new system that improved rather than slowed the business process.

Interviews

Interviews are most appropriate for eliciting requirements with one or two individuals at a time. These conversations allow the analyst to learn about the existing business and/or talk about possible improvements. For an interview to be successful, the analyst must carefully plan the questions and the focus of the conversation. An interview can be as short as 15 minutes or as long as 2 hours. The analyst must estimate how many questions can be covered in the allotted time. Having reviewed existing documentation, the analyst can develop very pointed questions to confirm his or her understanding of the overall business functions. Then he or she can ask more detailed questions on a particular topic. Planning ahead is critical for conducting productive interviews.

The BA should prepare an agenda for each interview. It may not be necessary to share the agenda with the stakeholder, but it is critical for the BA to plan the order of topics to be covered and to estimate the time to be spent on each one. The agenda or plan must include a clear objective—what you are trying to accomplish during the session. For example: "I would like to come away from the interview with a clear understanding of why the accounting department categorizes vendors and the list of categories currently used." Without a clear objective, an interview can turn into a conversation, meandering in many directions and not meeting project needs. Stakeholders are very busy, so business analysis professionals must make the very best use of their time. When a subject takes longer than the allotted time, ask the stakeholder for another appointment. Don't assume that he or she can spend more time with you than originally planned.

To prepare for an interview, the BA should familiarize himself or herself with the individual being interviewed. Where does the stakeholder report in the organization? What is his or her title? How involved has he or she been with the project? Will this work be significantly impacted by the project? Is he or she a decision maker? Understanding the position of the interviewee allows the BA to develop questions that are at the proper level (see Chapter 2).

Note taking during an interview is extremely important. Few BAs are able to remember the complex answers given by stakeholders. Develop a note-taking system that allows you to paraphrase or "shorthand" the information. One useful technique is to listen for the core requirements components (data, process, external agents, and business rules, which will be discussed further in Chapter 6) and jot those components down. Even a BA with an excellent memory should take notes. Note taking lets the stakeholders know that responses are being heard and recorded. This is a signal to them that their answers are important and that you are listening carefully. These skills are discussed in Chapter 7.

Following up after an interview is polite and often yields additional information. It also allows the BA to confirm his or her understanding of the topics discussed. The BA can phone or e-mail a quick "thank you" and ask the interviewee if he or she has any more thoughts after the interview. Often, people will continue to think about the questions asked and may realize that they didn't completely or accurately answer. It is common to hear a stakeholder say "Oh, I forgot to tell you about . . ."

Asking stakeholders for any follow-up thoughts may result in a requirement for exception processing or an unusual business transaction. These are the types of requirements that may have been missed in past projects, costing organizations thousands of dollars in rework or production problems.

BABOK Connection	
Knowledge Area	**Task/Technique**
Elicitation	Interview

Surveys and Questionnaires

Conducting a survey or questionnaire can be useful when the sources of information are in different locations or the number of participants answering a given question is large. Surveys and questionnaires may be administered to internal or external stakeholders.

Surveys and questionnaires allow the BA to ask exactly the same questions over a large group of stakeholders, removing any subjective interviewing bias. They may be conducted formally or informally. Formal surveys are usually designed and conducted by a market research firm or department. The BA will work closely with researchers to develop the questions and possible answers.

Informal surveys can be used to confirm the analyst's understanding of a process, assess the impact of a change, or generate solution ideas. Informal surveys are used for a small number of people and require less preparation than more formal surveys. They also may be used for brainstorming ideas or getting an initial feel for the needs of the stakeholders.

Content and distribution are factors that require considerable planning if the BA expects a high rate of return and useful results. The layout of the form or screen sent to the participants must be clear and very easy to use. Participants must be told why they have been asked to participate and how valuable their responses will be.

The shorter the survey, the more likely participants are to respond. The questions should clearly relate to the survey objective and be focused on at most two subject areas.

Another way to increase the number of responses is to offer an incentive. An employee incentive may be as simple as: "You will be entered in a drawing to win a free lunch in the cafeteria." An incentive for an external customer might involve the opportunity to win a free product or service.

Typically, closed-ended questions (i.e., yes or no, multiple choice) are used to allow answers to be tabulated and reported quickly. They must be carefully worded to minimize ambiguity. Be aware that you are forcing the participant to choose an answer. Closed-ended questions are limiting and can

BABOK Connection	
Knowledge Area	**Task/Technique**
Elicitation	Survey/Questionnaire

lead stakeholders to an answer with which they do not truly agree. Most analysts "test" the questions on a few stakeholders before sending out the survey. A useful resource for designing surveys is *An Introduction to Survey Research, Polling, and Data Analysis* (Weisberg et al., 1996).

Facilitated Sessions

A business analysis professional who needs to learn information from several stakeholders should consider conducting a formal requirements gathering session. This session is designed to bring together people from different areas of the business to focus on one particular process or topic. They work together to build a shared corporate understanding of the process and may also work to develop ideas for problem solving solutions. These sessions were developed by IBM and were originally called Joint Application Design™ (Wood and Silver, 1995). The technique was developed around an impartial, trained facilitator who conducted each session with specific rules and leadership skills.

Webster's New World College Dictionary defines the word facilitate as *to make easy or easier*. This is a very nice way of explaining why facilitation sessions are often considered during project initiation and requirements gathering. To make requirements elicitation *easy or easier* is a goal toward which all teams strive. A facilitator is one who is a planner, designer, helper, instrument, or agent.

Facilitated sessions are not *meetings*. They are very structured, planned, working sessions where every participant is carefully chosen and has a critical role to play. Planning and preparing for a facilitation session is a significant task that if not done well results in a poorly run session and a huge waste of time for the participants.

Knowing when to conduct a facilitated session is very important. These sessions can be costly in terms of the number of participants and the time required. They should be scheduled and conducted only when there are more than two viewpoints that must be represented. Every business analysis professional must be familiar with the steps required to conduct a session successfully. Ideally, a new BA will be able to observe several sessions before conducting one of his or her own.

Facilitated sessions are an excellent technique for project initiation activities. The newly formed project team of business and technical stakeholders can come together to clarify understanding of the reason for and objectives of the project. In addition, the team can help to develop the scope or boundaries of the project. Bringing together project participants at the beginning of the project creates team enthusiasm and synergy. Everyone feels a part of the planning and decision making. They agree to "buy into" the project goals and will be advocates for change in their departments. These initial project kickoff sessions are even more valuable when the project sponsor starts the session by telling the group the reason for initiating the project and explaining its important business value to the organization.

Facilitated sessions are also useful for detailed requirements gathering and elicitation. A particular business process or set of business rules may be the focus of the session, with participants providing content for and review of requirements diagrams or models. These sessions can also be structured as brainstorming sessions where participants generate ideas for process improvements or new software designs.

Facilitated information gathering sessions are led by a facilitator who is usually supported by a recorder and a timekeeper. The session is carefully planned by this facilitation team. Topics on the agenda, participants, meeting location, and length of sessions are all carefully considered and documented.

Facilitated sessions are a great way for BAs to gather business requirements and help their business teams understand and articulate needs. Using facilitated sessions to gather and analyze requirements is a key task of many BAs.

It is important to recognize that a BA acting as a facilitator on his or her own project is not independent or completely objective, as traditional professional facilitators are. The BA brings his or her business area knowledge, understanding of techno-

BABOK Connection	
Knowledge Area	**Task/Technique**
Elicitation	Requirements Workshop

logical options, and understanding of the organizational environment to the session, making him or her not only the facilitator but also a valuable member of the group.

Why Use a Facilitated Session?

There are several reasons why a facilitated session might make gathering requirements easier:

- ◆ **Multiple vs. individual input**: As stakeholders listen to other stakeholders describe their requirements, they all may be reminded of additional requirements that might have been missed with one-on-one interviews.
- ◆ **Resolution of differences**: Individual interviews with stakeholders often result in different answers to the same question. This causes the BA to reinterview people to try to resolve the discrepancy. By using a facilitated session with

all parties involved together, the BA can help them discuss their disparate points of view. Often, these differences result from something as simple as different use of terminology or different assumptions. When a requirement is discussed by the group, these differences may be resolved quickly.

True differences in requirements are identified immediately and the team becomes aware of issues that will need to be addressed. The entire group recognizes that the ultimate solution must be able to address a variety of needs. When it becomes clear that stakeholders have conflicting requirements, the BA and project manager may need to adjust the project plan to allow time to address these conflicts.

◆ **Balancing priorities**: Different stakeholders often have different priorities with respect to requirements. Leading the group through a discussion of priorities will result in everyone understanding other stakeholder needs. The facilitator can direct the negotiation among stakeholders to arrive at one shared priority list.

◆ **Scope the project**: A facilitated session is very beneficial at the beginning of a project as a way to develop the scope or area to be studied. This session is planned and prepared by the project manager and the BA working together and can increase the likelihood of project success by having all of the stakeholders understand and agree to the project boundaries.

◆ **Team building**: As with any well-orchestrated group work, team members develop rapport with each other and become more vested in the success of the project. Teams often behave dysfunctionally at the start of a project. Participating in group sessions increases team cohesiveness and helps to create high-performing teams.

◆ **Process improvement identification**: Occasionally, as people from different departments talk about how they do their work and exchange experiences, one may learn of a different procedure or policy that could solve a business problem right away. These business process improvements often can be implemented before a project is complete.

Challenges for the Business Analyst as the Facilitator

Because the BA cannot be completely independent or neutral during a facilitated session related to his or her own project, he or she must be very careful when conducting the session. The BA must allow the project stakeholders to provide the requirements and keep them within the project boundaries. The BA also must lead the session in the direction that makes the best use of the participants' time and meets the objectives of the project.

This often means that the BA must allow the group to explore areas that he or she knows are "going nowhere," allowing group members to figure that out for themselves. However, if the BA sees that the group is heading in a completely wrong direction, he or she can "facilitate" the group back on the right path. This requires excellent communication skills and a good sense of group momentum.

One way to minimize the challenges faced by a BA acting as the facilitator is to use two BAs to run the session. One BA can act as the facilitator and the other as the scribe. This is referred to as *BA pairing*, where two BAs work together on a project. In the ideal situation, one BA would have extensive business area knowledge and the other would have an IT background. This pair of BAs would be able to listen to requirements, quickly identify the areas that need further discussion, and then tailor and refine their questions to lead the group in the most productive direction.

Focus Groups

Focus groups are sessions with randomly selected individuals who represent a particular demographic or viewpoint. These individuals are asked questions and for opinions relating to a very specific topic.

Focus groups are typically used for external customers to give feedback on consumer products. A few customers are selected to discuss current products or discuss new product prototypes and ideas.

Focus groups are led by professional, independent facilitators who are skilled at observation and listening. The facilitator does not participate in the group discussion and does not attempt to influence any opinions. These sessions are often held in a special location, convenient for group members. Some market research companies have focus group rooms with two-way mirrors for observation and/or recording capabilities.

BAs don't usually conduct focus groups on their own. They work with an experienced market research professional who conducts the sessions. The BA helps the facilitator determine the appropriate partici-

BABOK Connection	
Knowledge Area	**Task/Technique**
Elicitation	Focus Group

pants based on the type of information needed. The BA also develops specific questions for the participants and analyzes the results. If possible, the BA can observe the focus group live or via recording later.

Competitive Analysis

Another method for learning about the enterprise as a whole is competitive analysis. A BA should always be aware of the competition. Individual departments focus on external competitors to the extent necessary for their work. Marketing, sales, and new product development areas are extremely aware of the competition and closely follow competitive trends. A BA working with these business units must familiarize himself or herself with the competition. Recognize that competitive analysis may be less important in business areas such as accounting. The human resources department may consider its external competitors to be other companies which employ people with similar skill sets. IT departments frequently view foreign IT service providers as competitors.

As a BA, you must be aware of who your stakeholders consider to be their competition. You don't need to be an expert on all the competitive organizations, but you must be aware of them. Find out if your company publishes any regular reports on the competition and try to get on the distribution list. This will help you keep informed about competitive changes.

Who are your company's competitors? Does your project assignment involve direct customer or product impacts? If so, you must understand the products and services that your competition offers. Does the organization lead its industry with state-of-the-art products or is it an industry laggard? How does the company differentiate itself from its competitors? Often, you can easily find competitors and their products and services by doing simple research. Review competitive marketing materials, just as you would your company's. How do they compare? Where are there areas for possible advantages?

Competitive analysis is the most important technique for a product manager. Product managers who support externally sold products are responsible for making sure that their products offer value superior to their competitors' products by constantly staying aware of competitive changes. Product managers must be in constant contact with current customers, listening for suggestions and for problems with their products and jumping on trends as quickly as appropriate.

BABOK Connection	
Knowledge Area	**Task/Technique**
Enterprise Analysis	Competitive Analysis and Benchmark Studies

Interface Analysis

When a project is intended to provide a technical solution, it frequently will need to interface or communicate with existing systems. Very few business systems operate in a vacuum. Interface analysis is a technique for identifying interfaces that may impact or be impacted by the current project and planning the changes necessary to smoothly integrate the new solution into the existing environment. Identifying existing interfaces

BABOK Connection	
Knowledge Area	**Task/Technique**
Elicitation	Interface Identification

also helps to identify stakeholders that use and support those interfaces. They will be important subject matter experts as you work to design the changes. Ideally, interface analysis will be done using system documentation and procedural manuals, but if these documents are not up to date, traditional requirements elicitation and analysis must be used. When the existing system involves software, you may want to use reverse engineering tools to derive a logical understanding from the actual program code.

LEARN THE CURRENT (AS IS) SYSTEM

A very common question among BAs at the beginning of a project is: "Should I learn and document the current business procedures before I start looking for a solution to the problem?" This is an excellent question that should be part of the business analysis planning work (see Chapter 7) on every project. The answer is not simple or straightforward and will differ depending on the project characteristics.

First, the BA must understand the business area in detail before even thinking about making any solution recommendations. One of the worst mistakes that a BA can make is to tell a stakeholder how to fix a problem when he or she doesn't really understand it. The stakeholder will be annoyed and lose faith in the BA. Think of how you would feel when you have been struggling with a technical problem for several hours and the person at the help desk suggests that you reboot the computer. You tried that in the first five minutes and know that it won't help!

Do whatever you need to understand the business as quickly as possible. If that means drawing workflow diagrams of current procedures, draw them. The diagrams may be rough, handwritten drafts, just

BABOK Connection	
Knowledge Area	**Task/Technique**
Elicitation	Reverse Engineering

enough to aid in learning and to generate follow-up questions. If you learn through understanding information or data, sketch a data model. If the business area has complex rules, make a list of business rules. The document/diagrams are the means to an end—

your understanding. Once you truly understand the current environment, these notes may simply be filed away. Remember that the business system is more than just the software. Sometimes an analysis of the existing software is needed. This is referred to as reverse engineering.

A second consideration is whether anyone other than the BA needs to understand the current procedures. If the answer is yes, then you need to produce some professional deliverables from this activity and plan carefully around what those deliverables should be. See Chapter 6 for suggestions on deliverables.

There are several reasons why a project team might decide to formally document the current or as is business system:

◆ Having a clear definition of the old procedure along with the new will help the organizational change specialists understand the extent of the change and its ramifications.
◆ It highlights processes that need further analysis by identifying gaps and problems.
◆ A clear solution has not yet been identified, so alternative solutions will be compared to the current state.
◆ During an interim period, the old system may continue to be used in conjunction with the new.

When you have the opportunity to brainstorm on possible solutions and make recommendations, be sure that you completely understand: (1) the core business requirements and (2) the current *how*—the system and procedures currently used to accomplish the work (see Chapter 6 for the core requirements components). Understanding the core business needs independent of how they are currently performed allows for creativity in solution brainstorming. Understanding the current procedures prevents you from redesigning the same system.

On the other hand, there are some analysts who are strongly against learning the current system. There is a concern that once you understand the current system, you will be unable to creatively design an excellent system.

Case in Point

I once was assigned to redesign a customer management system. The existing software was almost 20 years old and had been patched and updated thousands of times. In initial discussions with the business stakeholders, the IT manager became concerned that the project team would end up simply rewriting the existing system. Most of the organization had been using the old software for so long that everyone used its terminology and accepted its limitations as if they were business rules. The IT manager instructed the analysis and design teams not to look at the old software. She instructed us to elicit the true business requirements independent of the current how and design a brand new system that would support the business and allow for future flexibility. This was a challenging task because it felt natural to learn the business by learning the old system. It was also difficult because, as the IT manager predicted, all of the business workers understood the business through their use of the old software. We asked a lot of questions and worked to pull out the core or essential business needs (see next section) and designed a brand new software application. It expanded the capabilities of the entire company because we had ignored the limitations of the old system.

WHAT IS A BUSINESS PROCESS?

Many organizations use the phrase "business requirements" to mean high-level goals of the business. Excellent business analysis requires that business requirements, and in particular business processes, be analyzed at a much more detailed level. Analysts should work to understand as much detail as possible about each business process. These detailed business requirements should be documented in a business model that can be reused for future projects. This will be discussed further in Chapter 6.

To understand a business, you must understand the work that is performed. This work can be defined as a *business process*. There are as many different definitions for the word *process* as there are BAs and consultants! Most agree that a process is an activity—a verb—something that an organization performs. Since the word *process* and others close to it (activity, function, task, and even business use case) are used so inconsistently, the BA must be able to hear these words used inconsistently and interpret their meaning from the context within which they are used. The terms used to describe business activities and processes have subtle differences that are often lost when people don't understand what the original author/methodologist intended. Table 4.1 gives the proper usage and examples of terms commonly used to describe business processes.

Ideally, the BA will help an organization come to a common agreement on how the word *process* is used. Even in an organization with only 5 to 10 people, there will be inconsistent uses, so it is best to get comfortable with the inconsistency as opposed to

TABLE 4.1. Business Process Terms

Term	General Usage	Examples
Function	Generally considered higher level than a *process*. Functions are ongoing activities of the business. Names are usually nouns.	Human resource management, marketing, finance
Process	This can mean anything from a very high-level activity in the organization (e.g., *sell product*) to a low-level, detailed activity (e.g., *record order*). Some people use *process* to describe *how* work is done, and others use it to describe the goal of the work. Some use it to describe how software is developed (Rational Unified *Process*®). In business process management, it may be a high-level business transaction being managed across the organization. Names are usually verb-noun phrases. Processes should be named from the perspective of the business.	Receive order Validate order
Subprocess	A portion of a major process.	
Activity	Used interchangeably with *process, task,* or *procedure.*	
Task	Generally considered a lower level sub*process*. A task is usually defined as an individual unit of work that can be accomplished by one business worker in a short period of time. Names are verb-noun phrases.	Add new account
Procedure	Step-by-step activities that define how work should be done. Often, procedures are considered manual tasks (not entirely supported by software).	New employee procedure, hiring procedure, file a claim procedure
Use case	Defined as a *goal* of the business. The term use case is used inconsistently—some analysts define very high-level use cases, some (more technology-oriented analysts) define them as very detailed, and others create multiple levels. They are named from the perspective of the actor (person for whom the goal is desired). See Chapter 6 for more information.	Place order
Event	Something that happens—and causes the business to react. There are several types of events, primarily external and temporal. These requirements components are used in a technique called event partitioning. This will be discussed further in Chapter 6.	Customer requests product

trying to fight it. The way to deal with inconsistency is by listening carefully, asking clarifying questions, and always speaking precisely. These are things that BAs do very well anyway!

When learning about a business area, choose the terms that you will use from Table 4.1 and use them consistently. Make sure that other analysts on your project use the terms in the same way. If your organization has not used these terms in the past, include them in the project glossary.

BABOK Connection	
Knowledge Area	**Task/Technique**
Requirements Analysis	Specify and Model Requirements

Essential Analysis

In 1984, McMenamin and Palmer wrote a landmark book called *Essential Systems Analysis* in which they refined work on structured design developed in the 1970s (Stevens et al., 1974). It was radical at the time because they suggested thinking about "systems" independent of technology—the *what* vs. the *how*. Although they didn't use the phrase *business requirements,* they effectively recommended an approach to analyzing the business before designing the technology.

This conceptual approach to analysis is still the best approach for business analysis. Business analysis is about analyzing *the business,* not software or technology. The analyst should look at the business through "glasses" that filter out the technology. McMenamin and Palmer used the concept of perfect technology to help analysts don these "glasses."

Perfect Technology

The concept of perfect technology was developed to help analysts understand and analyze a business process—independent of *how* it might be done (McMenamin and Palmer, 1984). Perfect technology implies that there are no limitations and the business process can be built to be ultimately efficient and effective. To use this technique, the BA and business stakeholders imagine a perfect world within which the business process is performed. They *assume* the following:

- ◆ No storage limitations or constraints (infinite storage is available)
- ◆ Completely error-free processing is available
- ◆ No performance limits or constraints (infinite speed is available)
- ◆ Technology is available at no cost (unlimited funds are available)

When a business process is looked at free of these limitations, a very different perspective is revealed. By imagining a business process in its purest or most *essential* form, the analyst can name and describe the true business process without technological limitations.

No Storage Limitations or Constraints

When McMenamin and Palmer defined the concept of perfect technology, it was radical. In the 1980s, storing data in a computer system was costly. Over the years, storage costs have decreased so dramatically that this assumption is almost true. There are few limits on electronic storage capacity. The importance of this assumption is to remove an artificial IT constraint when analyzing the business. As a BA asks questions about business processes and the data that support them, he or she should never say "Oh, we don't have room to keep seven years worth of history." If the business requirement involves keeping historical data, it will be kept in some form. There are many data archive options. The analysis that should take place around data storage is learning why the data is important, how often it will be accessed, and by what criteria it will be searched. Working to define the best place to store the data and the best way to retrieve it keeps the analyst focused on the true business need as opposed to limiting the solution.

Case in Point

Mortgage applications, appraisals, and underwriting approval forms must be maintained through the life of a mortgage plus 7 years to comply with U.S. tax regulations. For a 30-year mortgage, this requirement is 37 years! For a mortgage servicing company with thousands or millions of loans, this requirement translates to a huge amount of paper. Solutions have focused on efficient boxing strategies, microfiche, and document management systems. Over the years, the core business requirement has not changed. Understanding this core requirement allows the analyst to imagine many solutions using current and future technology. Scan the documents and store them on DVDs? Copy digital images onto microchips?

Completely Error-Free Processing

This assumption, unlike storage limitations, has become more difficult to imagine as systems become more complex. It allows analysts to describe processes and consider creative business solutions without being concerned about whether or not they can be built properly. This assumption is very important when a BA is analyzing a very complex business area.

Case in Point

I was recently involved in analyzing a complex scheduling process that was being performed manually by a brilliant scheduler. When asking him to articulate exactly how he made decisions and judgments about which worker to assign to each unit of work, we initially worried that we couldn't create software logic that would accurately make the same decisions. It was natural for the software developers in the room to begin to suggest changes to the scheduling model to make it easier to automate, but we stayed with the discussion, assuming that we could build in the complexity as long as we completely understood it. Much of the scheduling complexity is now automated. This decreased corporate risk that only one person knows the business rules.

No Performance Limitations

This assumption requires the analyst to imagine the business process being implemented in such a way as to completely support the business regardless of the response time needs. For example, suppose a customer service representative says that he needs the customer account and history immediately available as he picks up the phone for that particular customer. Is it possible with current technology? In a perfect world, how would this be done? This assumption says that it doesn't matter if it is possible—it is a requirement. Using this assumption frees the analyst and subject matter expert to truly discover the requirements with respect to time and be aware of those requirements going forward. The ideal performance desired may not be possible, so it should be made clear to the business people that the team will negotiate something that is feasible.

Technology Is Available at No Cost

This assumption allows the analyst to think about possible solutions without being constrained by cost. Costs include purchasing technology, along with the people costs to design, develop, implement, and maintain the technology. Allow yourself to imagine the best solutions available. Once the ideas have been generated, the team can consider each one with realistic financial constraints.

Case in Point

One of my projects for a mortgage servicing company involved selecting individual mortgages (referred to as "loans") to place into mortgage pools. This activity was being done manually because everyone assumed that it would be too difficult and too costly to develop software to make the selection. We decided to suspend those constraints during a brainstorming/analysis session and just talked about how the portfolio manager makes the selection. First he looked for loans that had the interest rate desired by the pool. Then he looked at the loan type (FHA, VA, or conventional) because each pool was only allowed one type. Then he looked at loan amounts because each pool had an ideal total dollar maximum.

As we looked at each selection criterion, we realized that most of them would be very easy to automate by relatively simple programming queries. The data elements were all available and the selection parameters were fairly straightforward. There were pieces of the task that we could not easily automate, like reviewing the underwriting package to be sure that the repayment likelihood was high. We were able to develop an online function where the user entered the ideal pool parameters, the software selected and listed the loans that met the criteria, and then the user made the final decisions about which loans would actually go into the pool. We saved the user hundreds of hours of work by allowing ourselves to suspend reality for a few minutes and imagine perfect technology.

Summary of Perfect Technology

Perfect technology can be very useful for an analyst who comes from an IT background. Sometimes BAs get focused on *how* to fix a problem before completely understanding it. Another reason why these assumptions are important to understand is that many subject matter experts assume them naturally. People who have not been intimately involved with technology assume that it works correctly, is infinitely fast, and has no limitations.

On the other hand, as users become more and more experienced with software, and see its true limitations, they may have a hard time imagining perfect technology. A subject matter expert may unconsciously limit his or her own requirements because he or she doesn't think that technology will be able to support them. This limiting of requirements is exactly what BAs are trying to avoid. It is critical to elicit the true, full requirements even if you know that they can't completely be fulfilled at the time. Technology continues to evolve, and using one's imagination about what may be possible leads inventors to create even more sophisticated products. As an analyst, it is critical that a BA understand the way stakeholders think, since it influences the way they communicate. Also, make sure that the requested requirements are truly requirements.

The one caution about using these concepts of perfect technology is setting user expectations too high. No organization has perfect technology. The assumptions are used to facilitate analysis and help to get to the true requirement. Users must understand that once the requirements are understood, the team will determine the best solution based on known technology capabilities and the project budget. This will involve getting collective agreement on which requirements are included in the solution scope. As the solution is designed, the BA will keep subject matter experts informed about any requirements that may have to be compromised. For example: "We can display the customer's account history as soon as the telecommunications system identifies the customer phone number—but it may take as long as 10 seconds to display. Is this lag acceptable? Or we could display the most recent activity (last 6 months) with the rest of the history on another screen."

Essential Business Processes

An essential process is a core activity of a business that is described independently of how it is performed. These *core, essential* processes describe the business objectives and work in a way that remains relatively consistent over time. For example, one of the essential processes of a bank is to *accept deposits*. Over the history of banking, deposits have been accepted in many different ways: cash carried into a branch of a bank, funds wired from another bank, direct deposit from payroll systems, etc. Regardless of how this business activity is performed, it is and always will be an essential business process of the organization.

Much business analysis work depends on the ability to identify and clearly define processes. To understand the business architecture, BAs should look at the essential business processes. Business process improvement is performed by looking at how work is done in a business area and then pulling out the essential processes to find more efficient procedures to accomplish each one.

Case in Point

I recently met a man who is a business process analyst. I spoke with him about a new job opportunity that he was considering. He said that he didn't know what software application the company uses, but that it doesn't matter. He has specialized in the distribution business and enjoys coming into new organizations, observing their current procedures, and making

TABLE 4.2. Differences Between a Process and a Use Case

Process	Use Case
Business activity	Goal of the system needed by a particular actor
Named with a verb describing the work performed by the business (*validate order*)	Named with a verb describing the action taken by the actor (*place order*)
Defined without reference to who performs it	Tied to a specific role (the actor)
Defined so that it could be performed by any business worker and/or an external customer/supplier/vendor	Designed to be executed by the actor (often specified as a *conversation* between the actor and the software)
Always defined as independent of specific procedures or technologies	Business use cases may be independent of technology; system use cases describe how the software will support the activity

recommendations. He said to me: "You get an order, you pack it, and you ship it. How difficult can it be?" He had just named the essential processes in his business area. This was not meant to minimize the complexity of the distribution process. After working at many different companies, selling many different products, using different inventory and shipping software systems, he recognized that the core business processes are the same.

What Is the Difference between a Process and a Use Case?

Use cases have become very popular and are used by some project teams instead of processes or even in lieu of any other requirements components (see Chapter 6). Be sure to understand how your organization uses these requirements components. Because processes are defined independent of the *who* and *how*, they are more easily reused and allow for more design flexibility. Table 4.2 lists the differences between processes and use cases. Both should be defined independent of any current organizational structure or title.

Describing a Process

As each business process is identified and named, detailed questions should be answered about why it is done, what information it uses, and what business rules constrain or guide it. The successful analyst will delve deeply into each essential business process to make sure that its purpose and fundamental value to the organization are captured. Many of these questions may be difficult for subject matter experts to answer. The analyst must work with the business stakeholders to talk through the *whys* and *whats* of the process because only a deep, thorough understanding will give rise to improvements. By discussing each process in detail, the business subject matter expert thinks about the work in a new way. Often during analysis work, the subject matter expert comes up with a process improvement idea. This occurs because the process is being examined from a different perspective. Figure 4.1 is a template for describing a business process.

Naming processes is important yet is often done carelessly. Names should be chosen to accurately communicate the activity of the business (verb-noun), so that when the process is shown on diagrams, it is immediately recognizable. Process names should describe the *what,* not the *how.* Analysts can use the assumptions of perfect technology and the business glossary to help determine good business names.

Strong verbs to use in process names include:

- ◆ Accept
- ◆ Add
- ◆ Calculate
- ◆ Capture
- ◆ Communicate
- ◆ Delete
- ◆ Dispatch
- ◆ Generate
- ◆ Place
- ◆ Prepare
- ◆ Provide
- ◆ Receive
- ◆ Record
- ◆ Remit
- ◆ Request
- ◆ Send
- ◆ Submit
- ◆ Tabulate
- ◆ Update
- ◆ Validate
- ◆ Verify

Process ID:	1.a.i
Process name:	Add/update customer information
Detailed description:	This process accepts customer information and records it in our business area.
External agents involved:	Customer
What causes the process to occur?	Customer contacts Customer Service to place an order, change an order, cancel an order, request a catalog, or for any other inquiry.
What happens after the process is complete?	If a new customer has been added, then a catalog is sent immediately.
Business rules:	◆ If the customer does not exist in the database, then add all required customer information. ◆ If the customer is already in the database, then verify that the information is correct and make any necessary changes. ◆ If a customer is an organization, then there must be a contact person's name.

Data (attributes):	CRUD	Source
Customer name	CRU	External agent: Customer
Customer number	C	Internally created
Customer contact name	CRU	External agent: Customer
Customer contact phone number	CRU	External agent: Customer
Customer contact e-mail address	CRU	External agent: Customer
Customer mailing address	CRU	External agent: Customer

Additional notes:	
Information source:	Mary Smith

Functional requirement—AS IS	
List the group(s) that currently performs this process:	Customer Service
How is the process currently performed?	An online inquiry/update screen accesses a customer database.
Who uses the output?	Order Fulfillment, Shipping, Accounts Receivable, Marketing

Metrics (only required if the process is a candidate for re-engineering):	
How often is the process performed currently (i.e., daily, weekly, monthly)?	Daily
How many occurrences of the process are completed within the above time frame?	100
How long does it take to perform the process in the current environment (specify minutes or hours)?	1 min
Efficiency rating (1 to 5, 1 is lowest):	4

Functional requirement—Suggestions/notes for TO BE	
Anticipated future changes?	Customers should be able to update their own information via the Web site.
List the group(s) that may perform this process:	Customer via the Internet
Desired time to complete process (specify minutes or hours):	1 min
Anticipated future volume:	100–200 per day
Implemented in use case ID(s):	

FIGURE 4.1. Business Process Template

In addition to a strong, clear name, a description of the process must also be written. A name can only convey the basic information about what type of activity (the verb) is being performed on what type of data (the noun). A few sentences will elaborate on this name, providing all stakeholders with a clear, consistent understanding of the process. This description should explain why the process is important.

Analyzing a process includes understanding which, if any, external agents (organizations, people, and systems) interact with it. Most processes are performed in a business because an external agent has requested something. Understanding which externals are involved with each process provides additional information about why a process is performed.

During process analysis, it is important for the analyst to ask questions about sequence. What happens before this process (i.e., what *triggers* it)? What other processes are triggered by the completion of this one? And most importantly, why are processes performed in this order? One of the common mistakes made by new analysts is assuming that the current order of work is a *requirement* and must be maintained. This assumption locks the business into its current procedures and leaves little room for creative new solutions.

Each process must be examined for business rules. There will not always be a rule for every process, but most processes are guided by some type of a constraint (e.g., invoices are paid on the 15th and the last day of each month). As you are identifying business rules that are used during a process, think about whether each rule may also be used by another process. These shared rules should be defined consistently and their descriptions reused to save analysis time. Business rules will be discussed further in Chapter 6.

For each process, the analyst should think about the individual data elements needed to successfully perform it. These data elements may (1) come into the process from an outside source, (2) be created by the process, or (3) be retrieved from a storage facility (filing cabinet, database) inside the business. Businesses store a lot of data so that processes can use them whenever needed (e.g., customer addresses are stored in a database so that customers are not asked for their address every time they place an order). Process analysis includes verification that all of the data elements needed by a process are available to it. The importance of data requirements will also be discussed in Chapter 6.

While analyzing, naming, and documenting essential business processes are important work of the BA, understanding *how* a process is currently performed can sometimes be just as important. Often, when you are asking stakeholders questions about the core business activity and working to understand it independent of current technology limitations, they want to talk about the *how*. They feel that it is important for you to know, step by step, how they perform this business process. Listen carefully and make the notes that you need. Listen for gaps in the process or between processes. If you know that the technology currently supporting the process will be changing, understanding details about the current *how* may not be critical. Listen for problems and complaints to make sure that the new design will address the issues.

In addition, make notes about metrics. How long does the process take? How many times is it performed? Make sure you also understand who currently performs the process and who benefits from it. All of these things may change as your team brainstorms about alternative solutions. Understanding *how* the work is currently done prevents you from redesigning the same system. Finally, when talking with stakeholders about a process, listen to their suggestions for changes. They may have some great ideas about how the process could be made more efficient.

When the reason for a process is understood, as well as its constraints and data components, different creative approaches to accomplishing it can be imagined. In what ways could the business *receive an order*? Via a text message? In an e-mail message? On a handwritten note? Suppose the products being sold are car parts. Could the car itself send an electronic message when one of its parts is wearing out and place an order for a new one? Figure 4.2 shows an example of an essential process: *accept a customer order*. This core business activity may be performed successfully in many different ways (different *hows*). When business requirements and processes are documented independent of current technology, they can be reused on future projects in the same business area. This can save the BA a significant amount of time.

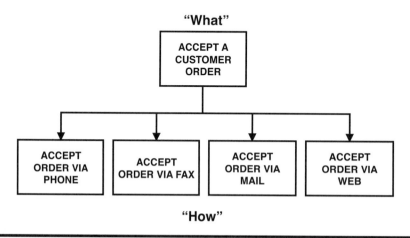

FIGURE 4.2. **Business Process:** *Accept Customer Order*

This is where an analyst's creativity can really shine. True innovation occurs when the innovator strips away the current procedures and looks at the base requirements. Then he or she can be creative in meeting those requirements. When you see a new product or service offered, think about how the inventor might have come up with the idea. Was it in response to a problem? Was it designed with the goal of increasing productivity or quality? Was it created to increase sales? Remember the primary business drivers (i.e., increase revenue, decrease costs). Any improvements made to an individual process roll up to help the entire organization.

In consumer product development, a brainstorming technique is used for package design. Think of an everyday common consumer product like soup. Now think of different types of packaging used for other items and imagine selling soup in that packaging. Soup in a box? Soup in a tube? Soup in a cylinder? Soup in a plastic jug? This technique illustrates the importance of finding the core business component and imagining it being presented in different ways. Once an essential process is understood, the analyst, business stakeholders, and solution team can imagine different procedures and systems that would support it.

Excellent BAs balance creativity with facts or metrics. Each process should be measured for its resource use, time to complete, efficiency, and number of times performed. Process improvements are evaluated by their improved metrics. Can the improved system get the process done faster? How much faster? Can the improved process allow the organization to handle larger volumes of transactions? How many? Will the improved process result in higher quality products or services? By how much? Excellent business analysis professionals ask these questions because they understand that measuring process improvement quantifies the success of a project.

BABOK Connection	
Knowledge Area	**Task/Technique**
Requirements Analysis	Indicators, Metrics, and Reporting

Six Sigma® is an approach to business process improvement that relies heavily on metrics. *Sigma* is a Greek letter assigned to represent the amount of variation or inconsistency exhibited by a measurable outcome. The name Six Sigma refers to the mathematical boundary within which errors are allowed. A Six Sigma capable process has a targeted quality performance goal of no more than 3.4 defects per million opportunities. The objective is to eliminate defects and variations in processes. When processes and their results are consistently measured, an organization can monitor improvements in efficiency and quality. It can also recognize decreases in productivity and respond more quickly. More and more organizations are using metrics to monitor performance. They are also building and buying complex business process monitoring systems and assigning process owners inside business units to monitor process effectiveness. To learn more about Six Sigma, read *The Six Sigma Way: How GE, Motorola, and Other Top Companies Are Honing Their Performance* (Pande et al., 2000).

When an essential business process is analyzed and described, this business requirement can be reused again and again. A business requirement is reusable when it is described independent of current procedures and technology. To help describe processes without embedding current technology, use the concept of perfect technology.

Seeing Things from the Top and from the Bottom

It is critical that a BA know as much about his or her business as possible. You may not be able to know everything, but the more you know, the better able you will be to identify problem areas and recommend effective solutions. This requires an understanding of the business at both a macro level and a micro level. In other words, you must be able to see the big picture: Why is the organization in business? How does the organization make money? You also must be able to see the detailed work that goes on inside the business: When a customer orders a product, how is inventory checked for availability? How do products get to the customer?

Being able to see the big picture (abstraction) *and* the low-level detail will make you a very valuable analyst. Most people in an organization cannot do both. Most of the executive-level people in an organization are very good at looking at the big picture. They can see opportunities for growth in the marketplace. They can see trends in the industry. They can envision the organization doing new things with new people. But most executives cannot or do not want to know about the day-to-day details of making the organization work. And realistically, they don't have time.

At the other end of the scale, individuals working in the business, performing individual tasks like customer service or claims adjusting, see work at a very detailed level. They know exactly which procedure is required for each type of transaction, but they may not understand how their detailed work fits into the big picture. They know which transaction code sets up the correct account in their software application. They know how to get around an approval requirement if the customer is important. Many of these people are very good at details but cannot or do not want to look at processes from a higher level. They are not comfortable with abstraction. This is where the BA comes in. BAs can listen to the broad, high-level plans and visions of the executives and imagine how the detailed work processes could support those plans. This is a skill that is never completely mastered but can continue to be improved.

A great diagramming technique to help analyze the business from the top and the bottom is the decomposition diagram. This is one of the best diagrams to use when you are analyzing a business area. It allows both high-level and subprocesses to be shown on one diagram and allows you to pull everything together for presentation and confirmation. The decomposition diagram allows the analyst to see things from the top down and the bottom up.

The decomposition diagram is a straightforward, simple diagram that is easy to use. It may be one of the first diagrams that a BA learns. Most people in business are familiar with an organizational chart, which is also drawn as a decomposition diagram. This familiarity makes the decomposition diagram easy to introduce to stakeholders. Figure 4.3 shows a decomposition diagram.

Implementation Planning

Part of knowing your business environment is truly understanding how the business area will be impacted by the solution designed for a project. Implementation or transition requirements describe the necessary actions to ensure a smooth transition of the project work (the solution) into the day-to-day operations of the business area. No matter how well built the solution is, a rough, unplanned implementation may be disruptive and negatively impact the business. It also may create a negative attitude in business stakeholders. These negative impacts can be avoided by implementation planning.

BAs are the *change agents* tasked with assessing the impacts of a change and planning the best approach to implement the change. Implementation planning involves analysis of the current (*as is*) business environment against the future (*to be*) business environment. The analyst identifies all aspects of the business that will be impacted by the change and plans each transition.

BABOK Connection	
Knowledge Area	**Task/Technique**
Solution Assessment and Validation	Define Transition Requirements
	Determine Organizational Readiness

Change impacts may necessitate training, setting specific rollout dates, and updating employee job descriptions, procedures manuals, and policies.

Training

Even a simple change to software should be accompanied by training. User help may be built into the software itself, or screen components like selection lists and message boxes

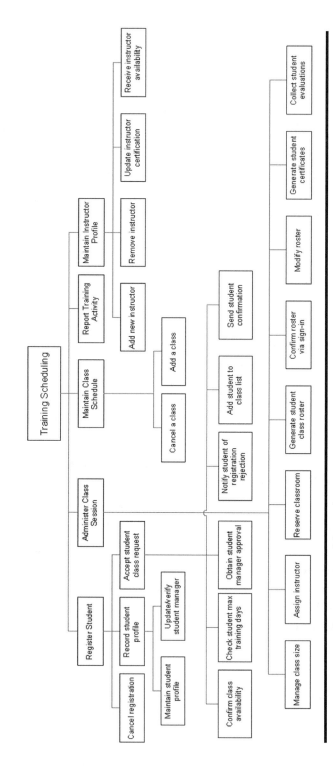

FIGURE 4.3. Sample Decomposition Diagram

may serve as the training mechanism. Users need to understand why a change was made and its value to their work. Some IT people underestimate the significance of a software change to a user. Even a change as small as repositioning a field on a screen has an impact on users. BAs understand the impact of changes because they have watched users at work and they understand the current business environment. They recognize that all of the individuals impacted by a change must be notified and prepared for it. Often, some of the people who will be impacted have not been involved with the project and don't know that a change is coming. BAs can design training to clearly explain the ramifications of the change to all of the parties impacted. BAs sometimes write the training materials and deliver formal training sessions.

Rollout Plan

A rollout plan details when, where, and how the solution will be made available to the business. Knowing the business environment allows the analyst to recommend the ideal time frame for the solution rollout. The rollout plan should be developed by the BA, the solution team, and the business stakeholders. It should include all of the technical steps necessary to implement any software changes, all of the business tasks necessary to transition to new procedures, and back-out or contingency plans in case there are problems during rollout. Table 4.3 shows a section of a sample rollout plan.

Schedule

When a solution rollout includes multiple business locations, a schedule for each location should be created. Different locations may request different times/dates for the change. The BA should help the business stakeholders think through the best timing possible. Obviously, don't schedule a change to the general ledger system at month end or year end. Don't schedule an upgrade to the Web site during its busiest hours of the day. These scheduling considerations must include both the business stakeholders and the solution team. The BA works to find the optimal time frame for the changes that will minimize business disruptions and maximize technical efficiency.

Metrics

The BA should identify metrics that can be used before and after the rollout to confirm data conversion and verify that the new system is operating within requirements. When

TABLE 4.3. Sample Rollout Plan

Date/Time	Task	Person Responsible	Notes and Back-out Contingency
Friday, April 3 noon	All users log out of the system after finishing the week's data entry work.	John Business area representative	If work cannot be completed, keep paper backup of information so that it can be entered into the new system after the cutover.
Friday, April 3 12:30–1:30 p.m.	Back up database. Print pre-conversion counts.	Jeff IT database administrator	Backup has been tested and timed at about 45 minutes.
Friday, April 3 1:30–5:00 p.m.	Convert production data to new database format.	Donna IT development	Conversion programs have been tested and timed at about 2 hours.
	Review error report from conversion and make corrections.	Donna IT development John Business representative	Data cleanup should take no longer than 1 hour.
	Finalize conversion. Print post-conversion counts.	Donna IT development	Pre-conversion counts should match post-conversion counts. If not, find the discrepancy and correct if possible. If more than 10% errors, rollout will be canceled and rescheduled for the future.

data is being converted, counts of the number of customers or number of orders should be exactly the same after the conversion as before. Exceptions should be identified before the rollout date during conversion tests and data cleanup completed as early as possible.

Metrics that measure system performance and other non-functional requirements should be collected before and after implementation (e.g., how long it took to process an order in the old system vs. how long it takes in the new). All of these measures of success provide quantitative ways of evaluating progress and alert the team to possible problems.

Procedures/Organizational Changes

All necessary changes to procedures, policies, and job descriptions should be made prior to rollout. Employees must be informed of these changes and be given the expected date of implementation. The more significant the changes, the earlier they should be communicated. Preparing business people for a change allows the change to proceed more smoothly.

BAs work with human resources personnel and organizational change specialists when employee responsibilities are impacted. BAs can provide these employment professionals detailed descriptions of the changes being made and the reasons for them. Business area management is also involved, working with human resources if pay grades or employee work hours are impacted.

SUMMARY OF TIPS FOR LEARNING YOUR BUSINESS

To get started knowing your business environment, take advantage of existing resources and experts in your organization.

1. Do you know your company's mission statement? Your division or business unit's mission? If not, find it and post it on your wall.
2. Read your company's Web site as if you were an external customer. What message does it convey? Is it easy to understand and use?
3. Look at a few of your competitors' Web sites. What differentiates your company from them?
4. If your company is publicly held, get the current financial report and look through it. Familiarize yourself with things like number of employees, total revenues, profit margin, and market share. Read the footnotes; they are often the most interesting part of the report.
5. If you haven't already done so, read employee/system procedure manuals for the business area of your current project. Even if the procedures are old and rarely referred to, you may gain an insight into how the old system was intended to work.

SUMMARY OF KEY POINTS

To act as a true advocate for the business, the business analysis professional must understand the business terminology, objectives, and processes of the business area within the scope of each project.

- ◆ When the BA is organizationally placed inside the business area, he or she understands the employee's perspective and can easily advocate for the business. When the BA is organizationally assigned somewhere outside the business area, in IT for example, this is a more challenging step.
- ◆ The BA should be comfortable using various elicitation techniques and should be able to select the most appropriate approach for each situation.
- ◆ Essential business process analysis is a core skill of the business analysis professional and requires the BA to be able to see through current procedures and software support to find the core business activity.
- ◆ The BA must not assume that software or technology is the answer to every business problem. Business analysis involves research to completely understand a problem, and its root cause, before suggesting a solution.
- ◆ The BA is also responsible for solution implementation planning. Rollout plans may include organizational/personnel changes, business policy changes, procedural changes, or software or technical support.

Business analysis involves eliciting business requirements from various stakeholders whose viewpoints are different. The BA confirms his or her understanding by learning from various sources, filling in gaps, and developing complete business models.

BIBLIOGRAPHY

Constantine, Larry L. and Lucy A.D. Lockwood (1999). *Software for Use: A Practical Guide to the Models and Methods of Usage-Centered Design.* Addison-Wesley.

Hertzel, Bill (1993). *The Complete Guide to Software Testing.* Second Edition. Wiley-QED Publication.

Kit, Edward (1995). *Software Testing in the Real World.* Addison-Wesley.

McMenamin, Stephen and John F. Palmer (1984). *Essential Systems Analysis.* Yourdon.

Myers, Glenford J. (2004). *Art of Software Testing.* John Wiley and Sons.

Pande, Peter S., Robert P. Neuman, and Roland R. Cavanagh (2000). *The Six Sigma Way: How GE, Motorola, and Other Top Companies Are Honing Their Performance.* McGraw-Hill.

Robertson, Suzanne and James Robertson (1999). *Mastering the Requirements Process.* Addison-Wesley.

Stevens, W., G. Myers, and L. Constantine (1974). Structured design. *IBM Systems Journal.* 13(2), 115–139.

Weisberg, Herbert F., Jon A. Krosnick, and Bruce D. Bowen (1996). *An Introduction to Survey Research, Polling, and Data Analysis.* Third Edition. Sage Publications.

Wood, Jane and Denise Silver (1995). *Joint Application Development.* Second Edition. John Wiley.

Yourdon, Edward and Larry L. Constantine (1979). *Structured Design: Fundamentals of a Discipline of Computer Program and Systems Design.* Prentice Hall.

5

KNOW YOUR TECHNICAL ENVIRONMENT

Technical awareness of the *possible* is one of the values that business stakeholders expect from business analysis professionals. It is important that you stay current on what technology is being used for what purposes. Business stakeholders expect business ana-

BABOK Connection	
Knowledge Area	**Task/Technique**
Underlying Competencies	Software Applications

lysts (BAs) to recommend technology that supports the business requirements and helps the business operate more efficiently and effectively. IT stakeholders expect BAs to communicate requirements in their "language" and not overpromise to the business stakeholders. Often, business stakeholders will hear of a new technology and ask if it could be used in their business area. The more you are aware of technology, the more valuable you will be to your stakeholders, even when your answer to them is no. Sometimes the new technology is in its infancy and not yet ready for production use. Sometimes the technology is too expensive for the business area being addressed. Maybe the new technology holds promise for the future and should be included in the business's strategic plan. Even if you are not an IT expert, you should be able to talk intelligently about the possibilities.

Case in Point

I personally don't know how wireless technology works. It amazes me that I can turn on my laptop in a Starbucks and have access to the entire world via the Internet! Rather than understanding how it works, when helping my business stakeholders solve business problems, it is important that I:

1. Understand the basic technical terminology (know that wireless means being unable to ignore e-mail messages when on a business trip!)
2. Know how the technology can be used (customers can order products to be delivered to their homes while sitting in an airport)
3. Know the limitations of the technology (not every hot spot works and some are costly)
4. Imagine uses for the technology in the business (people can have access to the Internet in their meetings no matter where they are held)

A BA's background drives the way that he or she approaches analysis projects and thinks about business solutions. When your background is IT, you may be in the habit of thinking about how to automate and integrate repetitive tasks and provide more sophisticated data for decision making. When your background is business, you may be thinking about new ways of doing business, how to better support customers, and how the business can be more successful. These two modes of thinking are both very useful and valuable in business analysis work. A business analysis professional who combines these two perspectives is the most valuable of all. In developing your skill set, look at your personal background to determine your primary thinking patterns and work to develop others. Much of this chapter is dedicated to business analysis professionals who come from the business side and don't have much hands-on experience with technology. Learn as much as you can about technology and its possibilities.

WHY DOES A BUSINESS ANALYST NEED TO UNDERSTAND THE TECHNICAL ENVIRONMENT?

Since BAs play a liaison role between business and IT, they need to be able to work in both worlds. Technology supports much of the work of organizations. The more a BA understands the enterprise IT assets and how to leverage them, the better he or she will be able to understand how they can be used to improve the business. Understanding what technology can and cannot do is critically important when trying to solve complex business problems. There are three reasons for a business analysis professional to *get familiar with* and *stay familiar with* technology capabilities.

First, learning about the current business requires the BA to understand *how* technology is supporting work today. When a BA begins talking with business stakeholders about their work, the business stakeholders will describe the technology and manual procedures using their terminology. Descriptions of technological components may not be exactly accurate; non-IT business stakeholders may use words to describe the system that are technically wrong. Many people have picked up technology words and phrases and use them inaccurately. For example, a data entry activity may be described as "putting the numbers into the PC," or a business person may confuse data with process and say something like "the database decides if the loan application is complete and gives us a report." The BA must be able to interpret unclear descriptions of current technology use.

BAs who understand technology know that most databases do not make decisions; there must be a software module that evaluates the data in the database and creates a report (actually, there are probably a large group of objects and/or modules that do this work). When eliciting requirements to learn about a business process, the BA must be able to hear descriptions and determine how accurate they are. This can be very challenging. As discussed in Chapter 4, BAs are listening to find core, essential business processes, business rules, data elements, and system interfaces. The accusation that "users don't know what they want" could be expanded to "users don't know what they have," and that is alright. Business stakeholders should not have to understand *how* their current application software *works*. But as a BA who is looking to recommend changes/improvements to a business system, you need to gain an understanding of both *what* the business is working to accomplish *and how* it is currently done. You need to ask questions, read software documentation, and talk with technologists to understand how the software supports the current work environment before suggesting changes. You also need to determine how effective the current software application is in meeting current or future needs.

The second reason why a business analysis professional must understand technology is to allow him or her to make feasible recommendations. To help formulate recommendations for changes to business systems, the BA must be aware of the possible options. Again, this does not imply that you need to know how to build the software/hardware components, but you need to know what can be built and what will work in the environment. Each organization operates within many constraints and limitations (i.e., budget, resources, regulation, standards). When considering new technology for a business area, consider the environment into which it would be deployed. Thus the question is not only "Can it be done?" but "Can it be done *here*?" Sometimes the answers to these questions are very different. The more a business analysis professional understands the current environment and enterprise technical architecture standards, the quicker he or she will be able to answer user questions about why certain changes may not be feasible. A question like "Can't we just add a column to this report with the current market price?" should trigger a whole series of thoughts in the BA's head:

- ◆ "Where would the system get the current market price to print on the report?"
- ◆ "How often does the price change?"
- ◆ "What external agent or company would provide the price changes?"
- ◆ "Who else would use this?"

The BA should be able to respond to the business user with follow-up questions or offer to investigate an idea. The BA should not say "Great idea!" and give the user the expectation that an idea is feasible and will be implemented unless it truly is.

The third reason why a business analysis professional must understand technology is that he or she must be able to see possibilities beyond the solution to the immediate problem. An experienced BA will always be looking at both tactical (short-term) and strategic (long-term) business solutions. The current project may be a small enhancement to an existing system and not require any detailed analysis. An experienced BA will think about this small change within a larger context. Maybe he or she assisted with several of these small change requests and begins to see a pattern that might be addressed with a larger, more strategic change. Are holes in an old tire constantly being patched instead of buying a new one? Maybe a new technology would provide a breakthrough in efficiency, but it is not yet cost effective. Get to know an enterprise architect from whom you can learn about upcoming changes. The business analysis professional stays aware of upcoming features and capabilities and works to move the business in a direction where these new capabilities will be feasible in the future.

Technology is changing at a faster and faster pace. Keeping up with the current capabilities and limitations is an important part of the ongoing professional development of a BA. Subscribe to IT newsletters and magazines. Stay close to people in IT. Attend lectures and webinars. Experience new technologies as often as possible (ask your child to teach you how to use an iPod® and show you how to use Facebook). Don't allow your knowledge to get stale. Successful BAs need to be aware of current trends and terminology. Read business analysis and technical blogs to learn what other organizations are doing.

Understand Technology, But Don't Talk Like a Technologist

For those who have worked in a technology role, it is important not to talk like a geek! This is the number one reason why the BA role was invented. Most business people tune out a person who starts talking at a very technical level. You will never be successful as a BA if you can't get yourself out of the technology enough to communicate with average business folks.

This is not a problem that is unique to IT or business. Have you ever had a doctor explain an illness to you and end up feeling like you have no idea what is really wrong? How about when your financial planner explains why he or she is rebalancing your portfolio based on the recommended market share penetration and capital ratios? Every profession has its lingo, which is very important and necessary inside the profession. Doctors can talk to each other very efficiently because they have a common vocabulary which is very precise. They don't say that the patient has a pain; they describe the symptom using clinical language that pinpoints the source and cause of the problem.

Case in Point

Several years ago, I took a family member to the Mayo Clinic in Rochester, Minnesota because she had a cancer that was very difficult to diagnose and even more difficult to cure. There was a surgeon there who had specialized in this particular cancer, and we were told that if anyone could help, she could. Upon arriving, we were introduced to a doctor who sat with us and explained the entire process that we would go through. First there would be preliminary tests and then more specific procedures to assess the extent of the problem. Finally, we would meet with the surgeon and she would give us her opinion and recommendations. This first doctor we met would be our "guide" throughout the process. He explained to us that we may not clearly understand what the surgeon or other medical professionals would be telling us, but he would be available to "translate" the medical jargon into something understandable to us. He was our BA. I was immediately struck by the fact that this guide was a doctor. He was not an administrator or a social worker. He was a highly trained medical professional whose entire job was to communicate with patients.

I believe that recognition of the importance of this communication with the patient and his or her family is one of the reasons why the Mayo Clinic is one of the best medical facilities in the world. The Mayo Clinic recognizes that expert professionals (like our surgeon) do not have time to focus on clear communication skills and compassionate bedside manner. The surgeon spends her valuable time diagnosing and treating as many patients as she can. Her assistants handle the communications and patient questions. This is an efficient use of this highly skilled resource. In the course of our 2 weeks at the Mayo Clinic, we spoke with the surgeon for only about 15 minutes. She walked into the examining room where we were waiting and efficiently explained the extent of the problem, her recommended treatment, and the probability of success. Then she walked out. It felt like a whirlwind of foreign facts and opinions. Our guide was there before and after the surgeon and spent time explaining and answering questions, consoling, and helping with treatment scheduling. Without him, we would have been lost. He was our "translator."

In most environments, technology professionals may be utilized in much the same way. Technical people should spend their time designing and architecting technology, not trying to explain its ramifications to lay people. Similarly, business stakeholders don't have time to explain the complexities of their business to an IT person. Translating or bridging this gap is the work of business analysis. BAs should expect that IT people speak a different language than the business. When a business analysis professional is not available, the technical person is expected to make the translation and will utilize business analysis skills.

WHAT DOES A BUSINESS ANALYST NEED TO KNOW ABOUT TECHNOLOGY?

There are some fundamentals of technology that every business analysis professional must understand. Regardless of your background, keep learning more; keep asking questions. You must have a high-level understanding of how things work in order to be an effective analyst. The better your understanding, the more likely you are to make excellent suggestions for changes and improvements.

Areas/terminology with which you should be familiar include:

◆ Software development/programming terminology
◆ Software development methodologies
◆ Technical architecture

◆ Operating systems
◆ Computer networking
◆ Data management
◆ Software usability/human interface design
◆ Software testing

Software Development/Programming Terminology

Know your developer's programming language

Does a Business Analyst Need to Know How to Develop Software?

At one of the first industry conferences for business analysis professionals, held in 2005, Business Analyst World™, a speaker listed *programming* as a skill needed by the BA. This caused quite a stir at the conference as BAs were asking each other, "Do you think that we need to know how to program?"

Many industry experts quickly said no, but the answer is not that simple. In the current business environment, can you think of any business today that is not utilizing technology? Many business activities are supported by technology, so a BA must have more than a superficial understanding of what technology can do and how it is built. Without some fundamental understanding of programming, a BA will have a difficult time communicating with his or her IT team members and may miss excellent solutions to business problems.

While writing *The Guide to the Business Analysis Body of Knowledge®* (BABOK®) for the International Institute of Business Analysis (IIBA™), the committee listed technical awareness as a core BA competency. There was unanimous agreement that BAs need to know something about technology to be effective. But how much? BAs who have not worked in a technology area should use this chapter as a guide to continuing education for career development. You don't have to be a "programmer," but you should have a high-level understanding of what programmers do and why they do it.

To help you understand the complexity of the work involved with programming or coding, think of the analogy of writing a series of documents that must fit together to form a cohesive package (e.g., a book with chapters or a requirements package with sections), as illustrated in Table 5.1.

Thinking about this analogy helps to understand why a developer's product is not correct the first time or even the second time. It also helps us to understand why it takes so long to complete a deliverable. If you have never written or reviewed any program code,

TABLE 5.1. Comparison of Writing Software to Writing a Document

Writing a Series of Documents	Writing a Software System
The entire document cannot be written in one sitting. It takes many hours to write and revise.	A developer cannot write a whole system in one sitting.
When you change a concept or term in one place, you have to go back and review the entire document for inconsistencies.	When a developer changes the definition of a data field, it may need to be changed in several places.
Making sure that each chapter or section leads to the next requires complex integration.	Integrating complex object components can be very difficult.
As the author, it is difficult to see grammatical errors in your own writing.	Developers have a tough time finding defects in their own code.
Even after many reviews, there are often "bugs" (typos, grammar errors, inconsistencies).	Even after extensive testing, software often contains defects.
Readers will not recognize the diligence required to put a document together.	Users often do not appreciate the complexity of their requests.

ask a developer to show you one of his or her programs for a specific business feature that you understand. Ask the developer to walk through each line of code and explain its function and relationship to the rest of the software. You will only have to listen for a short time to get a quick understanding of how complex software development is. You will probably be overwhelmed and want to get away from this code as soon as possible! This will re-enforce the reasons why requirements must be detailed. Programming languages and software systems do not assume anything or do anything automatically. If you want a field on the screen to be highlighted when the user forgets to fill it in, the developer has to write several lines of code to tell the screen to display a highlight. When the user enters the information on the screen, the developer has to write code to tell the screen to turn off the highlight. Every single action that a user wants must be coded exactly. How can developers do all of this detailed work when they are not given clear direction about what is needed? It is the BA's role to communicate this direction with an appropriate deliverable like a use case.

The most important work of the BA is communication. If you can't talk with a developer in his or her language, he or she may discount your value, and this will undermine your creditability. If you worked in the construction industry, you would have some understanding of how things are built; take the same approach with IT.

Take time to learn if your developer is working with a procedural language like COBOL or an object-oriented language. Learn object-oriented terms like encapsulation, inheritance, and abstraction. When you hear a term that you don't know, find a high-level definition. Find out if your organization has programming standards, screen design standards, and other governance policies to which your developer must adhere. These standards impact the developer's time to complete work, which should be factored into project time estimates.

Software Development Methodologies

Know your developer's process or methodology

Methodology/Software Development Life Cycle

Methodology is a word that was applied to IT software development in the 1970s. Early developers recognized that just sitting down to write code without any preliminary planning or requirements did not result in the best solution and often required a lot of time for rewrites. A methodology, as the name implies, is simply a structured, repeatable process. It may contain very specific instructions on how to develop software. Early methodologies were based on the software development life cycle, which recognized distinct phases in software development: plan, analyze, design, code, test. This fundamental structure is the foundation of every methodology, development process, and approach used in software development today. The word "methodology" has lost favor because some of the commercial methodologies sold in the 1980s and 1990s were massive, multivolume manuals which were difficult to follow. Organizations that purchased these methodologies often felt that the required deliverables took too much time. Teams began to skip steps or take shortcuts.

Over the last 30-plus years, there have been many attempts to write a cookbook approach to software development. IT managers yearn for a clear, simple process that their teams can follow to ensure success. Unfortunately, software development cannot be defined that neatly. Understanding business needs and turning them into software solutions is complex, non-linear, difficult work. It requires expert practitioners (project managers,

BAs, architects, developers) and some guidelines about how the work will be done. Since every project is different, every team will work differently.

Compare an IT development project to the work of making a movie. No two movies are exactly alike; even sequels have significant differences. Each movie has a unique set of people (actors, director, editor, makeup artists, costumers, set designers) and a unique plot. Each is shot at different locations and in a different order. Movies take months and sometimes years to make and cost millions of dollars. Sometimes they are canceled in the middle of production. Sometimes they are released and then flop. There are very few blockbusters. Although movie-making sophistication has increased over the years, so has the sophistication of the audience. Expectations are higher, so doing what you did on the last movie will not be good enough. This is very similar to IT development, which faces the same challenges and odds against success. Every project is different, with different stakeholders. The technology available continues to evolve and become more complex. Users continue to increase their sophistication and expectations. Using a software development process or methodology provides guidelines for the team based on best practices both inside and outside the organization. But no matter how good the process, having competent, trained team members will always be the key to the success of a project. Blind adherence to a process will not necessarily produce the correct product. This section gives a brief overview and history of software development methodologies.

Waterfall

First structured approach to software development
Introduced the concepts of phases, tasks, roles, and deliverables

The *waterfall* approach to software development is so named because it has distinct phases that are meant to be done in order, and high-level project objectives and requirements "fall" through from one phase to the next. The waterfall methodologies also introduced the concepts of team roles, deliverables, and sign-offs. The roles of team leader, programmer, and user were the first specified. Deliverables or software design documentation was introduced as a method of getting user agreement on work before the work was done. Sign-offs were introduced to get user "buy-in" to the work.

All other software development methodologies are based on the waterfall. Most of the concepts of the waterfall are still important and are included in subsequent methodologies. Figure 5.1 shows the classic waterfall approach.

In the waterfall approach, each activity or phase is dealt with once and completed for the entire system before the next phase is started (e.g., all analysis activities are completed

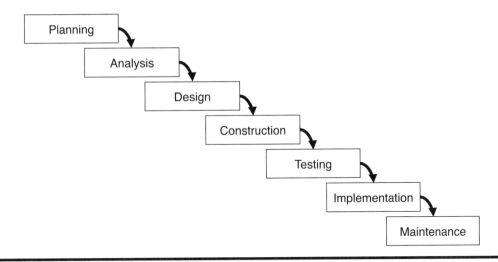

FIGURE 5.1. Waterfall Approach to Software Development

before the design phase is started). This structured, sequential approach is the one aspect of the waterfall approach that limited its success. Teams often spent too much of the project time in early phases and then had to rush through the rest of the process. It is unfortunate that the waterfall approach has suffered from negative publicity because the tasks and deliverables recommended by the approach are necessary and useful. The fundamental idea behind the waterfall approach—analyzing *before* designing and designing *before* coding—is still the most effective route to success (Royce, 1998).

Methodologies that were built around the waterfall approach acknowledge the importance of first planning the work, gathering/understanding requirements, and laying out a software design plan before starting to write code. Early developers did all of this work themselves. Prior to the concept of a *software development life cycle* or *methodology,* developers spoke with subject matter experts briefly and then began coding. This approach is often still used on maintenance projects. As projects became more complex, software became more complex. Coding without an overall design plan was problematic, like trying to build a house without a blueprint.

Planning Phase

The planning phase is intended to help the IT team ask high-level questions of the executive sponsor to determine the true project objectives. This was the first formalization of setting customer expectations for the IT work that would be done. It is also intended to help IT people understand business needs and priorities.

Analysis Phase

Definition of the analysis phase was really the beginning of business analysis work. The waterfall approach recommended that software requirements be written down and reviewed. This was a radical idea in the 1970s, when most developers only wrote code. This phase was created because developers had been creating software that didn't really perform functions the way that subject matter experts needed. Initial requirements were very brief and were all functional—they described what the software should do.

Design Phase

As software supported more and more business activities, developers created many programs and files to perform different functions. Programs have to know how data is stored in files to be able to share information. Early software systems were much like patchwork quilts, with random pieces sewn together. Development was slowed for several reasons: (1) early programs were not documented, so developers had to read each other's code to be able to share data; (2) as more and more programmers were working on the same systems, original programmer knowledge was not available; and (3) early programming did not follow any programming standards, so every program was different.

For all of these reasons, the waterfall approach suggested that someone in IT (a systems analyst or architect) draw a design of the programs and files needed by the system before coding started. These designs also began to document file exchange formats so that different programmers could be working on different yet related programs at the same time. The design phase also included documents called "program specifications," which described to the developer what his or her program was expected to do. These were initially very brief and evolved into more complete documents over the years.

Construction Phase

Only after completion of the first three phases did coding or construction begin. This was another radical concept at the time. (It is interesting to note that although most IT professionals have always agreed that planning, analysis, and design should be done before coding—in practice, this is still one of the industry's biggest weaknesses!)

Testing Phase

Early software didn't reside in test vs. production states. When coding was done, the user was given the results. If the results were not correct, the code was changed. Methodologies recommended that code be tested before being used by business people. This was another radical concept.

For today's BAs, the concepts introduced in the waterfall probably seem very obvious. Despite some negative publicity, many organizations still use waterfall or a modified waterfall approach very successfully. All later software development approaches and methodologies are measured against this original standard. No other approach has introduced as many key development precepts as the waterfall.

Information Engineering

Adds the importance of requirements models and introduces a data-centric focus
Utilizes JAD to bring business stakeholders into design discussions

In the 1980s, several methodologies (built on the foundations of waterfall) moved the IT industry toward a more data-centric approach. The volume of data that was being collected and managed by organizations forced IT managers to focus on better strategies for data design and management. In addition, the relational database structure was becoming commercially available and promised to make data inquiry easier (Martin, 1986).

Information engineering (IE) was so named because it recommended a data focus and a more structured "engineering-like" discipline for software requirements and design. It brought together several diagramming techniques: entity relationship diagramming, data flow diagramming, flowcharts, decomposition diagramming, and structure charts (see Chapter 6 for information on these techniques). IE introduced the concept of traceability (although it wasn't named until later) by showing how the various diagram components could be related to each other (e.g., a data store on a data flow diagram could be linked to an entity relationship diagram). These networks of linked diagrams were called a *model.* This was the beginning of business modeling, information modeling, object-oriented modeling, etc. IE also encouraged an "analyst" role and continued to suggest better requirements communication with business people. IE planning and analysis phases advocated the use of business language in models and requirements. IE's popularity was driven by the availability of CASE (computer-aided software engineering) tools. The complexity of these tools drove them to virtual extinction, and therefore IE is rarely used today.

IDEF

Developed at the same time as IE but from a government perspective
Reinforces the value of modeling requirements

The U.S. government, in managing large software development projects, evolved a series of software methodologies from manufacturing/engineering techniques. These approaches were also based on the waterfall approach with phases, deliverables, roles, and sign-offs. IDEF was a product of the Integrated Computer-Aided Manufacturing (ICAM) initiative of the U.S. Air Force. IDEF initially stood for ICAM DEFinition language; the Institute of Electrical and Electronics Engineers (IEEE) standards recast IDEF as "Integration DEFinition." Like IE, this approach acknowledged information (data) as a key requirement component and used models to represent requirements. IDEF requires a more formal review and sign-off process than IE. Several methods were outlined for IDEF. Four of them were used for business analysis: IDEF0 (functional modeling), IDEF1 (information modeling), IDEF1X (database modeling), and IDEF3 (process description capture). IDEF0 functional modeling diagrams are still in use and supported by a few graphical diagramming tools.

Joint Application Development/Design

Emphasizes user involvement with software design

Joint Application Design™ (JAD) evolved in parallel with many of the software methodologies. "Joint" work became important as IT systems expanded to support multiple business areas. This became very important as organizations began to recognize that data values could be shared. Separate business areas were brought together to develop a shared understanding of their information. As IT departments became larger and more sophisticated, they also became more isolated. Joint design acknowledged that the IT team members needed to work closely with business subject matter experts (Wood and Silver, 1995). Using JAD or *facilitated information gathering sessions* for requirements elicitation was discussed in Chapter 4.

Rapid Application Development

Adds prototyping and faster development concepts

Rapid application development (RAD) approaches typically used JAD to speed up the development process. They were developed as an alternative to the structured waterfall/IE, documentation-heavy approaches. With RAD came prototyping and a focus on involving users in the development/coding work. Groups of business people were brought together for extended JAD workshops where prototypes and system designs were agreed upon and quickly rolled out (McConnell, 1996). This approach is the forerunner to the latest group of methodologies known as *agile*.

Iterative/Incremental Development Approaches

Recognize the value of revisiting phases to catch missed requirements
Break projects into smaller deliverables that can be implemented faster

Iterative is so named because *to iterate* is to repeat and rework based on the work from the first iteration. The phases are still used, but this approach recognizes that one phase of a project may not be completely finished before the next is started. It gives permission for the team to revisit earlier work to pick up missed pieces. *Incremental* approaches recommend breaking large products into pieces and building each piece to fit with the existing whole. Pieces are integrated as they are completed.

These development approaches have been very well accepted by most IT departments. Iterative approaches recognize that all requirements may not be completely discovered and detailed during the first attempt. As IT architects begin to design solutions to meet business requirements, they will find holes or inconsistencies. The iterative approach allows time for the BA to go back to requirements elicitation to fill in the pieces that are missing or unclear. Incremental work requires that an overall plan is developed and then broken into small, more manageable-size pieces. This approach allows functionality to be delivered to business people faster and helps the team to prioritize the most important work first.

Object-Oriented Analysis and Design

Introduced reusable components in program code
Utilizes the concept of encapsulation, making software components more independent

Building on the concept of IE and data-centric design, object-oriented (OO) techniques and approaches were developed. OO design creates software systems that are built in a modular fashion, allowing relatively independent pieces of code (*objects*) to communicate with each other (Jacobson, 1992). This approach caused a radical change in software coding. Programming languages (previously procedural) were created, allowing developers to build objects (small, independent pieces of code) that could be reused in other systems. Introducing true reusability into software development rapidly increased the speed at which software can be created. Once OO programming languages were proven successful, software analysis and design techniques were developed to make a smooth transition for IT teams. OO analysis models include class diagrams and use case descriptions. The Unified Modeling Language (UML) has been developed to provide consistency for OO analysis and design (www.uml.org).

Unfortunately, OO development has not met the promise of reusability. The emergence of service-oriented architecture (SOA) concepts is another attempt to increase the reusability and maintainability of software components.

In addition, OO analysis has not proven useful to most BAs. OO analysis diagrams are too technical for most business stakeholders. In addition, the transition from analysis (business requirements) to design (functional requirements) is still one of the most difficult tasks in the software development life cycle. Many methodologists have tried to develop methods and techniques for automating and easing this transition, but it remains a very complex, manual task that is best accomplished by a team of knowledgeable business analysis professionals and software architects.

Rational Unified Process

The most well-known OO approach to software development

Currently owned by IBM, the Rational Unified Process® (RUP) is a commercially available development process. The process includes descriptions of team roles, tasks, and deliverables. It is a customizable approach and recommends iterative and incremental development and deployment. Its popularity has made the acronym RUP almost equivalent to an industry term.

Agile Development Approaches

Focus on small, co-located teams
Decreased focus on formal requirements

Every new software development approach grows out of experience with previous approaches, both good and bad. Most new approaches share one goal—faster development of useful business software to the business users. The word *agile* means being able to move quickly and easily and is used to describe an approach to software development that is fast, flexible, and effective. The agile style utilizes both the iterative and incremental characteristics.

Agile projects are gaining popularity and have been very successful in many organizations. Initially, some agile experts downplayed the need for a BA on the agile team. Instead, they utilized a developer to elicit requirements directly from the business stakeholders. An experienced BA will add significant value to the team. When a business analysis professional is not available, developers are expected to perform analysis and communicate directly with business stakeholders. Developers effectively wear two hats: that of the BA and that of the developer.

Characteristics of an agile project include:

◆ Short iterations (two to four weeks) with scope based on highest business value
◆ Small dedicated project team working closely together (ideally, the team is working in the same physical location)
◆ Full-time business stakeholder(s) assigned to the team
◆ JAD/facilitation sessions to quickly elicit requirements
◆ Daily "stand-up" meetings to keep the project on track (10 to 15 minutes)
◆ "Design as you go" approach to the software design
◆ "Demo as you go" approach to user requirements
◆ "Test as you go" approach to the software
◆ Requirements are communicated very informally
◆ Teams become self-managed

There are some really great things about using an agile approach:

1. Business value is delivered to business stakeholders very quickly.
2. Daily "stand-ups" and constant reviews keep all team members' work on track and focused.
3. Because iterations typically run between 10 and 30 days, there is no formal change control process required during an iteration. Once the iteration scope is agreed upon, no changes are allowed (unless the scope is not feasible). Changes to requirements are considered for a subsequent iteration.
4. No voluminous requirements documents are written. BAs don't have to spend hours fine-tuning every word in the requirements package in long document review sessions. Requirements are confirmed during demos of the product as it is developed or on white boards in the team workroom.
5. Working prototypes evolve from design artifacts to the production software so business users can see their requested changes and developers can easily make the changes to improve usability as the project moves along.
6. Dedicated team involvement including a full-time business stakeholder means everyone stays focused on achieving the objectives within the specified time frame.

These benefits are only achieved by a very high-performing team that understands the agile approach and commits to the process. Including a high-performing business analysis professional on the team increases the likelihood that the resulting product will meet true business needs and fit in well with the current business environment. If an experienced BA is not available, at least one team member must have extensive business analysis training and experience (Carkenord, 2007).

An Organization's Formal Methodology

An organization may have adopted one or more formal methodologies that define deliverables. This usually takes the decision about which requirements deliverables to use out of the hands of the team members and forces consistency from project to project. Unfortunately, many methodologies do not provide much detail on requirements elicitation and analysis from a business perspective. The business requirements document may be a single deliverable within the methodology. A business requirements document is made up of a set of requirements components and should be viewed as multiple deliverables.

If you are assigned to a project using a formal methodology, your first task should be to review the methodology for its handling of requirements deliverable(s) and determine if it meets the needs of the stakeholders. Part of your planning effort will be to add items to the formal methodology as needed for the project.

Using a methodology has its advantages and limitations. On the positive side, the BA can read the methodology and know exactly what is expected. The project plan is easier to develop because milestones are stipulated and defined.

The limitations of this scenario are obvious. Even the best methodologies cannot anticipate the circumstances of every project or the nuances of an individual organization. The prescribed deliverables may not work well for a particular project and you may find yourself forcing *round* requirements into a *square* hole. Create the required deliverables as best you can, and then use some additional deliverables that make more sense for the project needs. Few methodologies forbid you from creating more deliverables than prescribed! Although these additional deliverables may require more time, if they are beneficial in representing project needs, the time will be well spent. If a prescribed deliverable doesn't make sense for your project, petition the standards board to omit it.

Why Don't Most Methodologies Detail the Business Analysis Approach?

Most application development methodologies have limited coverage of requirements because most methodologies were developed by software developers and are focused on how to *develop software*. It makes perfect sense for a software development methodology to focus on development, but the assumption is that business requirements are well understood and available. This assumption usually is false. Methodologists have spent years trying to speed up the development process and steer developers toward techniques that will produce high-quality code that is easy to maintain. They have not focused their efforts on making sure that the team truly understands the business need before designing the software. This is where the BA needs to step in and enhance the methodology. *Business analysis must be done before software development* (see Figure 5.2).

Most of the business analysis and requirements techniques that BAs use have been around for a long time. Why haven't methodology authors incorporated them into their approaches? The simplest answer is that every project is different and deciding which techniques and approaches to use is not a simple task. Even the most experienced BA must spend time thinking about a new project assignment and finding the techniques that meet the needs of the team and the characteristics of the project. A smart methodology would need an expert system to ask hundreds of questions about a new assignment and based

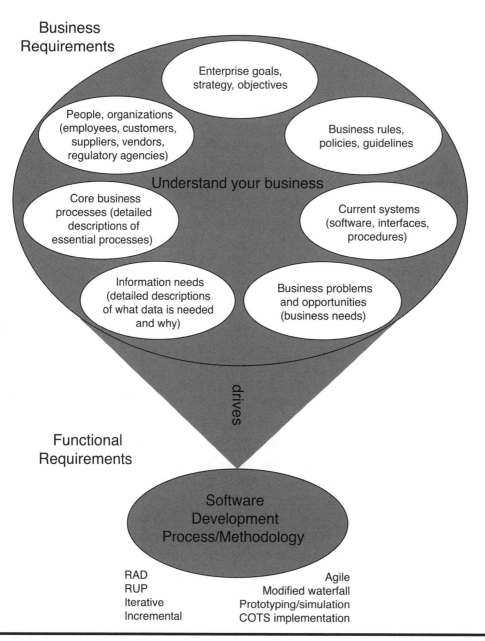

Business Requirements

Enterprise goals, strategy, objectives

People, organizations (employees, customers, suppliers, vendors, regulatory agencies)

Business rules, policies, guidelines

Understand your business

Core business processes (detailed descriptions of essential processes)

Current systems (software, interfaces, procedures)

Information needs (detailed descriptions of what data is needed and why)

Business problems and opportunities (business needs)

drives

Functional Requirements

Software Development Process/Methodology

RAD
RUP
Iterative
Incremental

Agile
Modified waterfall
Prototyping/simulation
COTS implementation

FIGURE 5.2. Business Requirements Come before Software Development

on those answers tell you exactly which techniques to use. This expert system currently exists only in the minds of experienced BAs.

An Organization's Informal Standards

It is more likely that an organization does not use a formal methodology. An organization may have one, and may profess to use it, but if it is frequently ignored, then it virtually does not exist.

In the absence of a formal methodology, the BA should examine the informal standards and processes that have developed inside the organization and consider them when planning his or her analysis work. Many informal standards and processes are very successful because they have been developed over time by trial and error.

If you take an informal survey of stakeholders about their previous experiences with requirements, you will hear things like: "That thing John wrote was unbelievable. It was 100 pages long and he expected us to read every word!" or "Mary didn't make us look at anything from her last project, but then the screen didn't really work the way we needed it to. Hmm—maybe we should have looked at it." or "That consultant who was here last year—what was his name—Kevin? He drew a really great flowchart of our whole process and then highlighted in red the areas that were going to change. We all really liked that. I still have it tacked to my office wall!" These types of statements, while ignored by 99% of the corporate population, are like gold to the BA. They hold clues to what the stakeholders liked and what they didn't. Success breeds success, so if Kevin was successful, take advantage of his technique and use it. You might even tell the subject matter experts: "I learned this technique from Kevin and he said that it worked well." Don't be shy about giving credit and using other people's ideas. The whole point here is excellent communication. BAs need to communicate in the most efficient way possible.

Technical Architecture

Know your organization's standards and basic architecture

There are many components that make up a software system. The foundation of the computer system is often referred to as *architecture*. This is a great way to describe the design and construction of a system because people can visualize a building's architecture. A BA does not need to understand every possible component or architecture that is available. He or she needs to understand that software is made up of a group of objects or components that work together to accomplish a goal. These components may be built by an internal development team, built by an outsourced team, purchased or acquired and used as is, customized, rented or leased, or accessed remotely. The interconnection between these components is much of what makes a software system so complex. Each component interfaces with others and expects the others to perform. Many of the components are very small and on their own do not appear to do anything or have any purpose. When combined with other components, however, they provide powerful functionality. The advent of more and more independent, reusable components makes software development faster. Developers can use pieces of code from various sources and combine them into a new, working product. A simple analogy would be the inventory of a hardware store. Each customer who shops at the store may buy a different combination of parts, lumber, and fasteners and go home to build a completely different product. There are an infinite number of products that can be built with the components that are available.

One of the important things to understand about software architecture is that there is no one common design. Each organization's technical architecture has evolved over the organization's history and is unique. Often, there are many different brands and versions of hardware, networking software, operating systems, communication systems, and packages all running simultaneously to support the organization's goals. BAs should consult with IT architects at the beginning of their projects to discuss the feasibility of solution options. BAs who are aware of the complex web of old and new technical components will make more intelligent recommendations and more clearly communicate the possible ramifications of changes to their business stakeholders.

Business stakeholders use software *applications.* A software application is a software system that supports a particular business area or function. Common examples are enterprise resource planning (ERP), customer relationship management (CRM),

BABOK Connection	
Knowledge Area	Task/Technique
Underlying Competencies	Software Applications

and general ledger. When you are learning about an application, your first questions should focus on when and where the application was designed. Knowing the operating system on which it runs, the language used to develop it, etc. will give you valuable information about how difficult it will be to change or interface with. Software systems have lasted much longer than anyone anticipated, so in a large organization it is not unusual to find an application that is 20 years old running next to an application that is 5 years old and another that is brand new. This collection of different architectures makes IT maintenance an expensive and time-consuming function in many companies. Most IT organizations have an architectural "road map" which describes their long-term strategy for building and maintaining software. Learn as much as you can about this plan, and work to incorporate all of your projects into the plan.

Operating Systems

BAs need to be involved in infrastructure changes to assess user impacts

An operating system manages computer resources and provides applications with an interface to access those resources. A BA needs to be aware of the operating systems used in his or her organization. Common operating systems are Microsoft Windows®, Linux, Mac OS X®, and Solaris. This knowledge is important on projects where the operating system becomes part of the requirements. For example, when searching for packaged software applications (commercial off-the-shelf), the vendor response to a Request for Proposal must specify the operating system(s) on which the package runs.

Operating systems are occasionally changed or upgraded. Operating system changes are usually prompted by the increased functionality available in the new version. These changes are often implemented in a project referred to as an *infrastructure project*. Infrastructure projects implement changes to the underlying IT architecture to improve system characteristics like performance, security, or reliability. Ideally, the infrastructure changes are transparent to the business users, and because of this assumption, business analysis professionals are often not assigned to these projects. This is unfortunate because many times infrastructure changes do impact end users. A simple change like a new system menu impacts business workers and should be communicated before the change is made. Encourage your management to include business analysis in all infrastructure projects. A BA is the best person to assess the impact of a change on the business community. The BA can communicate changes to the business and prepare users for any possible issues.

Case in Point

As a project manager on a vendor-supplied commercial off-the-shelf upgrade project, I faced an operating system issue. The version of the application that was currently in production ran on Microsoft Windows, and the newer version was available to run on Windows or IBM's Operating System/2 (OS/2). The IT manager had decided that we should use the OS/2 version because it was reported to be faster and more reliable. When I joined the project, which was already under way, the focus of the analysis effort was on the updated functionality. We knew that many new features would be available to business users and were documenting and testing those changes. The operating system change had not been analyzed or evaluated. We were conducting tests on the Windows version of the software.

As I began documenting the project and business risks, I learned that this organization did not have any current applications using OS/2. We needed to add tasks to the project plan to include purchasing a new server, purchasing the OS/2 software, and training an IT support person to maintain this system. I listed this as a risk since the company had no prior experience with this operating system. I suggested we order the new server and software immediately and begin testing in this environment. I knew from prior experience that even though a vendor tells you that an application works exactly the same way on both operating systems, there are often subtle differences. As we began the research into what type and brand of hardware were needed, we began to learn that OS/2 had specific requirements and some limitations. Research also prompted us to investigate the cost of all of the new equipment. If we decided to stay with the Windows platform, we could use the existing server and avoid significant costs. Once we put together all of the facts along with the risks of maintaining another IT architecture, we reversed the decision and stayed with the Windows version.

Computer Networking

BAs must appreciate the complexity involved in technical networking

A computer network is an interconnected set of computers. This simple definition belies the complexity of the networking systems used in most organizations. A network of computers is created using a sophisticated combination of hardware, operating systems, networking software, and communication protocols. There are many different types of networks: *LAN* (local area network), *WAN* (wide area network), *intranet* (internal closed network), *extranet* (internal network with controlled access by outside parties), and *internet* (an interconnection among or between public, private, commercial, industrial, or governmental networks). There are IT professionals who specialize in setting up and maintaining networks. These professionals should be consulted on any projects that will utilize networking. Business analysis professionals should be aware of potential networking changes and work with the IT professionals to learn about the ramifications for the project and, most importantly, the business environment.

Data Management

A key technical awareness—BAs must be aware of the importance of information in information systems; ignoring data requirements will guarantee project failure

Every successful organization in the world needs information and a lot of it. Organizations can't make intelligent decisions about launching a new product without knowing the characteristics of potential customers. Organizations can't adhere to government regulations without being able to report financial statistics along with descriptions of where those numbers come from. Organizations can't offer employees benefits without knowing important data about their families. So how do organizations keep track of all of this data? Much of it resides in sophisticated software databases and files that fill billions of bytes of storage on PCs, servers, and mainframes. BAs must understand the importance of data, how it is stored, and more importantly how it is accessed. A BA who does not understand fundamental database concepts may struggle.

To this end, it is imperative that every BA get formal training in data management and database concepts. You don't need to be able to build a database, but you must know what a database looks like, how it is created, how it can be changed, and how it is used. This fundamental knowledge is the building block upon which much of your technical awareness will rest.

New BAs should familiarize themselves with their organization's data management approach and with concepts like data integrity; conceptual, logical, and physical data modeling; relational database structures; data dictionary; data warehouse and business intelligence systems; data mart; database access methods; and data security issues. Find out which database management systems are in use in your organization (e.g., Oracle® or SQL Server®). It is not critical that you understand a particular database management system, but it is important that you know what a relational database looks like (see the next section) and where they are used in your organization.

BAs will be asking questions like:

◆ Who owns the data? How is this ownership maintained?

◆ How is the data used? Why is it maintained?

◆ What volume of data is expected?

◆ What is the data's "golden" source? How many places is this data stored?

◆ How is data mapped after a merger?

◆ How will data be converted from a legacy system to a new Web application?

◆ How often does data change?

◆ How often is data in the data warehouse refreshed? Is real-time data needed?

Relational Database

BAs must understand the terms tables, rows, columns, and keys in the relational database

A relational database is a place to store data. Almost every piece of information that is important to an organization is stored in a relational database. It is really amazing that this one approach to storing information has been universally accepted and maintained. Although it is not important that a BA understand the underlying details for its universal success, it is based on a solid mathematical model that has stood and will stand the test of time. In other words, there are very good reasons why everyone uses it! It is a fundamentally sound approach to organizing and understanding data requirements.

The good news about this method of storing data is that at a high level it is relatively easy to understand. Data is stored in *tables*. If you have used a spreadsheet with rows and columns, then you understand the basic structure of a relational database table. See Table 5.2 for an example. Each *column* represents a data element and each *row* contains the data

TABLE 5.2. Sample Relational Database Table

Customer Table

Customer Number	Name	Phone	E-mail Address
103	Smith	383-3839	smith@yahoo.com
104	Jones	495-0059	jones@hotmail.com
105	Carkenord	232-2020	bcarkenord@b2ttraining.com

TABLE 5.3. Sample Relational Database for Customer Related to Order

Customer Table

Customer Number	Name	Phone
103	Smith	383-3839
104	Jones	495-0059
105	Carkenord	232-2020

Order Table

Number	Date	Customer Number
292938	04/12/20xx	103
292939	04/12/20xx	103
292940	04/12/20xx	105

values for each data element. This simple structure is used to store and report on very large and complex types of information.

Every table has a *primary key*. A primary key uniquely identifies a particular row in the table. In the sample customer table in Table 5.2, the customer number is the primary key. A primary key is made up of one or more columns.

Database complexity is introduced by the relationships between the tables. Tables are related to each other via *foreign keys*. A foreign key is a primary key from the related table. Take the time to learn the basics of foreign key *migration* because these relationships between tables are critical for accessing data. Table 5.3 shows two related tables. Note that the customer number column exists in the order table as a foreign key. You can learn about relational databases by reading a book like the *Handbook of Relational Database Design* (Fleming and von Halle, 1989).

Deciding which pieces of information should reside in each table and how many tables are appropriate is the work of a database designer or architect (see Chapter 2).

Structured Query Language

BAs need to understand the purpose of basic SQL statements

Structured query language (SQL) is a query language used to access and manipulate data in a relational database. It was originally designed using English language statements to allow business people to query their data for ad hoc reporting. The hope was that IT developers would be free to focus on developing new complex software while business users could develop their own reports. Unfortunately, the complexity of most databases has prevented all but the most sophisticated users from becoming independent of IT support. SQL is used for almost every database management system based on the relational model. There are hundreds of books/publications available from which you can learn SQL. There are two primary statements with which the BA should be familiar: SELECT and JOIN.

Like relational database concepts, the basic building blocks of SQL are relatively simple concepts. The statement or code that tells the computer to retrieve information out of one of the database tables is a SELECT statement:

SELECT CUSTOMER NAME FROM CUST_TABLE

This statement tells the database management system to look at the table called CUST_TABLE and retrieve the customer names. You will often hear developers talk about the SELECT statement because it is the most used statement in all of SQL. If you find incorrect data in a report, the developer might say something like: "My SELECT statement only pulled customers who are active." The SELECT statement for a complex request may be several lines or even a page long. They are very complex to write and change. A simple change in a SELECT statement can result in a completely different result. See Figure 5.3 for an example of a complex SELECT statement.

The other statement with which you need to be familiar is JOIN. In SQL, the word JOIN refers to the task of bringing together information that is stored in two or more different tables. It is not critical that you understand the intricacies of the JOIN statement, but you should understand its basic purpose so that you can better communicate with developers.

Since most software applications manage large amounts of data, there are usually many tables. Almost any search of a database requires that at least two tables be joined together to find the requested information. See Figure 5.4 for a sample JOIN statement.

For example, if a business area wanted to see a list of all of the orders placed by a particular customer, the SQL code would JOIN the two tables together to provide a list (printed or on screen) showing the customer name and all of the order numbers, with any other details needed. Like the SELECT statement, a JOIN can become very complex and may be at the root of an erroneous report. Be prepared to listen to developers talk about the complexity of their JOIN when trying to diagnose problems. To learn more about SQL, refer to a book like *Sams Teach Yourself SQL in 10 Minutes* (Forta, 2004).

```
Select concat( ifnull(concat(first_name, \' \'),\'\'),
last_name, ifnull(concat(\'\\n(\',title,\')\'),\'\')) Name,
concat( ifnull(concat(\'(H)\',phone_home,\'\\n\'),\'\'),
ifnull(concat(\'(M)\',phone_mobile,\'\\n\'),\'\'),
ifnull(concat(\'(W)\',phone_work,\'\\n\'),\'\'),
ifnull(concat(\'(?)\',phone_other,\'\\n\'),\'\'),
ifnull(concat(\'(F)\',phone_fax,\'\\n\'),\'\')) as \'Phone
Numbers\', concat(address_street,\'\\n\',address_city, \'
\', address_state, \', \', address_postalcode) as Address,
concat( ifnull(concat(email1,\'\\n\'),\'\'),
ifnull(concat(email2,\'\\n\'),\'\')) as Emails from Users
where status = \'Active\' and deleted = 0 and id not in
(401,402,403,301,302,2000) order by last_name;
```

FIGURE 5.3. Sample Complex SELECT Statement

In cases where you are asking a developer to make a change to a data access, be aware that if the developer did not write the original SQL, he or she is going to need time to become familiar with the existing code before attempting to change it. As stated earlier, a simple one-word coding change can result in a significant change in the result. *This points out one reason why understanding the current or as is system is important.* A developer may make a change that answers the new requirement but negatively impacts an old requirement that still exists. The BA must understand what pieces of the existing system need to remain, along with the new functionality that is required.

```
SELECT * FROM order
JOIN customer
ON customer.customer_number = order.customer_number
ORDER BY order.order_date;
```

FIGURE 5.4. Sample JOIN Statement

Software Usability/Human Interface Design

Usability should be designed into solutions

Usability refers to the ease with which people can employ a particular tool or other human-made object in order to achieve a particular goal. It is important for BAs to understand the principles of software usability to help design usability into all of their project solutions. If your organization employs usability professionals, request their involvement on your project early. If possible, include them in requirements elicitation so that they can learn about the business needs and the business environment as you do. If your organization expects usability design as part of the role of the business analysis professional, learn about the principles and concepts. Jakob Nielsen's *Usability Engineering* is a great resource (Nielsen, 1993).

The International Organization for Standardization has defined a set of standards that detail the usability or *dialogue principles* of human/system interaction (ISO 9241 Part 110). Existing software interfaces can be assessed against these principles to determine the relative usability of existing software. As you read the principles, think about a software application with which you are familiar (e.g., Amazon.com). How well does it follow the principles?

1. **Suitability for the task**: This principle recommends that software functionality should be designed for the particular task the user is trying to accomplish based on the work required and the user's skill level. This includes facilitating logical workflows and the software's ability to work with other applications.
2. **Self-descriptiveness**: The interface should be intuitive and make it clear what the user should do next. Adherence to this principle eliminates the need for help systems and online procedure manuals.
3. **Controllability**: The user should be able to control the pace and sequence of the interaction and must be able to easily exit from the system whenever desired.
4. **Conformity with user expectations**: The software should behave consistently and as a user would expect. Whenever the software reacts differently than the user expects, there may be a usability issue (e.g., a user who clicks on a cancel button expects to be released from the current transaction).
5. **Error tolerance**: The software should be forgiving and be prepared to handle any user error. Error messages must be very clear and written in the user's

language. They should explain what error was made and how the user can correct the problem. In the most usable systems, software is built to anticipate and prevent user errors.

6. **Suitability for individualization**: The software should be customizable (i.e., menus, screen look) for individual users. Novice users should be provided help and expert users should be able to be highly productive.

7. **Suitability for learning**: The software should be simple and support learning so users can become more efficient and productive. It should use clear business terminology and minimize the user's memory load.

Software Testing

BAs support testing professionals to validate that the product meets business needs

One reason why you need to understand the technical environment is that you will probably be involved in testing solutions. Many BAs and many other project team members dislike testing because they don't understand it fully and because it has always been low on the IT priority list of areas to improve. A successful business analysis professional appreciates the importance of quality assurance practices and is able to step in and help when necessary.

Testing software programs and components has been done since software was first invented. Testing strategies and tactics are actually much older than software. Other disciplines perform testing: electrical systems are tested, architectural designs are tested, and the engineering discipline involves significant testing. As in many other respects, these disciplines, which are much more established than software development, can give great insights into testing approaches. Testing professionals use test plans, test cases, test procedures, and automated testing tools to plan and execute efficient, effective tests. A great introductory resource on software testing is *The Complete Guide to Software Testing* by Bill Hertzel (1993).

Many software testing practices can also be used on manual procedures and processes. Testing should not be limited to software. When a project solution includes new employee procedures, *test* them just as you would software. Design test cases for usual and unusual situations.

BABOK Connection	
Knowledge Area	**Task/Technique**
Solution Assessment and Validation	Validate Solution

Case in Point

I learned to enjoy testing when I starting conducting seminars on quality assurance. In the past, most of my testing had been on my own programs. No one enjoys finding problems with their own work, but when I started studying the core concepts of software testing, I realized that it is a sophisticated profession which brings great value to every project. There are very structured approaches to designing test cases so that they cover as many requirements as possible. When I began developing workshops for my seminars, I enjoyed designing the test plans, and students really enjoyed exercising the tests because when they found defects, they felt successful. This is when I realized why testers should be objective people who have not been involved with the software development work. Finding defects is like going on a scavenger hunt—the more you find, the better. Quality assurance professionals become very adept at designing clever test cases to try to fool the software and trick it into making mistakes. This is a valuable skill for an organization because it ensures better quality products.

Understanding the testing process helps the BA in requirements elicitation and analysis. The BA must make sure that each requirement is excellent by making sure that it is "testable" or "verifiable." The classic example of a requirement which is not testable is: "The system should be easy to use." There is not a clear test that could be designed to validate this requirement. When an analyst thinks about how each requirement will be tested, he or she writes more detailed, precise requirements. The experienced analyst also considers performance requirements when helping to design a solution. Specific performance requirements must be elicited by the analyst even though they will often be difficult for subject matter experts and users to articulate. "It needs to be fast" is not a useful requirement. The BA uses questions and examples to help users determine their performance tolerance: "If the query request was returned within 30 seconds, would you be satisfied? Let's sit here quietly for 30 seconds to see what that much time feels like." "Would 45 seconds be too long?" "Would you accept a system that returned short, simple queries in an average of 15 seconds, while complex queries might take up to 60 seconds?"

BAs are involved in test planning and in designing realistic, useful test cases. BAs also are key team members as defects are found and corrected. Since BAs understand the requirements and the solution design, they often see defects and know from where

BABOK Connection	
Knowledge Area	**Task/Technique**
Solution Assessment and Validation	Defect and Issue Reporting

they originated. BAs often report defects and research them to determine the cause and the correction.

Most software development testing approaches used today are based around the standards set by the Institute of Electrical and Electronics Engineers (www.ieee.org). This professional organization dates back to 1884 and has a lot of experience and knowledge from which to draw. What software developers discovered early is that testing software applications is similar to testing electronics products. Each individual component is tested separately (unit testing), then connections between pieces are tested (integration testing), and then an entire product is tested together (system testing). Finally, the product is tested by the end users (user acceptance testing) to allow them to be confident that the product does what they need. One of the reasons why use case descriptions (see Chapter 6) have become such a popular analysis technique is that a use case leads directly to a test case. Software quality assurance (SQA) professionals can quickly understand the requirements and understand how best to the test the software against the requirements.

SQA professionals and the approaches they recommend always involve quality activities at the beginning of and throughout a project. An SQA professional should be involved with project scoping, reviewing requirements, reviewing designs, and testing to be sure that the product works and that it meets user needs. All too often, due to resource constraints, an SQA person is added to a team after it is behind schedule to quickly test the product and get it ready for production. Coming onto the team in a late stage does not give the SQA professional much chance to influence the quality of the outcome. It simply puts that person in the position of testing and identifying defects.

Many BAs are expected to perform all of the business analysis tasks along with all of the SQA tasks. If testing will be part of your responsibility, get formal training in standard SQA practices and work to incorporate these standards into your organization. When you are assigned to a large project, talk with your project manager about bringing on an SQA professional. Explain that an objective quality professional will be more valuable and allow you to focus on the business analysis work.

Software Testing Phases

BAs need to understand the testing process

Even if not responsible for planning and executing tests, every BA should understand the common testing phases and practices. When a project's solution is in the testing phase, the BA should be closely involved. As tests are executed and defects found, the BA is a

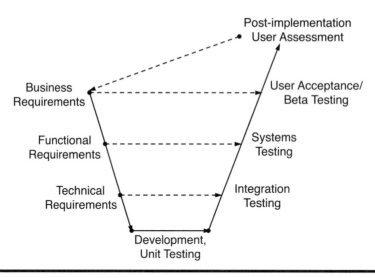

FIGURE 5.5. Sample V Model for Software Testing

great resource to help determine the cause of the defects and to help with ideas for correcting them. Some of the problems found will require business stakeholders to make decisions, and the BA can help with these. The BA should also be watching for errors that were caused by poor requirements. BAs can significantly improve their elicitation and analysis skills by learning from prior mistakes. Look upon these mistakes as *lessons learned.*

Software testing approaches are based on the *V model.* There are many variations of the V model, but the fundamental concept of this model is that software testing should begin as soon as a project is initiated. The V model recommends that the software testing team be independent from the development team. This independence fosters more thorough and unbiased evaluation of product quality (Kooman and Pol, 1999). During each phase of the software development life cycle, there is a corresponding phase of software testing. These phases are called unit testing, integration testing, systems testing, and user acceptance testing. See Figure 5.5 for one version of the V model.

Unit Testing

Unit testing is usually the first level of testing and is performed by the developer. A unit is a small piece of the software that can be tested individually. The objective of unit testing is to find problems in the smallest component of a system before testing the system in its entirety. BAs may assist developers by identifying test cases and reviewing unit test results.

Integration Testing

The next level or phase of testing is referred to as *integration testing*. Integration testing requires the individually tested units to be integrated and tested as a larger unit or subsystem. The objective of integration testing is to find problems in how components of a system work together. These tests validate the software architecture design. The development team or quality assurance team performs integration testing. BAs may assist by identifying test cases and reviewing test results. Inadequate integration testing, often due to waiting too late in the development process, is one of the main causes of project failure.

System Testing

The next level or phase of testing is called *system testing*. System testing is the last chance for a project team to verify a product before turning it over to users for their review. The objective of system testing is to find problems in how the software meets the users' needs. These tests validate that the software meets the original requirements. BAs are involved with system testing by making sure that the software meets the business requirements.

There are several types of tests that may be performed as a part of system testing. Table 5.4 provides some examples.

Regression Testing

Regression testing is a specific type of testing with which a BA must be familiar. The concept is simple: after any software change, retest functions of the software that have not changed to be sure that the results are still correct. As simple as the concept is, it is one of the biggest areas of failure in the testing discipline. Why? Because who wants to test something that has already been tested? It is not glamorous or exciting, it often does not expose any defects or quality enhancements, and it can be very tedious and boring. Having acknowledged these issues, regression testing *must* be done. Software is very complex, and a small change can easily "break" something else that was previously working fine. Regression testing is performed throughout all of the other testing phases when changes are made after the initial testing has been completed.

TABLE 5.4. System-Level Tests

Test Type	Purpose
Requirements validation	Makes sure that system logic supports the business and functional requirements
Performance testing	Measures the speed of response
Stress testing	Pushes the software to its limits in terms of number of users and rate of input
Volume testing	Uses high-volume transactions to verify that the software will handle all growth projections
Security testing	Makes sure that unauthorized users cannot gain access to confidential data and that authorized users can effectively complete their required tasks
Installation testing	Important for software that will be shipped to users and requires local installation
Configuration testing	Determines how the software will perform on various types of hardware, operating system, networks, and in conjunction with other software packages running on the same system
Usability testing	Verifies that the software has been designed for the users within the principles of usability

Case in Point

A good analogy for regression testing is the electrical system in your house. Let's say that you hire an electrician to install a new outlet in the wall where you want to hang a flat screen TV. When he is done, you plug a small lamp into the new outlet to test it before you pay the electrician. The lamp works. Later in the day, you turn on the switch for the ceiling fan in the room and nothing happens. Did the electrician cut a wire to the ceiling fan? Did he simply reroute the ceiling fan wire to the new outlet? You probably didn't explicitly say that you still expected the ceiling fan to work after the TV was installed! It was an existing requirement that you didn't feel the need to restate.

After you hang the TV on the wall and your family settles in to watch a movie, your daughter decides to make microwave popcorn. There is a loud pop and all of the power on one side of your house goes out! The electrician may have put the TV on the same circuit as the kitchen, which is not powerful enough to handle everything on it. Did you *specify* that you wanted to be able to use the microwave while watching TV?

Business stakeholders experience these same frustrations when a new requirement is fulfilled but the old functionality suddenly behaves differently. They didn't specifically say "all of the existing screens should still work the same way after the new one is installed." But this is an implied requirement that is verified through regression testing.

User Acceptance Testing

Most BAs are involved in user acceptance testing (UAT). UAT is the final phase of testing. Users test real-life scenarios to verify that the software will meet their needs. UAT is an important step in validating that the end solution meets the business needs. This conformance testing is named as such because the intention is that the users of the software will run the tests and accept the product. As software continues to become more complex and less procedural, testing becomes more complex. Testing software is challenging for even the most experienced SQA professionals. If it is difficult for them, think about how overwhelming it may seem to users. This complexity is why many organizations ask BAs to get involved. Typically, when software is sold outside of the development organization, UAT is referred to as *beta testing* and allows users to try out a new version of the software before its general release.

Why should users do UAT? Ideally, users are executing tests and building their confidence that the product does what they hoped it would do. Unfortunately, assigning a BA to this task often gives users the idea that they don't have to participate. They feel that they have told the BA all of their requirements, so the BA should be able to accept the software. Don't allow this to happen. Losing stakeholder engagement at this critical junction in a project may create dissatisfaction with the solution implemented. This is a dangerous situation and one that every BA should work to avoid. There are a couple of common reasons why this occurs, so beware!

1. Users, like everyone else, are very busy. If they think that the BA can do the work for them, they will be happy to let him or her do it.

2. Testing is hard work, and most users have never been trained in how or why they are doing it. No one likes doing something that they don't really know how to do well.

3. Users often do not realize the likelihood of errors in developed software. This is not a negative statement about developers. It is a fact that developing software is difficult and discovering defects is a normal part of the process. Users may not be aware of the risk if a defect is not found.

4. Finally, users do not realize the significant impending change that the software will have on their work environment and they need to get prepared. When users actually work with the software during UAT, they realize how their corresponding procedures are going to have to change.

Although there are a few obstacles to overcome when trying to get users more involved with UAT, the benefits are enormous. Users who actually participate in UAT are usually more satisfied with the end product than those who do not. They are not shocked

BABOK Connection	
Knowledge Area	**Task/Technique**
Solution Assessment and Validation	User Acceptance Testing

by the change after deployment, but rather are gently prodded toward the change during UAT. Users who are committed to the entire software development process are more likely to get the product they need (Kupersmith, 2007).

Post-Implementation User Assessment

Post-implementation user assessment is an evaluation of the effectiveness of the software after it has been thoroughly used in the business area. This is an important part of the testing life cycle but is often missed. The objective of post-implementation user assessment is to find out how well the solution meets user requirements. BAs, project managers, and/ or quality assurance analysts perform the assessment by observing users at their jobs or asking well-designed questions and conducting a follow-up session.

The real proof of whether a system fulfills the needs of the business area will only come as it is being used. This is the final validation. After training and a settling in period, BAs should discuss with users the

BABOK Connection	
Knowledge Area	**Task/Technique**
Solution Assessment and Validation	Evaluate Solution Performance

usefulness of the system. BAs may also take measurements to determine if the system is performing as expected and to determine if the original objectives of the project were met.

WORKING WITH IT

Communicating with Developers

Some developers are not accustomed to receiving excellent requirements and as such don't expect them. They may have been handed poorly written requirements in the past and don't think that it is worth their time to read them. They may be accustomed to working without clear requirements and have experience iteratively developing and redeveloping them based on feedback. In some environments, this agile method of development works very well.

Work with the developers to encourage them to review requirements by walking through your requirements with them, helping them to see that they are getting useful information. If the developers aren't accustomed to using or working from requirements, you may want to give them a small piece of a requirement, schedule a walkthrough over the phone or in person, and lead them through the document. You may want to present a use case or a subset of the data model. As you walk through the document, section by section, ask if they have questions or comments. As they begin to develop the software and come back to you with questions, point them back to the document if a question is one that you have already addressed. You want to get them in the habit of looking at the requirements package when they have questions. As they begin to see that you have already thought about things like exceptions and alternate paths, they will become more confident in your documents and more willing to read them.

Most developers are creative and enjoy offering suggestions. Whenever possible, ask developers for ideas within the limitations of the requirements. This is another reason why written requirements are so useful. If you give a developer clear guidelines within which he or she can be creative, you will often get a great design. When not given clear boundaries, a developer may create something that looks great but can't be used because it doesn't meet user needs. This can be discouraging for the developer. Be specific about the functionality that is needed and the business rules that must be adhered to.

Some developers will be interested in understanding why the business needs a particular function, while other developers will be satisfied just to build it. For developers who ask why, share business information. This will help them better understand the reason for their work and often make them more committed team members. For developers who aren't interested in understanding the business reasons for a function, don't give them too much information. Many developers are very "black and white": "Do you want the *source* data field converted to a data field called *lead source*? Yes or no?" Answer questions directly and concisely. (A three-paragraph dissertation on what a source is and how the business people use sources to generate more business is too much information for many developers.)

Communicating requirements is complicated by the use of outside and/or offshore developers. Utilize the best communication technology available and increase the formality and detail of your requirements for offsite team members.

BABOK Connection	
Knowledge Area	**Task/Technique**
Underlying Competencies	Communication Skills

When to Get IT Involved in a Project

One of the steps in business analysis planning is to think about when it will be appropriate to involve the IT stakeholders in a project and which of them to involve first. As with most business analysis questions, the answer is "it depends."

On a small, maintenance project where you anticipate only a minor change to an existing application, there may be no reason to get IT involved until you are prepared to provide a detailed description of the change. Examples of this type of change would be moving a field on a screen to a new position or changing the format of a report.

On large or brand new development projects, an IT architect should be involved from the very beginning of the project because there will be many decisions to be made. For example:

◆ On what platform will the new application be run?
◆ Which database management system will hold the data?
◆ What constraints will be faced from the interfacing applications?
◆ What type of technical architecture is needed?

On medium-size projects, involve IT as needed. The following guidelines may help in making this decision:

◆ When the solution will need new information (data) to be stored electronically—involve IT early (specifically data management people)
◆ When the business user community is large and their daily work will be changed—involve IT or help desk management early
◆ When you hope to automate complex business rules—involve IT early
◆ When large volumes of data are to be reported on or queried—involve IT early

Err on the side of caution and talk with the IT stakeholders as early as possible just to make sure there is not a major technology issue in your path. The earlier the IT architect knows a change is coming, the more time he or she will have to plan for it. The IT architect also may be aware of other related projects that are going on that need to be coordinated with yours.

In addition, asking IT for suggestions, confirmation, and buy-in early in the process improves relationships and will smooth the implementation process. No one wants to be surprised by a change at the last minute and no one wants to be told to make a change. People would rather be *asked*. Involving IT early means that you can ask for ideas before the requirements have been written and improve the quality and accuracy of the requirements.

IT Corporate Culture

Every IT organization has a culture and a unique environment. It is important for BAs to be aware of this culture and environment to adapt work styles to fit the organization. Consultants have known this for years. When a consultant walks into a new organization, he or she immediately begins to get clues about the culture of the company. Most people automatically perform this type of assessment during an interview for a new job. What do the employees wear? Is the office generally quiet or noisy? Are people working calmly or is there a sense of panic and immediacy? These initial clues tell us a lot about how projects are going to be run in an organization.

Understanding the technical environment also involves awareness of how an enterprise views technology. Is technology a key driver for the organization, as in the case of a software vendor? Or is technology a support mechanism that allows the organization to fulfill its true mission, as in the case of a hospice company where patient care and personal service are the important products and technology is used to support the people providing the core service?

SUMMARY OF KEY POINTS

Effective BAs understand technology concepts and constraints. They can talk intelligently with technical stakeholders when discussing solution options. They appreciate the complexity of the IT environment and properly set user expectations.

◆ Excellent BAs must be constantly vigilant for new opportunities for technology usage so that they can assist with implementation of new technologies that will most benefit the business. Read about new technology in periodicals, vendor white papers, and product reviews. Subscribe to online magazines and communities and review main articles frequently.

◆ Technology is changing every day in new and unpredictable ways. It is very exciting, but it can be very intimidating and overwhelming to try to stay on top of everything that is going on.

◆ It is important for BAs to understand the software development methodologies, and their requirements deliverables, used in an organization.

◆ Business analysis professionals don't need to understand the underlying architecture of technology, how it was created, or how it is maintained; however, they must know key terms in order to communicate with IT architects, developers, data managers, and infrastructure support personnel.

BIBLIOGRAPHY

Carkenord, Barbara (2004). Why does a business analyst need to worry about data? *the bridge* magazine, B2T Training. Fall/Winter (www.b2ttraining.com).

Carkenord, Barbara (2007). How Does a BA Add Value to an Agile Project? White Paper. B2T Training. Fall (www.b2ttraining.com).

Fleming, Candace C. and Barbara von Halle (1989). *Handbook of Relational Database Design.* Addison-Wesley Professional.

Forta, Ben (2004). *Sams Teach Yourself SQL in 10 Minutes.* Third Edition. Sams.

Hertzel, Bill (1993). *The Complete Guide to Software Testing.* Second Edition. Wiley-QED Publication.

Jacobson, Ivar (1992). *Object Oriented Software Engineering: A Use Case Driven Approach.* Addison-Wesley Professional.

Kooman, Tim and Martin Pol (1999). *Test Procedure Improvement.* Addison-Wesley.

Kupersmith, Jonathan (2007). Putting the user back in user acceptance testing. *the bridge* magazine, B2T Training. Fall.

Martin, James (1986). *Information Engineering.* Savant.

McConnell, Steve (1996). *Rapid Development: Taming Wild Software Schedules.* Microsoft Press.

Nielsen, Jakob (1993). *Usability Engineering.* Morgan Kaufmann.

Royce, Walker (1998). *Software Project Management: A Unified Framework.* Addison-Wesley Object Technology Series. Addison-Wesley Professional.

Schwabler, Ken (2004). *Agile Project Management with Scrum.* Microsoft Professional Publishing.

Wood, Jane and Denise Silver (1995). *Joint Application Development.* Second Edition. John Wiley.

6

KNOW YOUR ANALYSIS TECHNIQUES

Business analysis professionals spend the majority of their time working with requirements: eliciting requirements from business stakeholders, analyzing requirements, presenting them to business stakeholders for review, and presenting them to the solution team for execution. *Presenting* requirements refers to communicating the requirements to the appropriate stakeholder in the most appropriate format. Business stakeholders must review and confirm business requirements before they are used to design solutions. Depending on the individual business stakeholders, the appropriate presentation may be a formal requirements package or a working simulation of the potential software. IT architect stakeholders and solution designers must review functional requirements to understand the needs of the business and the desired solution functionality. These stakeholders may prefer to see requirements in diagrams or models that mirror software design specifications. Developers must review technical requirements and specifications to build the solution. They often prefer prototypes of screens, report layouts, and use case descriptions that show expected user interaction with the software. Any of these requirements may be presented formally in a traditional requirements package or informally in a slide presentation or handwritten on flip charts or white boards. *Regardless of the level of formality and materials used to present the requirements, requirements must be analyzed and presented.* The business analysis professional makes decisions about how to best analyze, understand, and communicate requirements to best support stakeholders and stay within the project time frame.

Because requirements are so important, everyone on the project team should understand and agree upon what a requirement is and how requirements will be expressed and presented. This chapter discusses the organization and categorization of requirements, identification of core requirements components, useful analysis and presentation techniques, and the criteria to use when deciding how formally requirements should be presented.

Experienced analysts have found diagrams, models, prototypes, simulation, and tables to be more useful than pure text. Business analysts (BAs) must work to learn these visual communication techniques and sometimes educate stakeholders on the value of these presentation formats.

There are many techniques for analyzing and presenting requirements. Each technique focuses on particular core requirements components. Each technique has a history and was developed to meet a particular need. Over time, these techniques have been used by thousands of analysts, and some individuals have altered the techniques depending on the circumstances. There is no wrong way to "analyze" or "think." These techniques are simply tools to help the analyst see a problem or situation from a different perspective. Most projects will benefit from the use of several techniques.

The totality of requirements and analysis work is referred to inconsistently among business analysis and software development professionals. Requirements management, requirements engineering, software engineering, and systems analysis all refer to the development of requirements using different definitions and terminology. Requirements drive all project work, so their importance cannot be overstated. The challenges for business analysis professionals come in deciding how to best analyze and communicate the requirements.

Case in Point

I was consulting with an organization that was looking for some process improvement suggestions. The work was very manual, and as the volume increased, workers were asked to put in more and more overtime. The business process involved returns of a consumer product that were repackaged and distributed to a discount outlet center. Each product returned (a pair of shoes) had to be inspected for wear and readiness for resale at a discount store. Workers had to make sure that both shoes were the same style and size and that there was a right and left shoe! As a worker opened a returned shoe box, he or she made several decisions and then acted based on those decisions: Does the box need to be replaced because it was damaged? Does the tissue paper surrounding the shoes need to be replaced? Are the shoes damaged or worn? Do the shoes match?

I taught the analysts about workflow diagrams. I showed them how to use Microsoft Office Visio® to produce the diagrams professionally. We practiced representing a couple of business processes using common flowcharting shapes and discussed the use of off-page connectors if a process diagram required more than one page. We drew a geographic workflow diagram of the work area showing the location of new shoe boxes, tissue paper, tags, etc. I left the assignment for a few weeks feeling confident that the analysts would be able to document their current processes and begin to look for areas of improvement before my scheduled return.

On my next visit, I planned to review their as is workflow diagrams and facilitate the process improvement brainstorming sessions. When I arrived, I was surprised to hear that the analysts weren't ready for me. They had not finished their as is workflow diagrams. As I began talking with the analysts and reviewing the work that they had done, a clear pattern emerged. The analysts had studied their processes and taken detailed notes. Each one had begun creating the workflow diagrams in Visio, and this is where the problem occurred. They had spent hours and hours moving shapes around on their screens, attempting to create the perfect diagram. Decisions about where to place each symbol and how best to attach a flow line became paralyzing. It was almost as if they were creating great works of art that couldn't be unveiled until every detail was complete. They had spent weeks focusing on aesthetics and never once thought about how the business processes might be improved. They were so distracted with the result of the technique that they forgot to analyze. This is a common problem with new analysts and one of the reasons why mentors are so important. New analysts often do not want to show anyone a requirement deliverable until it is perfect. This is a mistake. Early reviews of rough drafts will keep you moving in the right direction.

CATEGORIZING AND PRESENTING REQUIREMENTS

Collecting and Managing Requirements

A BA must be organized in order to collect and maintain requirements information. As you perform business analysis work, you will collect a considerable amount of information. Much of this information is given to you verbally, but additionally you will receive e-mail messages, documents, forms, example reports, files, old requirements documents, and much more. One of your critical skills as a BA is the ability to organize all of this information, consider its importance to your project, and maintain it in a retrievable, usable form. You are effectively the repository for the project requirements.

If you do not have a sophisticated requirements management tool to serve as your repository, you need to have your own system. Many analysts use filing systems and notebooks to keep and organize this information. Having a standard requirements package is very helpful because you can add information to the package as you receive it and put it exactly where it belongs. This makes review and retrieval much easier.

In addition to requirements, there is other project information that the BA must maintain: meeting minutes, history of interviews, outstanding issues/questions list, current project schedule, etc. You must be able to find and refer back to project docu-

BABOK Connection	
Knowledge Area	**Task/Technique**
Underlying Competencies	Behavioral

mentation quickly when needed. The only way to do this is to have a system for organizing and storing the information when you receive it.

What Is a Requirement?

Every experienced BA has his or her own understanding of what a "requirement" looks like, but the profession does not have a shared understanding. According to the International Institute of Business Analysis (IIBA™) *Guide to the Business Analysis Body of Knowledge®* (BABOK®), Version 2.0 Draft 2008:

> A requirement is a condition or capability needed by a stakeholder to solve a problem or achieve an objective.

Another way to define a requirement is *anything that is important enough to discuss, analyze, document, and validate.* A requirement can be documented and presented as:

- ◆ A sentence ("The system shall . . .")
- ◆ A structured sentence (as in a business rule)
- ◆ A structured text template
- ◆ A table or spreadsheet (list of stakeholders)
- ◆ A diagram (workflow)
- ◆ A model (entity relationship diagram with associated details)

◆ A prototype or simulation
◆ A graph
◆ Any number of other formats

The format or representation does not qualify something as a requirement; it is the *intent* and the *stakeholder need* that make it a requirement. There is debate among BAs about what qualifies as a requirement. Is a screen layout a requirement? Is a business rule a requirement? Is a test case a requirement? *The business analysis profession should broaden the term requirement to include everything that BAs produce to communicate with their stakeholders to accomplish the completion of a product.* Make sure that your organization, or at least your team, agrees on the definition of *requirement.*

BAs often create diagrams, notes, spreadsheets, scribbles, etc. that they use to analyze and think through a particular problem. These "work products" may not be presented to stakeholders, but they assist the BA in his or her work. They are analysis tools that help the analyst understand the requirements.

Categorizing Requirements

Most BAs agree that requirements need to be categorized. Categories are needed because when requirements are correct and complete, they are usually very detailed. Most projects include a large number of these detailed requirements. When there are

BABOK Connection	
Knowledge Area	**Task/Technique**
Requirements Analysis	Organize Requirements

a large number of "things" to keep track of, organizing these "things" into logical categories allows them to be found easily and used quickly.

Case in Point

Think about how people keep track of books: fiction, non-fiction, biography, children's, etc. When we walk into a bookstore or library looking for a particular book, the categories help us find the book for which we are searching. Some books are very easy to categorize. For example, biographies are shelved in alphabetical order by the subject of the biography (e.g., biographies about Thomas Jefferson are shelved under J). Other books are more difficult to categorize. Where would a book on World War II be shelved? It could be in history, historical fiction, biography, sociology, or American studies. Categorizing requirements presents this same challenge. Deciding on categories and placing specific requirements into these categories is as much an art as it is a science. Each person who looks at a requirement may categorize it in a different way. There may be more than one category that is applicable to a particular requirement.

Over the years of book publishing, some general guidelines have been developed for categorizing books. Libraries in the United States use the Dewey Decimal Classification® system. Many bookstores generally follow these guidelines but make changes as appropriate for their customers, publishers, authors, and employees. Having general guidelines makes the search for books much easier.

If you owned a bookstore, even a small one, how would you categorize books? Would you use a system that makes sense to your employees, so that they could quickly shelve new stock as it arrives? Would you use a system that makes sense to your customers, so that they can quickly find the books they want? Would you use the Dewey Decimal System? What if a new book is published that doesn't belong in any of your categories? Would you create a new category? Would you reorganize all of your categories once a month? Once a year? Never? Develop a consistent approach to categorization and communicate it to all of the stakeholders.

Why Categorize Requirements?

The most obvious reason for categorizing requirements is to keep them organized and easy to find. When a project generates a large number of complex requirements, the only way to manage them is to separate them into categories and uniquely identify them. To build consistency into the analysis process, the same categories should be used on every project. Any team member on any project will know the categories and be able to organize and review requirements quickly.

The second and maybe most important reason for categorizing requirements is to separate them by audience. Remember that the only reason why requirements are formally documented and presented is to communicate and confirm understanding (and to decrease reliance on people's memories!). Different types of requirements will be reviewed and approved by different stakeholders. Business stakeholders review business requirements to make sure that the true business needs are understood and that nothing has been missed. Developers review detailed functional requirements. This points to the practicality of categorizing and presenting like requirements together. Using the same logic, technical requirements are rarely reviewed by business stakeholders and as such should be categorized separately and presented specifically to the technical team.

A third reason for categorizing requirements is reusability. True business requirements will outlive software applications and procedures. When business requirements are created from the *what* perspective, they can be used on other projects. Reusing requirements saves time and encourages enterprise-wide consistency. These are excellent results of the business analysis discipline. Functional requirements may be reused when enhancements are requested to existing software. The original functional design can be used to show the change. Technical requirements become important documentation for software implementers, support people, and the maintenance team. In addition, a successful technical design may be copied and reused for another application.

Finally, a reason to categorize requirements is to facilitate impact analysis for managing change requests. Impact analysis refers to the assessment made to determine the ramifications (impact) of a proposed change. Impact analysis relies on requirements traceability. After a solution system has been deployed and is being used successfully, changes are often requested. Maybe the business has decided to offer a new type of product or service. Business leaders will ask: "What is the impact of this change? How much will it cost to change our systems?" Impact analysis requires the analyst to review existing systems to determine what changes need to be made. Having requirements clearly categorized and organized provides the analyst with the material needed to quickly assess the impact of a change.

Deciding on categories is time consuming and challenging, so it is inefficient to develop a new set of categories every time you start a project. An organization will be most efficient if it decides on one general categorization scheme and uses it consistently. A consistent system will increase BA efficiency, even if it is not perfect. Review the system periodically to make adjustments. The following are some suggestions for setting up your own system.

Developing a System for Organizing Requirements

There are many factors to consider when designing a requirements categorization system. You must balance these factors to create the best system for your organization. Understanding *why* you are documenting requirements will help you decide how to best categorize them. Think about the following questions:

Should requirements be separated by type? Business vs. functional? This is a great question and one that initially seems very obvious. The business requirements (business needs that are independent of technology) may be listed separately from functional requirements (behaviors of software), but for some requirements components this results in repeated information (i.e., description of a piece of business data listed in the data model and with screens where it is used).

In what order will the requirements be gathered? This is the least useful approach to organizing requirements even though it may initially appear to be the easiest. Unfortunately, requirements are often not elicited or gathered in a logical order. Business stakeholders don't always talk about their needs in a straightforward, linear fashion. In addition, the iterative nature of requirements development means that the BA will often be presented with unrelated requirements and then have to figure out where to "put" them. Imagine if a publisher delivered a large box of books to your bookstore that were not in any particular order. Simply placing them on the shelf as they come in will not be useful when a customer is looking for a particular book.

Who will review each requirement? A BA's most important job is to clearly communicate with stakeholders. Often, several stakeholders will be reviewing the requirements document and it would be most efficient for the BA to present the requirements in an order that will make reviewing as easy as possible. Is a stakeholder from accounts payable who only needs to review a few key financial requirements required to read the entire package and search only for the items in which he or she is interested? On the other hand, do many of the requirements that affect accounts payable also affect other stakeholders?

How is each requirement used? This consideration is important when the requirements relate to software development. Most developers are not anxious to read volumes of business requirements. They want to know exactly what you want the software to do. They also prefer the requirements to be separated by the technology needed. For example: put all data elements together to assist the database designer, or list all users together to make the security access design easier (see the section on core requirements components later in this chapter). Are the developers on-site or offshore? How often will you be communicating with them? These factors will also play into your decision.

How are the requirements related to each other? Tracing requirements to each other is a very important technique to ensure completeness and decrease change management time. There are very few requirements that are not related to at least one other requirement. These relationships between requirements make their presentation more complex. This aspect of requirements argues for a unique name or number for every requirement.

These unique identifiers are invaluable for tracing (see the section on traceability matrices later in this chapter). This is one of the many areas where a requirements management tool is very beneficial.

Should the same requirement be presented in different ways for different stakeholders?
Ideally, the answer to this question is no. It is not efficient to repackage the same information in multiple ways. However, a BA's most important job is to clearly communicate with stakeholders. If a requirement is clear to one stakeholder in a graphical format and clear to another stakeholder in a sentence, then it may have to be presented in multiple versions. If this is necessary (make sure that it is *absolutely* necessary), then both versions must be kept up to date when there are changes.

Which requirements are reusable? Many requirements are reusable on future projects, and it may be helpful to document them together. Business requirements that are technology independent can be reused on future projects and as such should be kept together in a format that allows other analysts to access them. Data requirements are reusable and most easily referenced when they are documented in the same format, in the same place. This is another area where a requirements management tool is very helpful.

If your organization does not have a consistent categorization schema—implement one. Create one, try it, and revise as you learn. Any system is better than none. Most projects have a large enough number of requirements to justify categorizing them into groups. These groupings make the requirements easier to document, double check, and review.

IIBA BABOK Categories

The IIBA BABOK committee discussed categories of requirements for hours, each member bringing his or her own system to the group. Although there was general agreement on most topics, this one was not easily resolved. In the end, the group decided that there is not one *right* system that will work for all organizations. All of the committee members agreed that any logical system will work if used properly. The BABOK lists a few example categories as common practices: business requirements, stakeholder requirements, solution requirements (functional and non-functional requirements), and implementation or transition requirements. (The latest version of the IIBA BABOK definition of each is available at www.iiba.org.)

A Recommended Categorization System

If you are just developing a categorization system, it is recommended that you use three main categories to organize requirements: *business, functional,* and *technical.* An additional section of requirements called *non-functional* will support the functional category. These categories are fairly common and are used by many organizations. Organizations are most successful when they initially implement a simple system with a small number of categories to get the people in the organization used to the categorization idea.

Business Requirements

Business requirements are the detailed descriptions of information, business activities, business rules, and external interactions needed to accomplish the business mission. They are described using business terminology and presented in formats that are easy for business people to review.

Business requirements address business problems, needs, and goals independent of *how* they might be solved and accomplished. Business requirements include the project initiation components (statement of purpose, objectives, risks, etc., discussed in Chapter 3) and the core components of data, process, and business rules. These components are described using business terminology and together comprise a picture of the business which may also be referred to as the *business model. Business requirements should be understood in detail. A common misconception is that business requirements are high level only.* This view causes analysts to miss critical business needs. These requirements are elicited and analyzed to gain a complete understanding of the business in order to recommend effective solutions. If the business is not understood—in detail, solution recommendations may be inappropriate and not solve the business problem.

Business requirements do not describe *how* work is done but rather *what* work is accomplished. This *what* vs. *how* difference is very important. Business requirements are elicited, analyzed, and documented by business analysis professionals. BAs must be able to differentiate between a business need (*what*) and a procedural or software function (*how*).

To understand the difference between a *what* and a *how,* look at a business process like *sell product.* This process is a business requirement because it is a core business need (refer to the section on what a business process is in Chapter 4) and is named to describe the business goal without indicating *how* the goal is accomplished. There could be many ways that this business process can be performed. Once a product is sold in a store with a customer and salesclerk talking face to face, the customer could pay for the product with cash, a check, or a credit card. The clerk could record the sale in a ledger book, on a cash register, or with a scanning machine. The customer could carry the product out of the store or request that it be delivered. Another way the business process could be accomplished is the product could be sold via the Internet. A customer in a remote location could select the product from an online catalog, pay through an online service, and request shipping. The "salesclerk" in this case may be a fulfillment worker who boxes the product and gives it to the shipper. If the product can be transferred electronically, another possible sale could be a download to the customer.

All of these possible procedures support the core business process *sell product.* Business requirements are those core, fundamental components of a business that don't change much over time. They are the most important requirements because all procedures, software, solutions, etc. should support the core business requirements. Identifying the true fundamental business needs allows many possibilities for delivery or distribution. These possibilities are the *hows* or functional requirements.

Functional Requirements

Functional requirements describe how work will be done. How will data be collected and stored? How will business rules be enforced? How will communication with people, organizations, and systems take place? For each business requirement, there may be several functional requirements that support it. When software is used to support the business requirements, functional requirements describe what the software will "look like" to the end user. How will the software *function* (this is the root of the category name) or *behave*? For business requirements that are not supported by software, functional requirements include employee procedures, forms, workflows, policy documents, and guidelines that describe *how* the work will be done.

Functional requirements describe observable behaviors the system should exhibit. They are a view from the user's perspective of *how* the system or process will work. Functional requirements are typically used to describe software applications, although many of the functional analysis techniques are also useful for describing process changes. Functional requirements typically include a design area scope description which shows the boundaries of the software to be built. This scope may be shown on a use case diagram, with a list of processes or features, or in a narrative. Once the scope of the software is defined, functional requirements are developed to describe the functionality. Functional requirements include descriptions and diagrams showing how the user will interact with the software. This will include screen designs, report layouts, and warning messages based on business rules. To design these components, analysts and technical architects will often develop a list of potential users, indicating each user's needs and goals (called a use case). In addition to describing *how* the software will interact with users, functional requirements also include detailed data definitions. These definitions are developed directly from the business data requirements and describe how the business data will look, be entered, be validated, and be reported on.

Functional requirements are typically documented by BAs. Deciding how a solution will be designed is a collaborative effort between the business people and the technology staff. The BA facilitates discussions with individuals from various stakeholder groups to come to consensus on a design that meets business needs and is technologically feasible.

Non-Functional Requirements

Solution requirements are typically broken down into functional and non-functional requirements. Different methodologies refer to non-functional requirements as supplementary requirements, constraints, or quality of service requirements. *These requirements are only created when a software solution is being developed. They are requirements for the software that may not be directly related to particular business needs, functions, or behaviors.* These are requirements that the software must meet to fulfill the user's needs. Some examples include:

◆ Accessibility
◆ Audit and control
◆ Compatibility
◆ Effectiveness (resulting performance in relation to effort)
◆ Efficiency (resource consumption for a given load)
◆ Extensibility (adding features and carry-forward of customizations at next major version upgrade)
◆ Legal and licensing issues
◆ Maintainability
◆ Performance/response time
◆ Quality (e.g., faults discovered, faults delivered)
◆ Reliability

- Resource constraints (processor speed, memory, disk space, network bandwidth, etc.)
- Safety
- Scalability (horizontal, vertical)
- Security
- Stability
- System availability
- Usability and learn ability

These non-functional requirements may be elicited and documented by the BA in conjunction with IT resources.

BABOK Connection	
Knowledge Area	**Task/Technique**
Requirements Analysis	Non-functional Requirements

Technical Requirements

Technical requirements include detailed descriptions of the technical architecture framework, database definitions, business rule engines, program logic, development objects, application interfaces, network architecture, security components, and many other of the technical specifications of a solution. These technical requirements (also referred to as *specifications*) specify how the solution should be built and integrated into existing systems in the organization. The technical requirements are developed based on the functional and non-functional requirements agreed upon by the business stakeholders and sponsor. They include hardware descriptions, database designs, programming standards, and guidelines. They may include specific product names of software development tools that will be used. In addition, the technical requirements will include a description of how interfaces to outside systems will be accomplished. These descriptions include data sent to, or received from, other applications and any required conversion algorithms. BAs rarely write technical requirements (unless a BA is also playing the role of IT architect or systems analyst), but may be asked to review them. This review process allows the BA to confirm that the technical plans support the true business needs (via the functional requirements).

Stepping through the categories of requirements and their relationship to each other shows the importance of identifying complete requirements from the beginning. When business requirements are used as the basis for solution design discussions (as they should be), they must be complete. A missed business requirement will result in several missed functional requirements and may drive the technical architecture design in a way that prevents the business need from being easily added later.

CORE REQUIREMENTS COMPONENTS

After using and understanding many business analysis techniques, a few common core components emerge. Each analysis technique looks at a requirement or set of requirements from a unique perspective. Looking at a requirement from different perspectives is like picking up an object (e.g., a cell phone or a can of soda) and examining it from different sides, at different angles and in different lights. If the object has moving parts, you move them to watch how the object changes. Carefully examining the object gives you information about its construction and its uses. Looking at a requirement from all "sides" helps the BA more clearly understand it. Breaking a requirement into its core components opens the moving parts and lets you examine it from the inside out.

The core requirements components are data, process, business rules, and external agents. The techniques and approaches used to analyze a project must encompass these four components or you will miss an important part of your analysis. Figure 6.1 shows an example of these components.

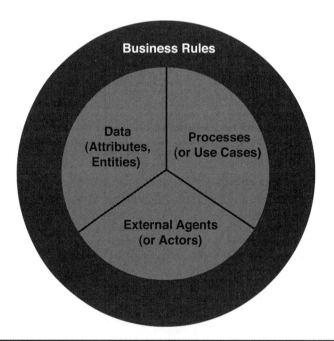

FIGURE 6.1. Core Requirements Components

Breaking requirements into these core components is a strong analysis technique that should be constantly practiced by the business analysis professional. This is a fundamental analytical skill that should become automatic over time. Experienced analysts begin to identify these components as soon as a business person begins describing his or her business.

Overview of Core Requirements Components

Data (Entities and Attributes)

Data is the *information* used by a business to do work. It is the fundamental component upon which all systems are based. The phrases "information systems" and "information technology" both acknowledge the importance of information or data to any system, whether automated or manual. A business analysis professional must understand that information can come in many different formats and can be manipulated, changed, and presented in an infinite number of ways. But missing data requirements is a fatal flaw. The most sophisticated software in the world will not be useful if it does not manage the information needed by the user.

Processes (Use Cases)

Processes are the activity or work that is done by a business. They are the second fundamental component upon which systems are based. Data and process are the two most important components to identify and break out. One can rarely exist without the other (business processes were discussed in Chapter 4). Every true process uses data. Every important piece of data is used by at least one process. (*Note*: Many people use the phrase *use case* to mean process.)

External Agents (Actors)

External agents are people, organizations, or other systems that interact with the area of a business being discussed. No business area operates in a vacuum. Each business area must interact with at least one external person, organization, or system. These requirements components are relatively easy to find because they are your users, your customers, the government, vendors, suppliers, other departments, and outside software/hardware systems. When use cases are the requirements technique, external agents are referred to as *actors* (people who *use* software systems are also sometimes referred to as user classes).

Business Rules

Business rules are constraints or guidelines under which a business operates. In Figure 6.1, business rules were shown to encircle the other three components. This is because business rules frequently involve data, process, and external agents. When you identify, name, and define the data, processes, and external agents, you can then document business rules by using the related component names.

These four core requirements components exist in each category of requirements: business, functional, and technical. They provide critical perspectives of each requirement. Breaking every requirement into these components helps to simplify a complex business area and builds a strong foundation upon which to document very detailed requirements.

Case in Point

Suppose a business stakeholder requests that a new field be added to a screen. Many analysts would see no need to write a requirements document or do much analysis. But even in this most simple scenario the four key requirements components exist: the field is *data*, the screen functionality is *process*, decisions about when to use the field and how to edit it are *business rules*, and the users who enter it, change it, delete it, and read it are *external agents*. A good analyst is not deceived by a simple business solution. He or she always looks for the core requirements and thinks through their importance and the implications of their change.

This doesn't mean that a simple change like a screen change requires hours and hours of requirements gathering and documentation. An analyst who is already familiar with the business and the application may be able to do a thorough analysis in just a few seconds in his or her head. *The important point is that you do the analysis.* You need to be sure that the business solution you are going to help implement makes sense for the current business problem and for the overall organization.

If your organization doesn't have any standard requirements package or format, this is a very basic way to introduce some consistency. Document your requirements, grouping them by the core components. A very simple structure could just include a list under each component. See Table 6.1 for a simple list of core requirements components.

Core Requirements Component: Entities (Data)

Data requirements are most commonly analyzed using the entity relationship diagramming technique. This technique defines three data components: entities, attributes, and

TABLE 6.1. Sample Core Requirements Components

Data	Customer name
	Customer address
	Customer phone
	Order number
	Order date
	Order items
Process	Place order
	Accept payment
External agents	Customer
	Shipping
	Accounts receivable department
Business rules	Orders over $50 receive free shipping

relationships (business rules). Every business analysis professional should be familiar with the entity relationship diagramming analysis technique and understand why data requirements are important. One of the best and most readable resources on entity relationship diagramming is *Data Modeling Essentials* by Simsion and Witt (2005). Business analysis professionals should include it in their library.

An entity (in *entity* relationship diagramming) is a uniquely identifiable person, thing, or concept whose information is important to a business. These *entities* are the big, important things that the business manages. Common examples include CUSTOMER, PRODUCT, and ORDER. When working in a Unified Modeling Language (UML) or object-oriented (OO) methodology, these would be referred to as *objects* or *classes*. Entities are named with nouns or noun phrases. The names are very important because these entities will be referred to frequently in other requirements. Names must be clearly defined in a glossary and, most importantly, used consistently. One of the most common mistakes made by inexperienced analysts is inconsistent use of terminology.

Traditionally, entities were elicited and documented in requirements because they represented data or information that needed to be stored in a database for software development. But there is a more important reason for performing data analysis. *Understanding the information that a business area uses to accomplish its goals ensures the BA knows the "materials" and "products" of the business.* Little business work can be done without information. To ignore business information and focus only on process and business rules is like trying to build a table with only two legs. It will not stand up.

Unfortunately, people who do not understand the meaning and importance of the words *data* and *information* often ignore these requirements because they "already have a database" or "are not building software." When a project involves an existing application, a vendor package, or a process change, data requirements seem like a logical task to skip. *However, ignoring business data requirements almost always leads to problems.* Business people need information constantly. They want it on reports, on display screens, and on forms. They want it to be accurate, available, and flexible so that it can be manipulated as needed. Regardless of the type of project to which you are assigned—*don't ignore the data.* See Table 6.2 for an entity list template.

Core Requirements Component: Attributes (Data)

Attributes (also from entity relationship diagramming) represent pieces of information that further describe entities. In other words, when you recognize that CUSTOMER information is important to the business, its attributes become obvious: FIRST NAME, LAST NAME, MAILING ADDRESS, E-MAIL ADDRESS, PHONE NUMBER. These individual data elements describe the important characteristics of each entity. Attributes, like entities, are named using nouns or noun phrases because they represent things (in UML and OO diagrams, they are also referred to as attributes, characteristics of objects, or classes). See Table 6.3 for an example of an attribute template. (Attributes and their descriptions may also be collected in a data dictionary.)

Attributes are everywhere in the business infrastructure: reports, screens, forms, phone systems, procedures, guidelines, policies, etc. It is imperative that the analyst identify and document all needed attributes during requirements elicitation.

As recommended for entities, attributes should be carefully named and defined. Business terminology must be used—not IT terminology. Names like NEW CUSTOMER INDICATOR or CUSTOMER FLAG are meaningless to business stakeholders. The excellent analyst discusses the meaning and description of each data element and names it appropriately. This does not imply that the common name used by a business is always the best name. Common names or phrases used in business areas are occasionally inaccurate and have evolved over time in a way that is no longer meaningful. An expert in business analysis will help business stakeholders name each attribute accurately without including past or future technology bias.

TABLE 6.2. Sample Entity List Template

Entity ID	Name	Unique Identifier	Number of Occurrences		Owner/Author
			Current	Future	
E1	CLASS SESSION	Class session number	10/mo	15/mo	Owner: TA
E2	COURSE (Content)	Course title	15	30	Owner: TA
E3	COURSE EQUIPMENT	(Course title + Course equipment type)	25	40	Owner: TA
E4	INSTRUCTOR	(Instructor last name + instructor first name)	5	7	Owner: TA
E5	INSTRUCTOR QUALIFICATION	(Instructor first name + Instructor last name + Course title)			Owner: TA
E6	LOCATION	Location name	2	3	Owner: Facilities
E7	REGISTRATION	(Student number + Class session number)	200/mo	350/mo	Owner: TA
E8	STUDENT	Student number (same as human resources employee number)	1000	3000	Owner: HR

For data that is already stored in a database, the analyst's questions should be: "Where and in how many databases?" Many organizations store an important piece of business information (an attribute) in tens or hundreds of places. Think about an attribute like CUSTOMER NUMBER. How many files, databases, or spreadsheets in your organization store this piece of information? Redundant data storage often results in an ongoing data integrity problem. If there are names and addresses in multiple places, which occurrence of the customer name and address is the correct one? Are they all kept

TABLE 6.3. Sample Attribute Template

Name	U	M	R	Date Type/ Length	Valid Values	Default Value	Owner	Definition
ID: Class session number	Y	Y	N	Number	1–999999		Training management	Unique number assigned to each class session for tracking purposes
Class session start date	N	Y	N	Date			Training management	Classes are only held on business days
Class minimum number of students	N	Y	N	Number	5–20	5	Training management	Least number of students that the class session will be held for
Class maximum number of students	N	Y	N	Number	5–20	14	Training management	Largest number of students that the class session will be held for
Class current number of registrations	N	N	N	Number	5–20	0	Derived	Tally of the number of registrants to date
Class setup	N	N	N	Char (50)			Training management	Description of any setup required for the class
Class session room number	N	N	N	Char (3)			Corp. meeting room system	The number of the room where the class will be held
Course title	N	Y	N	See COURSE for attribute characteristics				
Location name	N	Y	N	See LOCATION for attribute characteristics				
Instructor last name	N	N	N	See INSTRUCTOR for attribute characteristics				
Instructor first name	N	N	N	See INSTRUCTOR for attribute characteristics				

U = unique, M = mandatory, R = repetitions.

in sync? Who maintains them? With data stored in existing databases, data requirements become even more important because instead of defining what data is *needed,* the analyst needs to be a detective, searching out all of the possible places where a piece of data is stored and then determining which of the many locations holds the correct value for this particular solution.

In addition to naming and defining each attribute, there are detailed characteristics to be considered by the analyst. These characteristics further describe the attribute, helping the analyst to more completely understand the business need. They often uncover business rules and reveal more detailed and complex requirements that might otherwise be missed.

Attribute Uniqueness

Whether or not an attribute is unique tells the team if it should be used to look up, search, and find a particular set of data. For example, if CUSTOMER NUMBER is unique, it can be used to search the database for a particular customer. If the CUSTOMER PHONE NUMBER is not unique, a search on phone number may result in two or more customers. Understanding how data can best be searched and accessed is a very important part of business analysis. In addition, specifying uniqueness helps with ongoing data integrity. If the EMPLOYEE NUMBER attribute was defined as unique and another employee is added with the same number, there is a data problem.

The uniqueness characteristic of each attribute helps the analyst ask a very specific question about the business requirements: *Is a value of this attribute unique among all values?* Frequently, the business stakeholders will be able to answer this question easily and without reservation. Occasionally, however, the answer will not be simple. Analysts should listen for phrases like "Well, it is usually unique but we have had a couple of duplicates when . . ." or "I think it is unique, but I am not sure how it is assigned, so it may not be." Answers like these must be followed up with more detailed conversation.

Mandatory or Optional

Another important question that should be asked for each attribute is: *Is the attribute mandatory?* When the answer to this question is no, the analyst must always follow up, looking for one or more business rules that guide its collection. For example, if a subject matter expert (SME) is asked if a CUSTOMER E-MAIL ADDRESS is mandatory, the answer "it depends" leads to business rules. When a customer places an order via the Web site, an e-mail address is required. But when a customer places an order by phone, it is not. This business rule can easily be missed if attributes are not thoroughly analyzed.

Attribute Repetitions

Can there be many occurrences of a particular attribute? For example, can a customer have more than one phone number? More than one e-mail address? Eliciting requirements around possible repeating attributes helps to open up discussions about possible values and their relevance to the business. Often, old application systems only had room for one phone number. Users with more than one phone number were forced to choose which one to enter. Valuable data has been lost because the existing database didn't have a place for it. Sometimes users put extra information somewhere else in the database. "If the customer gives me a second e-mail address, I put it in the customer title field on the screen because we don't usually enter titles." These discussions point out specific problems with current business systems and will help analysts design better solutions for the future. In addition, they highlight current data integrity problems that may negatively impact new reports when existing data elements are used.

In addition to finding limitations with the current business system, the questions about attribute repetitions help the analyst to walk the SMEs through some what-if analysis. For example, if a customer has three e-mail addresses, will they all be stored? For what would they be used? How would which one to use to send the order confirmation be determined? Would it be sent to all three? Who will maintain these addresses?

Core Requirements Component: Processes (Use Cases)

A process is a business activity that transforms input (data) into outputs. Many BAs and systems analysts now use the phrase *use case* interchangeably with process (processes were discussed in Chapter 4). From the perspective of most business stakeholders, processes are the most important requirements. Processes, as a requirements component, are much more difficult to name and define than data. It is easy to recommend that process names start with a verb and include a noun (data), but verbs are much more ambiguous than nouns and activities are much more difficult to describe than things (data). Consider a simple example like *receive order*. What does the word "receive" imply? Would *record order* be more descriptive? *Receive* is passive, whereas *record* is active. But does either word really describe the work that is done in the business? Would *validate order* be clearer, or is *recording* a completely different activity from *validating*? There are many subtle nuances in the English language, from which these verbs are taken. Deciding which one is the most meaningful for a particular project is very subjective, but there is no denying that processes are one of the most important of the core requirements components.

Process descriptions are important for almost every project in which a BA is involved. The title *business analyst* comes from the focus on understanding and representing the business, processes being a key component. Processes are analyzed using decomposition diagrams, data flow diagrams, workflow diagrams, and use case descriptions.

Core Requirements Component: External Agents (Actors)

An external agent is a person, organization, or system with which a business area interacts. These external agents are known by many different names: actors, externals, or interfaces. The word *external* as part of the name is important. BAs must be aware of the scope of a requirements area. Actors are external to the software solution in UML diagrams and are used in use cases.

It is important for analysts to identify external agents for several reasons. Ideally, they are identified during project initiation because knowing all of the external interfaces helps with project planning and estimating. Each external agent must be represented in a project by a stakeholder. These stakeholders are key resources for requirements elicitation. They may be external to the company or just external to the project. When they are external to the company, the analyst may have limited access for requirements elicitation. The larger the number of externals, the longer requirements elicitation, reviews, and approvals will take.

Another important reason to identify external agents is that they may interface with the solution or final outcome of a project. Because their issues and concerns must be addressed in the solution design, their needs (requirements) are very important.

Externals also must be considered when security of data or process is important. Many of the nouns defined as entities will also be external agents. For example, a *customer* is an external agent because he or she is outside the project, and *customer* is an entity because there is important information about customers (attributes) that must be stored (first name, last name, etc.) Be sure to use the nouns (i.e., *customer and vendor*) consistently.

Internal vs. External

There may be people, organizations, or systems that are inside the scope of a project. They would also be considered stakeholders. They can provide requirements because they operate within the business area under study. Systems inside the scope may include existing software applications and manual procedures. It is important to differentiate between external agents and internals because a project does not control the externals but may change the role of the internals. In other words, employees who are inside the business area may have their work changed by a project solution. Roles may change, procedures may change, and systems may change. External agents are called *external* because they cannot be changed by a project. Customers, vendors, and government agencies are examples of external agents that are not under the control of a project. This is a critical distinction and one that should be made during project initiation activities (project initiation was discussed in Chapter 3).

Core Requirements Component: Business Rules

A business rule is a condition that governs the way work is done. Business rules are typically described with a sentence or two. They may be named or numbered to allow them to be linked or traced to other requirements components. They may start out high level or detailed; either way, the analyst should ask questions to refine the rule to be very specific and clearly written. Business rules are a key requirements component because they frequently tie the other requirements components together. When the rule "an order over $500 gets free shipping" is revealed, it brings together several other requirements components: data (order total amount, shipping charges), process (calculate shipping charge), and external agents (customer, shipper). A great resource on business rules is *Business Rules Applied* by Barbara von Halle (2003).

Some analysts consider business rules to be "requirements" and others do not. They argue that business rules are constraints of an organization, not "needs." This is another debate that is important to be aware of so that your communications with other team members are clear. It doesn't really matter whether or not you consider a business rule to be a requirement. The important part of business analysis is that business rules must be elicited, documented, and confirmed. They may be included in the requirements package or in a separate document.

It is important for the analyst to write business rules carefully. References to data (nouns) must use the exact same nouns as defined in the data requirements. Similarly, verbs must be used consistently with their use in process and use case names. There are some commercially available syntax sys-

BABOK Connection	
Knowledge Area	**Task/Technique**
Requirements Analysis	Business Rules

tems for documenting business rules, such as RuleSpeak (Ross, 2003). In addition, there are software systems called business rule engines that store and execute rules. Rules are very complex, and each organization should have some standards around documenting rules. *Rules are often reused* in an organization by different departments. This argues for a rules administrator and shared repository. Rules are frequently changed in many organizations, so it is important to clearly define rules and maintain them separately from business processes, use cases, and data structures. While some rules will logically be represented in a data model (entity relationship diagram), most must be described with more detail than can be shown in an entity relationship diagram.

Finding Business Rules

Because business rules define constraints or rules about a business, they can be thought of as *decision points*. Each rule helps a business stakeholder make a decision. The rule has been articulated to ensure consistency in making these decisions. Imagine a business area where each employee makes decisions based on his or her own opinions. Customers would get a different response depending on with whom they spoke ("But the woman I spoke with yesterday told me that I could return this item").

Identifying, documenting, and confirming business rules improves the consistency of a business area even if the rules are never codified into software. Often during a requirements workshop focused on business rules, two different business stakeholders will realize that they had a different understanding of a rule. Exposing these unknown discrepancies is the value of analysis. Business areas realize improved communication and increased consistency immediately.

Often, business rules are exposed during requirement elicitation around processes and data. Many business rules are "data-related business rules" and are documented with the data model as a relationship (in the entity relationship diagram). Most business rules rely on at least one piece of information (data).

As business SMEs discuss their work, listen for decision words like "verify," "validate," "check," "determine," and "assess." When a person or system makes a decision, they are enforcing a business rule. That rule needs to be articulated, reviewed, and documented. Business rules are an important requirements component that should be managed and maintained after the implementation of a solution. Once implemented into software or procedures or processes, these rules drive the work of the business and should be easy to review and change when the software has been designed with rules in mind.

ANALYSIS TECHNIQUES AND PRESENTATION FORMATS

There are many techniques for analyzing and presenting requirements. Each technique focuses on particular core requirements components. Each technique has a history and was developed to meet a particular need. Over time, these techniques have been used by thousands of analysts, and some individuals have altered the techniques depending on the circumstances. There is no wrong way to "analyze" or "think." These techniques are simply tools to help the analyst see a problem or situation from a different perspective. Most projects will benefit from the use of several techniques.

It is important for a successful business analysis professional to be familiar with many analysis techniques. The more tools you know how to use, the more flexible you will be. Imagine a plumber with only a wrench in his or her toolbox. Although the wrench is an important tool, it may not always be able to solve the problem. Over time, a plumber adds more tools to the toolbox as he or she confronts new problems and situations. As he or she builds a toolbox, the plumber builds his or her skill set and ability to add value to any situation.

Learn each technique as it was originally developed before trying to change it! Each technique has a specific intent. It is important that you learn a technique thoroughly before trying to modify it. You will be tempted to make up your own techniques, and as an experienced analyst you may succeed. But new analysts will be wise to use well-established techniques as they were intended until they have gained enough experience to feel comfortable making an adjustment.

Completing a technique in its entirety ensures that you have not missed portions of the requirement and that you have asked the right questions. The diagram, template, or screen layout helps develop questions as you work to complete it. If you can't finalize a diagram or description, then you have not completed your analysis. The power in completing the techniques is in knowing that you have fully analyzed a problem from each technique's perspective. A wonderful side benefit is that your analysis or thoughts are captured in a logical documentation or presentation format. Yet, completing a technique does not have to result in a long, formal requirements document. Analysis can be done informally, as long as it is done completely. Make sure that you understand the business needs and problems. Then decide how to present requirements (document, white board, presentation, etc.).

Every technique in this section has been described in other books and publications. References are recommended for you to learn more. As you learn to use each technique, you will come to appreciate the ability to present complex requirements in simple formats.

Try using a variety of analysis techniques on the same problem to see what new information is exposed. It is amazing how well some of the older techniques work. Don't ignore tried-and-true techniques (e.g., data flow diagramming) just because they have been around for years. Many analysts still use these successfully on their projects. Presenting complex requirements simply and clearly is an essential skill for a business analysis professional. This section gives a brief overview of each technique and the reasons for using it.

Glossary

An important component of strong communication is the consistent use of terms and phrases. It is easy to forget how dependent human beings are on language. Every conversation involves a common understanding of terms. When someone uses a term that you have never heard before, or uses a known term in a different way, the message is incomplete. Your brain may even get distracted thinking about the unknown term and miss the rest of the communication. Understanding the importance of terms is critical to successful analysis. Analysts must be precise when discussing and presenting requirements. The accurate use of terms, especially terms that are unique to a business domain, will ensure successful communication of requirements.

This points out another important lesson for the business analysis professional. You must be able to use the terms from the business even when they are foreign or unfamiliar to you. This is where a glossary can help. The analyst should begin jotting down important terms from the very first meetings with stakeholders. Terms that seem common and well known should be confirmed. Each term should be defined and the definition should be agreed upon by all project stakeholders. Undefined terms create ambiguous requirements.

An SME may describe a process as:

A customer purchases products by logging into the Web site and placing items in the shopping cart. When the buyer is ready to check out, the screen should display the total shipping charges and the total order amount.

Is the *customer* the same person as the *buyer*? Is an *item* always a *product*? What is the difference between the *shopping cart* and the *order*? Using inconsistent terminology in requirements often leads to mistakes in solution development.

Analysts must listen very carefully to the use of terms by stakeholders. As inconsistencies are found, they must be exposed. Be aware, though, that simply exposing an inconsistency will not correct it. If one department has been using the term *customer* and another department has been using the term *client,* you will not be able to quickly change either of their habits. You must first determine if they are using the terms in exactly the same way. If not, there may be two different words that are important and relevant here. Your job, as the analyst, is to point out the inconsistency, get agreement on the term definitions, and work to bring the group to consensus on shared language to be used in procedures and systems.

Workflow Diagrams

A workflow diagram visually details one or more business processes to clarify understanding or to make process improvement recommendations. Workflow diagrams (also known as flowcharting, UML activity diagrams, and process maps) are one of the oldest and most well-established analysis techniques. See Figure 6.2 for an example of a workflow diagram.

Workflow diagrams show *how* work is accomplished, including the sequence in which things are done. They can also show information flows through the processes and how business people and other external agents are involved with the process. They may be used to visually represent a current process (as is) or to represent a recommended future process (to be).

There are many variations of workflow diagrams. Almost every software development approach recommends their use for requirements. The American National Standards Institute (ANSI) (www.ansi.org) standardized symbols and shapes for use in these diagrams in the 1970s. A small subset of the standard is commonly used, and a few shapes (like the diamond for a decision) have become almost universally understood. A workflow diagram can be divided into sections to show departments or divisions within an organization. These sections are referred to as *swim lanes.* The UML shapes vary a bit from ANSI for use in the UML activity diagram.

The workflow diagram is one of the first techniques that a new analyst should learn. It is the most flexible technique, with few rules for its creation. The flexibility of the technique allows its use on many different types of projects. Its flexibility also makes it challenging for analysts. One of the decisions that an analyst will make when using this technique is whether or not a final diagram will be used as a formal deliverable. Although this decision is made for every technique, workflow diagrams are unique because they may be created at various levels of detail, for current or future systems, and for various audiences. When a workflow diagram is used as a formal deliverable, care must be taken to clearly communicate its purpose and its viewpoint.

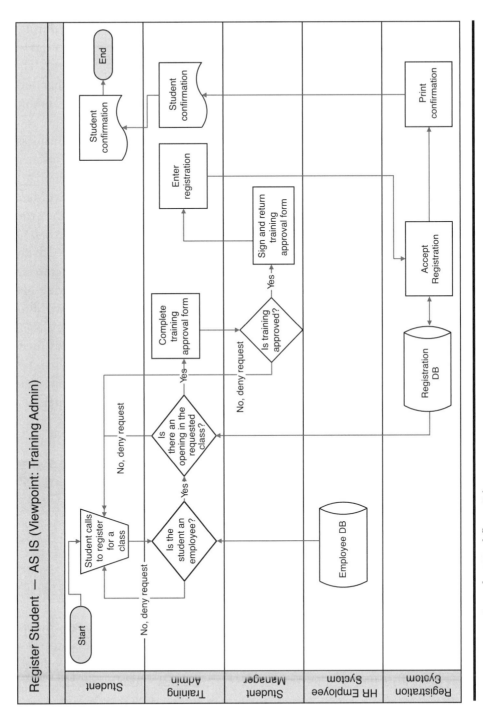

FIGURE 6.2. Sample Workflow Diagram

Workflow diagrams are a great tool for analysts to use for note taking during requirements elicitation. Business stakeholders frequently describe their work as a series of tasks, interjecting notes about worker involvement and current software support. The analyst draws a picture of the business process to help understand it and confirm that understanding with the SMEs. Using a workflow diagram as a conversation tool does not imply that it must become a formal deliverable.

A relatively new approach to creating workflow diagrams is called Business Process Modeling Notation© (www.bpmn.org). This notation was defined by the Business Process Management Initiative, a non-profit professional organization striving to standardize business process modeling techniques. This organization merged with the Object Management Group (www.omg.org), which maintains the UML standards. Together the groups hope to produce a seamless transition from business modeling to software design.

Another type of workflow diagram is found in the Six Sigma approach to process improvement. The Six Sigma workflow diagram is called the SIPOC diagram (Supplier, Inputs, Process, Outputs, and Customer) and is used to show a high-level view of an entire business transaction. A process on a SIPOC diagram may be decomposed into a more detailed SIPOC diagram. This Six Sigma technique is used to identify and measure current business activities (as is) and perform root cause analysis to find process inefficiencies (Pande et al., 2000).

Lean approaches use a technique called value stream mapping to analyze the flow of materials and information to bring a product or service to the customer. It includes standard symbols for supply chain entities. The focus is on improving processes and reducing waste (www.lean.org).

Workflow diagrams are also used for implementation or transition requirements. Employee procedure manuals, standard operating procedures, and rollout plans are all better communicated by including visual instructions rather than just text.

BABOK Connection	
Knowledge Area	**Task/Technique**
Requirements Analysis	Process Modeling

Why Use Workflow Diagrams?

Because workflow diagrams are so flexible and can be created using many different standards and notations, they are useful on many types of projects. Business process improvement projects rely heavily on as is and to be diagrams. Software development projects benefit from their use at either the business requirements level (*what* does the user do) or the functional requirements level (*how* will the user do it). They are also very helpful for enterprise-level projects like mergers and acquisitions. When two departments are being merged, it is worthwhile to analyze each of their current procedures (as is) and compare them. This allows the common activities to be identified and differences highlighted. The project team can also use metrics to identify best practices for recommending the merged to be procedures. Additionally, workflow diagrams have become very critical for organizations that are developing a service-oriented architecture.

Entity Relationship Diagramming

Data requirements are represented in an entity relationship diagram (ERD). This diagram along with accompanying descriptions and details comprise a "data model." This is a visual representation of the information requirements of a business domain or of an application software system. The technique uses the core requirements components of entities, attributes, and business rules. This analysis technique helps the analyst develop questions about information needs. The technique was developed in 1976 by Peter Chen at MIT (Chen, 1976) and has been used by data analysts, administrators, and database designers around the world. It is based on mathematical principles and includes specific rules and guidelines for its successful use. See Figure 6.3 for an example of an ERD drawn using Microsoft Visio Professional®.

The popularity and long life of this technique are attributed to its rigor and simplicity. The diagram can show a complex business domain in a straightforward, concise manner, making communications much clearer. The model shows not only information needs but also many business rules as they relate to data. The rules are the "relationships" in the name entity relationship diagram. When using an ERD to document business requirements, the diagram and related details combined make up a *logical data model.*

BABOK Connection	
Knowledge Area	**Task/Technique**
Requirements Analysis	Data Modeling

Why Build a Logical Data Model?

The most important reason to build a logical data model is to confirm the user's and analyst's understanding of the business data requirements and ensure that the software developed satisfies the business need. Logical data modeling provides the analyst with a

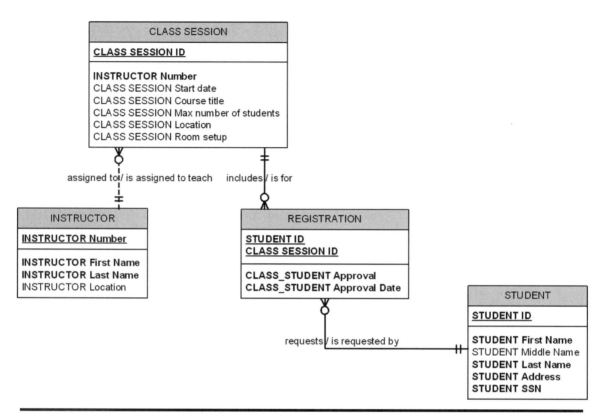

FIGURE 6.3. Sample Entity Relationship Diagram

structured tool and technique to conduct analysis. Most SMEs can articulate problems and possible solutions; unfortunately, their problems and solutions are often based on current system constraints, not true business needs. Asking business people to detail every piece of data (attribute) requires them to understand and articulate every aspect of their business. This approach allows the business to drive the system design, not the other way around. It also stimulates more detailed discussion and thoughts. By identifying and detailing data in a model, further requirements and problem areas arise and are dealt with long before software design.

It is an outstanding technique to help the analyst understand the business from a different perspective. Most business areas are defined by their processes: "This is what we *do*." But looking at the information used to accomplish work allows the analyst to understand processes from the other side. It also helps the analyst find significant business rules and ask detailed questions that lead to more hidden business rules.

Second, when a project involves creation of or changes to a database, the ERD is the preferred communication vehicle for people responsible for creating and maintaining data in IT. The diagram will be well understood and give the analyst a common language with which to communicate with a database administrator.

A logical data model also facilitates data reuse and sharing. Data is stable over time; therefore, the model remains stable over time. As additional project teams scope out their project areas, they can reuse the model components that are shared by the business. This leads to physical data sharing and less storage of redundant data. It also helps the organization recognize that information is an organization-wide resource, not the property of one department or another. Data sharing makes an organization more cohesive and increases the quality of service to outside customers and suppliers.

Data modeling is very useful on commercial off-the-shelf (COTS) projects. Understanding the business data needs and including them in a Request for Proposal is crucial for package selection. Reputable vendors should provide an ERD that represents their system's underlying data structure. Comparing the COTS data with the business data requirements, attribute by attribute, allows the selection committee to make an accurate assessment of how well each package would support the business. If a package cannot accommodate business data requirements along with their associated business rules, then it should be rejected. Missing data cannot always be rectified by custom programming.

There are data modeling tools that support the creation of an ERD and its associated details. Many of these tools are capable of using the ERD requirements to build a database design. These tools are used by data analysts, administrators, and database administrators to create, update, and maintain data structures used by application software. Most business analysis professionals do not have access to these tools, but the absence of a tool does not mean that one should ignore this technique. Microsoft Office Visio provides a stencil for data models which is robust enough to represent the information needs of most projects. Templates for documenting entities, attributes, and business rules may also be beneficial.

Business Process Modeling with the Decomposition Diagram

The decomposition diagram shows all of the essential business processes without showing any sequence or relationships between them. See Figure 6.4 for an example.

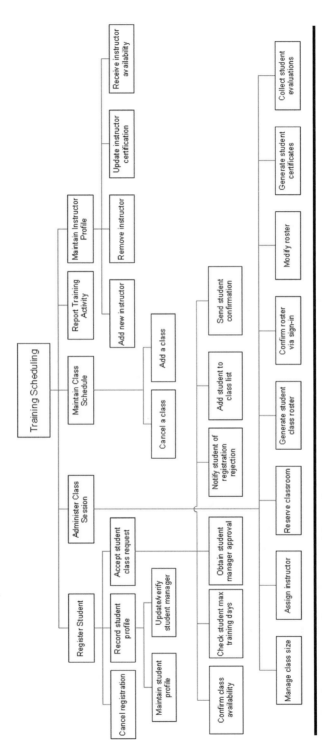

FIGURE 6.4. Sample Decomposition Diagram

Decomposition analysis is a proven approach for breaking a complex system into manageable pieces. Because the diagram itself follows the same general rules as an organizational chart, many business people are very comfortable reviewing requirements using this presentation. It is called "decomposition" because each process may be broken down into more detailed processes that further describe it (Martin, 1986). A strength of this technique is the separation of process from sequence. To truly understand business processes, it is useful to look at them as independent tasks. By isolating each one, you see the core building blocks upon which all of the complex business procedures and systems are built. Looking at them as independent units facilitates creative brainstorming around how they might be structured or be built to be done differently in the future.

The decomposition diagram can be used to present many different requirements and business components. Be sure to show only one type of component in each diagram (or label if different). Decomposition diagramming is often used in strategic planning activities, showing the breakdown of high-level corporate goals into lower level divisions and then department goals. The diagramming technique may also be used to show the breakdown of tasks on a project work breakdown structure.

As with many diagrams, the decomposition diagram is easy to review. This clarity deceives readers into believing that the development of the diagram is just as easy. *In reality, this is one of the most difficult diagrams to create.* There are few rules for its development, which leaves the analyst room for subjective representations. SMEs may feel great frustration if presented with an empty white board and asked to describe their organization's processes using a top-down approach. When using this technique, draft the decomposition diagram based on your project initiation documentation and your basic understanding of the business. SMEs will be able to more easily correct a draft diagram than build one from scratch.

Each process on the decomposition diagram must be further described with triggers, trailers, related business rules, and data. The diagram in combination with these descriptions is referred to as a "process model" or "business model" (Martin and McClure, 1985). (See the section on what a business process is in Chapter 4.)

There are a few key rules for building a decomposition diagram which enforce consistency and rigor. Having guidelines for requirements helps all BAs use them consistently and helps stakeholders who are reviewing them expect predictable patterns.

Rules for decomposition diagram are:

◆ Only one type of relationship between components is shown on the diagram: parent to child (shown with a line between boxes).

- ◆ Only one type of requirement is shown on a diagram (i.e., if you are decomposing processes, don't show any business rules; only show processes).
- ◆ Every parent has more than one child.
- ◆ No sequence is shown (no arrows).
- ◆ A child must be at a lower level than its parent (more detailed, finer distinctions).

Although there are specific rules for developing a decomposition diagram, no two BAs would create an identical diagram given the same set of requirements. Each decomposition diagram can represent a different perspective and contain varying levels of detail. Typically, the processes at the top and bottom of the diagram are easier to identify than the ones in the middle. Don't spend too much time discussing the middle-level process names. The diagram is useful for organizing and structuring analysis work. It gives the team a visual way to see each process within the context of the business and allows the group to then focus on one particular process at a time. It helps to set boundaries for detailed analysis work.

BABOK Connection	
Knowledge Area	**Task/Technique**
Enterprise Analysis	Decomposition

Why Build a Decomposition Diagram?

A decomposition diagram is a simple graphic display of a business area. It is easy to review and revise. A decomposition diagram can be created at a high level or detailed level. It can be used to design any type of solution: software, hardware, procedural, or manual. When it includes true, essential business processes, it is a lasting model of the business that can be refined and reused on future projects. A decomposition diagram can be used to organize many things—data, goals, problems, etc.

Use Case Diagram

A *use case* is a goal of a software system. It comes from the Swedish word *anvendningstall*, which means *situation of usage* or *usage case*. A use case diagram shows the main use cases along with the actors who are involved with them. The use case diagramming technique was developed to show functional requirements—how a software system interacts with its users (actors). It is typically used to present a future view of a system. The technique was developed in the mid-1980s and has become a very popular technique for documenting requirements (Jacobson, 1992). This diagram is useful for showing the scope of a project or a software product (see the discussion on scoping in Chapter 3).

Figure 6.5 shows an example of a use case diagram. Use cases are depicted as ovals and actors as stick people. Actors are people, organizations, or systems with which the software interfaces. In addition to use cases and actors, the use case diagram includes an automation boundary. This boundary delineates what the software includes and shows the interfaces to the software with the association lines. Associations to *people actors* represent

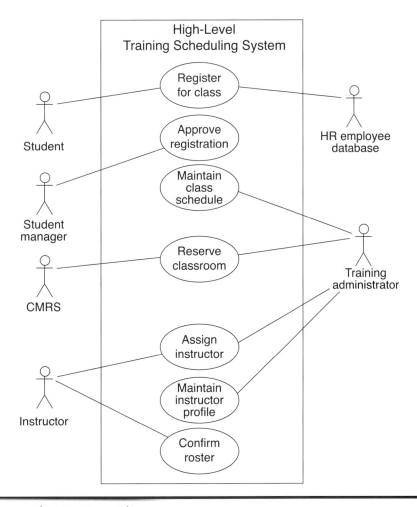

FIGURE 6.5. Sample Use Case Diagram

user interfaces like screens and reports. Associations to *system or organization actors* represent automated or electronic interfaces.

Although the use case diagram was developed as a software design technique, it can be used at the business requirements (non-technical) level. Use cases may be named and defined as independent of technology (referred to as business use cases). The automation boundary can be used to represent the business or project boundary. This allows the use case diagram to show the scope of the requirements or analysis work.

Use Case Descriptions

Each use case on a use case diagram is described in a use case description. The use case technique is popular because each use case description is a functional requirement deliverable that contains all of the requirements components for a particular software function. A use case description also includes a sequential set of steps that describe how the software and actors should interact to achieve a business goal. This dialogue presents a clear picture to business stakeholders of how they will use the new software before it is built. The dialogue also provides developers with detailed instructions about how to build the software.

Within the steps of a use case, analysts typically include a primary path (the happy path) along with alternate paths. These alternate paths show exception processing and error conditions. For each step, the analyst describes the action that the actor will take and the way the system should respond. This description may include detailed data requirements along with the business rules that apply (Cockburn, 2000). See Figure 6.6 for an example of a use case template.

As with all analysis techniques, developing the deliverable is more complex than it would initially appear. Organizations that have started using use cases as a standard requirement deliverable sometimes find analysts struggling with consistency and level of detail. There are stories of use cases that have grown to 100 pages. Is this a useful deliverable? To successfully use this technique, analysts must be well trained and the organization must have some guidelines about how it is used. When used in combination with other requirements deliverables (i.e., ERD, prototypes), use case descriptions can be created in manageable sizes and can be very useful.

One of the major weaknesses of the use case approach is that a use case description may contain several requirements components (data, process, business rules, external agents) instead of documenting them separately. Documenting components together makes it very easy to miss requirements and makes reusability of components very difficult. Most

System Use Case Description—Maintain Instructor Profile	
Use Case ID	UC-2
Use Case Name	Maintain Instructor Profile
Created By	Catherine
Date Created	1/15/08
Actor(s)	Training Administrator
Description	This use case allows the Training Admin department to add new instructors, delete instructors, and keep instructor information up to date.
Pre-conditions	The instructor must have been approved by Training Management to be included in the Instructor list.
Post-conditions	Instructor profile is correct.
Priority	Medium
Frequency of Use	2–3 times per week
Primary Path	Instructor profile exists and the instructor has been certified on an additional course.

Actor Actions	System Responses
1. Training Administrator selects **Instructors** from the main menu.	1. System displays **Instructors** screen with blank form.
2. Training Administrator selects instructor name from **Instructor** drop-down list.	2. Displays the instructor profile information in screen fields. The **Add** and **Update** buttons are disabled. The **Delete** button is enabled.
3. Training Administrator reviews the instructor name and current course certifications for accuracy.	3. No response
4. Training Administrator marks a check in the box next to the course that the instructor is now certified to teach.	4. System enables the **Update** button.

FIGURE 6.6. Sample Use Case Description Template

data elements in information systems are used by more than one process. When a data element is documented inside a use case, it must be redundantly defined in every use case that needs it. This leads to wasted time writing requirements and the possibility for a lot of errors. If a characteristic of a data element changes, you need to go to every use case that uses it to make the same change. If you miss one, your requirements are inconsistent and there will be errors in the software—guaranteed!

To make your use case descriptions more concise and consistent, define the individual requirements components separately (with unique names) and simply refer to them in the use case descriptions. This alleviates the need to change every use case description when a data or business rule requirement is changed.

BABOK Connection	
Knowledge Area	**Task/Technique**
Requirements Analysis	Scenarios and Use Cases

Why Use Use Cases?

The use case diagram is part of UML (see Chapter 5). It is a simple diagram for stakeholders to review and can help to ease the communication between business stakeholders and technical stakeholders. Like many analysis techniques, this one appears much more simple and straightforward than it is. The resulting diagram is not as important as the discussions and decisions that are made during its development. This is a great technique to use with business stakeholders, specifically decision makers, because it requires decisions about how people (actors) will work with the software. A simple line on this diagram between an actor and a use case could completely change a business person's job. It may necessitate job description changes, responsibilities changes, and new procedures.

Use case descriptions—especially the primary and alternate paths—are great for brainstorming with software users about design options. Working through the specific interactions between the user and the software helps design a system that more accurately mirrors the natural workflow of the user. Even when the team thinks it has a consistent vision of the solution, writing down these specific steps/interactions points out different views and allows decisions to be made before coding begins.

In addition to changing a person's job, design decisions often change external interfaces also. With almost universal access to the Internet, many organizations are putting more functionality in the hands of their customers. The customer is an actor whose role is changing significantly. Customers do not have job descriptions or procedure manuals.

They are not paid by an organization to do work. Be aware that shifting an interaction with software from a business worker to the customer is a significant change. It has occurred with banks (ATMs), retail stores (credit card scanners), order processing (over the Internet), and many customer service departments (voice prompt phone systems). Turning the processes of the organization over to the customer requires that the processes be very well defined and the software automation be extremely usable and intuitive. When the customer becomes your actor, new procedures need to be developed to support this actor. Employees shift their focus from the original process to answering customer questions and helping the customer navigate the technology.

Case in Point

I discovered the value of use case descriptions when designing a Web order processing system. Some team members assumed that customers would be required to log in before browsing the product catalog. The marketing stakeholders disagreed. They wanted to allow anyone to browse products without having to set up a login ID. This difference of opinion was discovered on the first step of the use case description: *order product.*

Prototypes/Simulations

A prototype is a model of a user interface in an automated system. It may be a screen layout, report layout, or data entry form. It is built as part of a software design to show the stakeholders what the software will "look like."

When a proposed solution (to be) involves the addition of or update to an online screen, analysts often create a prototype that shows the screen design, along with a storyboard or simulation that demonstrates how the screen interacts with other screens.

Along with the prototype, functional requirements must include a description of how data entry fields are edited and validated, along with business rules that should be enforced for users of the screen. Warning messages, error messages, and other informational text to be displayed must be specified by the BA in conjunction with the SME. Messages written by developers often are not understandable to business users.

A *storyboard* shows a series of screens and how the software user should be able to navigate between them. See Figure 6.7 for an example of a storyboard diagram created using the iRise Studio™ simulation tool. Each rectangle on the diagram represents a screen and has an associated screen design.

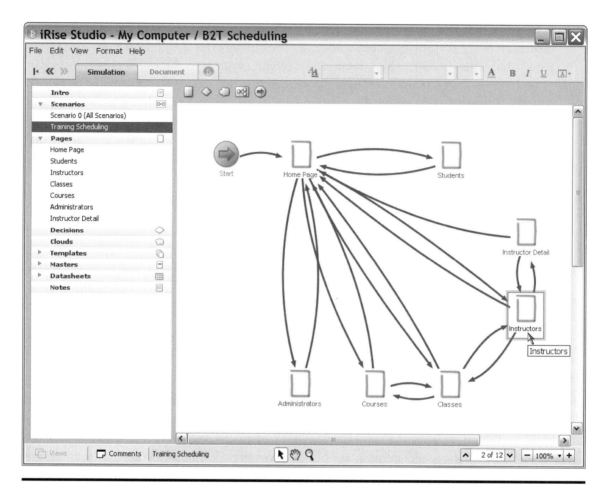

FIGURE 6.7. Sample Storyboard

A *screen layout* can be created using a simulation tool like iRise, a development tool like Microsoft Visual Studio®, a graphic design tool like Microsoft Visio, or simply on paper. The design should show data fields in their relative positions, field length, field labels, text boxes, menus, selection buttons, etc. The more detailed the prototype, the more accurate the requirement and the faster the reviews and development. See Figure 6.8 for an example of a screen layout.

Simulation means "something that looks or acts like something else." Simulating a screen or series of screens allows the user to actually enter data on screens, click on menus

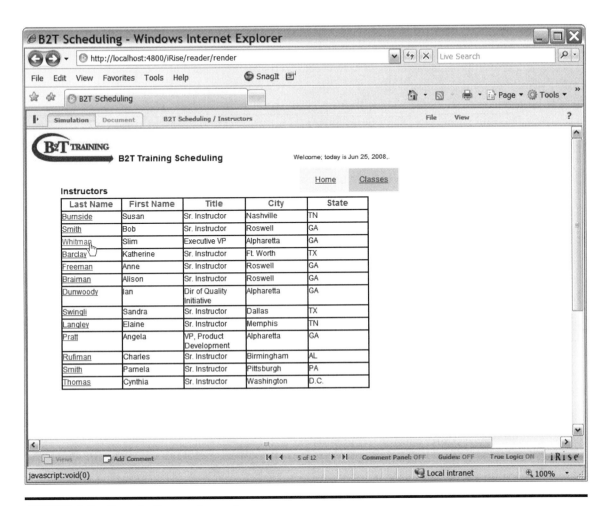

FIGURE 6.8. Sample Screen Layout

and selection fields, navigate between screens, etc. It mimics the desired online function-ality to confirm requirements with the SMEs and provide clear specifications to the developers.

Report layouts are similar to prototypes in that they show how software will interface with a user. The report layout specifies how data from the database will be presented to users, including formatting, column headers, and pagination. Report layouts are excellent communication tools for developers because they specifically show the end product expected by the user. Report layouts are accompanied by descriptions of the calculations, summarizations, etc., along with the names of the database tables and columns to be used.

Prototyping is such an effective requirements analysis and presentation technique that it is used on most software development projects. Even a simple screen change can be implemented incorrectly without a clear visual requirement. There are a few cautions when using prototypes. The first caution is not to create or present prototypes too early in a project. Business requirements should be clearly understood first, and the analyst should be sure that a software solution, specifically an online screen, is the most appropriate approach to answering the business need. When users start reviewing a prototype, they can get very distracted with its aesthetics and forget to review it for core business requirements. Prototypes may be presented early in a project when business stakeholders don't have any idea about what their potential solution might look like or when the team is working on the feasibility of an idea.

The second caution is to be careful not to set unrealistic stakeholder expectations. When a user sees a prototype on a computer screen, he or she may believe that the application is complete and functional. The user may assume that the project is nearing completion and anticipation may rise. BAs must be sure to clearly explain that the prototype is simply a picture or *mock-up* of the final software. An analogy would be the *Hollywood house.* When moviemakers need a particular style of home or building for a scene in a movie, they build a façade that looks exactly like the building in the story. But if you were to walk through the front door, you might see two long poles propping up the façade, with no ceiling or walls. This is a good description of a prototype.

Finally, a third caution relates to the application software development. Prototypes built by developers are often considered "quick and dirty." They often do not follow enterprise coding standards or best

BABOK Connection	
Knowledge Area	**Task/Technique**
Elicitation	Prototyping

practice software development principles. They are intended to be used as requirements deliverables and then thrown away. They are not production-quality software. Once the requirements have been approved, the development team should build the software based on the requirements using the standard tools and best practices expected. It may be tempting to use the prototype as a starting point for the software development because it would appear to save time, but when the prototype is used to *finish* the application, the resulting software is often poorly structured and difficult to maintain. Imagine building a real house around the Hollywood façade. Walls would be forced to fit into a front that wasn't designed as a part of the whole (van Duyne et al., 2006).

Why Use Prototypes/Simulations?

Prototyping is an excellent analysis technique for software development because it allows the business stakeholders, specifically the software users, to see the software design before it is built. Business stakeholders can easily decide if the design contains the necessary data components, has meaningful labels and descriptions, and make specific suggestions about the placement of screen items and aesthetics. A prototype is also an excellent requirements presentation deliverable for IT developers because they can see exactly what is to be built.

Other Techniques

Event Modeling

Identifying and analyzing events provides another valuable requirements perspective. An event is something that happens outside a business area, to which the business area must respond. The responses to events are business processes, so this technique is an alternative approach to identifying business processes. Various methodologists have named several types of events; external and temporal (driven by time) are the most commonly used (Yourdon, 1988). Events are named with the external agent who initiates them (e.g., *customer* places an order).

Entity State Transition/UML State Machine Diagrams

The state transition analysis technique recommends that the analyst think through all of the *states* a particular entity or object may be in. A state is a stage in the behavior pattern of an entity (Ambler, 2005). Example *states* for the entity ORDER would be new,

BABOK Connection	
Knowledge Area	**Task/Technique**
Requirements Analysis	Event and State Modeling

paid, verified, shipped, etc. State transition analysis requires the analyst to think through all of the states in which an entity can exist. Thinking about each state helps to identify processes (how does the state change), additional data, and business rules.

Object Modeling/Class Modeling

Object modeling and class modeling are UML/OO techniques for understanding a business or designing a system. The object or class represents a group of items that are important to the business. The concept of an object or class is broader than that of an entity. The object or class represents not only data but also processes (called behaviors or methods) combined into one requirements component. Object modeling and class modeling are used extensively for software design. These techniques have been used occasionally to elicit and present business requirements.

User Stories

User stories are a relatively new requirements technique derived from use cases. A user story is a specific description of something the software needs to do. User stories are used by some of the agile approaches to software development and with extreme programming (www.extremeprograming.org) to quickly gather requirements. The stories are usually documented very informally on index cards and not maintained as development progresses. They are not intended to capture detailed requirements. They just provide the overall needs of the software for use in prioritization and estimating. More detailed requirements are discussed by the developer and the user as the software is built. Read *User Stories Applied* by Mike Cohn (2004) to learn about user stories.

Traceability Matrices

A powerful analysis technique is traceability or the linking of requirements. By identifying which requirements components are related to each other, along with any characteristics about the relationship, the analyst will find missing or inconsistent pieces. Almost any two requirements components can be linked. Deciding which links will be useful for each project depends on the project type and risks.

As business requirements are further detailed in functional and technical requirements, they should be *traced*. When a business stakeholder describes a core business process like RECORD ORDER and the team designs a Web data entry page to allow customers to enter their order information, the business requirement RECORD ORDER is linked to the Web page design. Every component of the completed solution can be traced back to a business requirement. See Table 6.4 for an example of a traceability matrix.

Traceability is an important concept for BAs to understand because recognizing that

BABOK Connection	
Knowledge Area	**Task/Technique**
Business Analysis Planning and Monitoring	Plan Requirements Management Process
Requirements Management and Communication	Manage Requirements Traceability

TABLE 6.4. Sample Traceability Matrix

Business Process	Prototype		
	Web Order Page	**Payment Page**	**Confirm Page**
Record order	X		X
Accept payment		X	X
Check inventory	X		

requirements are related to other requirements is critical to complete understanding. Thinking about traceability helps develop complete requirements. When you identify a new requirement, ask questions about possible related components.

The most common link is referred to as the CRUD matrix: the link between data and process. The CRUD matrix assesses how each data component is affected by each process. CRUD (create, read, update, delete) refers to the actions that a process may take on data. The CRUD matrix may be built on high-level data and process components (entities and business processes) or detailed components (attributes to use cases or screens). See Table 6.5 for an example of a CRUD matrix.

Gap Analysis

Gap analysis is used to find specific gaps in either software or manual procedures. Gap analysis compares two or more systems using a structured documentation format. Most gap analysis is represented in a matrix or

BABOK Connection	
Knowledge Area	**Task/Technique**
Enterprise Analysis	Gap Analysis

table (see Table 6.6 for an example). Common uses of gap analysis include:

◆ Comparing business data requirements to a COTS application database (for package selection evaluation or conversion requirements)
◆ Comparing existing software application functions to a COTS application function list (for package selection evaluation)
◆ Comparing data, process, or business rules of two similar departments during a merger or acquisition (for determination of best practices for merging)

TABLE 6.5. Sample CRUD Matrix

Process	Data					
	Employee			Paycheck		
	Number	State Withholding Percentage	State Withholding Amount	Date	Gross Wage Amount	Net Wage Amount
Calculate gross wages	R			C	C	
Calculate state withholding	R	R	C		R	
Calculate fed withholding	R				R	
Calculate net wages	R					C

Data Flow Diagramming

Data flow diagramming is one of the oldest analysis techniques created for software development. The technique was pioneered by Larry Constantine in the mid-1970s to assist with program design (Yourdon and Constantine, 1979). The diagram's "bubbles" and "arrows" were extremely popular in the 1970s, 1980s, and even the 1990s when CASE (computer-aided software engineering) tools provided analysts with a graphical tool to assist with the creation and maintenance of the diagrams. The power of this technique is in its simplicity and structure. A "bubble" or circle on the diagram represents a process. Arrows show data flowing into and out of each process. The basic assumption is that a process must have at least one input and at least one output flow. This assumption serves as the foundation for all other process analysis techniques.

As software became more complex, data flow diagrams (DFDs) became large. Wall-size diagrams often decorated offices. The difficulty of creating and maintaining these large diagrams led to the development of a series of smaller related diagrams called "leveled DFDs." Processes are decomposed on a decomposition diagram and a separate DFD

TABLE 6.6. Sample Gap Analysis

COTS Database		Business Data	
Table	**Column**	**Entity**	**Attribute**
Table 1	Table 1 Key	Vendor	Number
	T1 NM		Name
	T1 PH		Phone Number
	T1 AC		Account Number
	T1 ADD1		Mailing Address Street 1
	T1 ADD2		Mailing Address Street 2
	T1 CTY		Mailing Address City
	T1 ST		Mailing Address State
	T1 CO		Mailing Address Country
	T1 PS		Mailing Address Postal Code
Table 3	Table 3 Key	Check Payment	Check Number
	T3 PYAMT		Amount Paid
	T3 DTE		Date Paid
	T3 MM		**GAP**
	T3 APRV		Approved by
	GAP		Bank Routing Number

is created for each *leg* of the decomposition diagram. This keeps each diagram a manageable size and allows analysis and review to be done on one particular area of the business at a time.

There are few software tools available to assist the analyst with creating and maintaining DFDs. Without a tool, leveled DFDs are awkward to create and almost impossible to maintain. Because a tool is not available, most analysts only use this technique for a subset of the analysis area when there is a particularly complex process. DFD analysis is a great thinking tool and can be done for individual processes very simply. As with all of the analysis techniques, DFDs give the analyst a different perspective on a problem and allow it to be presented in a different way.

One specific DFD which is used frequently by analysts is the context-level DFD (see the section on project initiation in Chapter 3). This top-level DFD is a great diagram for developing consensus on the scope of the analysis area or the scope of a solution design.

Choosing the Appropriate Techniques

A BA may choose one technique for his or her analysis and understanding and another technique for presentation to business stakeholders. Most projects will be supported by several requirements techniques/deliverables. This section provides some suggestions for making these selections. There are three main options for documenting or presenting requirements: text, graphics, or a combination of both. The main goal is to provide requirements in the format(s) that best communicates to the intended audience. A secondary goal is to present the requirements in a format that allows for fast, efficient reviews. This is one of the reasons why graphics (diagrams, tables, etc.) are so popular.

Using Text to Present Requirements

Text has been the traditional approach to documenting requirements. It has the main advantage of being easy to produce (no special software is needed) and can be written and reviewed by anyone (e.g., SME, BA, project manager, developer).

Unfortunately, textual requirements have many limitations. As requirements get more and more detailed, textual requirements get longer and longer. Since detailed requirements typically describe how software should work and look, there are many stronger analysis techniques that should be used in place of text. Prototypes, simulations, report layouts, data diagrams, class and object models, and state transition diagrams are just a few examples. Long textual descriptions of software are difficult to review and mistakes are often missed. The English language can be ambiguous; requirements are often unclear and misinterpreted. In addition, most software developers dislike long textual requirements and will tend to skim them rather than study them. This leads to code that only loosely matches the business needs.

Using Graphics to Present Requirements

Depending on the particular type of requirement, a visual or graphical representation of a requirement may be easier to review and approve than a textual description. As the saying goes, "a picture is worth a thousand words." Diagrams, screen layouts, tables, matrices, and structured text are all effective approaches to presenting and communicating requirements. Although diagrams are useful, there are disadvantages to graphical requirements. They require a more skilled and knowledgeable analyst to create and present them. Reviewers must understand the symbols used. Diagram symbols often force short names which may not be descriptive enough. Techniques for consistently diagramming must be well understood, and graphics software is required to create the visual deliverables. An advanced form of graphics is a simulation. The simulation allows stakeholders to "try out" the software design and evaluate the requirements in an active way.

Using a Combination of Text and Graphics

Most BAs use a combination of text and graphics to present their requirements. Diagrams are supported by labels and annotations on the diagram and attached textual descriptions. Textual descriptions are structured as much as possible to describe components of the diagram. In an excellent requirements development tool, a diagram would link directly to these supporting textual descriptions and related requirements components, providing a complete model of the requirements.

Choosing an Approach

There are some types of requirements that lend themselves to a particular representation better than others. Audience preferences should also be considered.

Case in Point

Think about the following examples of requirements (not software related) and how you would prefer to review them:

- ◆ How do you like to get driving directions? Some people prefer maps (visual), while others prefer a description of the route that indicates each turn (text).

◆ How would you review and approve a new home design? A floor plan (visual) and a drawing of the outside façade, along with dimensions (text)?

◆ When you review a menu at a restaurant, do you prefer a textual description or pictures of the food? Why?

◆ When you are shopping for a new car, do you read the brochure (text) or look at the diagram of the engine and drive train (graphic)?

There are specific types of requirements that are best presented in text: project initiation descriptions like the statement of purpose, list of objectives, and list of assumptions. There are some requirements which only make sense as graphics: screen layouts, report layouts, and database designs. Most requirements benefit from a combination of a graphic along with supporting text: an ERD is a diagram with detailed characteristics and descriptions attached to it, a business process may be shown on a decomposition diagram or workflow diagram and described by attached text, and a business rule may be diagrammed as a relationship on an ERD and have a more detailed constraint list attached. These combinations of graphics and text are often referred to as *models*.

Business Analyst Preferences

Most BAs have preferences about analysis techniques. You may prefer techniques that you learned first or those that have worked successfully on past projects. It is important as a BA that you know which techniques work best for you to analyze and understand the business. It doesn't matter whether your favorite diagrams or models are used by anyone else. If they help you understand and clarify requirements, use them. This is a very important point. *Use the analysis technique(s) that helps you understand.* It doesn't have to result in a deliverable that anyone else looks at as long as it helps you better understand the business and ask better questions.

Case in Point

I have a very strong affection for ERDs and can't imagine ever working on a project of any type without developing one. This is a technique that helps me see the world in the best way for my comprehension. For me, understanding the information (data) in a business area and how it relates to all of the other information is a core factor in my ability to understand requirements and see possible solutions. Even when an ERD is not an appropriate deliverable, I sketch one out to aid in my understanding and to help me develop detailed questions.

Subject Matter Expert Preferences

How do you decide which analysis and documentation techniques to use? This is one of the most important set of decisions that you will face at the beginning of a project.

First of all, think about your stakeholders. Start with the SMEs. Chapter 2 discussed the importance of knowing your audience. The SMEs are your customers, and they have effectively "hired" you to represent their needs to a group of technical people. They may not know what you are doing, but they like you because you listen to them and you communicate in business language. You want to present your findings back to them in a format that they will best understand.

The first thing to keep in mind is that your SMEs don't know why you have to use any requirements documents at all! They explain to you what they need and want, and they expect you to go away and magically get it done. *Business people often don't appreciate the complexity of their requirements and don't understand why requirements documents are necessary.* This attitude may change over time as SMEs learn to appreciate the value of reviewing requirements documents. Business stakeholders want the solution implemented as soon as possible, and it may appear to them that you are wasting time writing a fancy document instead of getting things done. Be sensitive to the fact that you are going to have to "sell" them on the idea of this work.

When IT analysts first started creating requirements documentation back in the 1980s, they often delivered truckloads of paper to the SMEs, along with a deadline for it to be reviewed. IT would either refuse to start development work until the document was approved or begin work and ignore any questions or changes to the document. This is part of the reason why many SMEs don't get excited when you tell them you are going to write a requirements document.

So, you are writing a document for a group of SMEs who don't see any need for it and who will not have any desire to review it! What is the best format for such a document? A requirements document needs to be as concise as possible so that stakeholder review time can be as short as possible. However, obeying the rules of excellent requirements, it also has to be complete, unambiguous, prioritized, etc. How do you accomplish all of these goals at the same time? Very carefully.

Consider everything that you know about one of your key stakeholders. Does the person like to talk about what he or she does? Does the stakeholder sometimes draw diagrams to explain his or her processes to you? Does he or she write long textual descriptions? Being aware of how the SME presents information will give you a clue as to how the person would like to see information presented back to him or her. If you are working with an SME who is a financial, accounting, or numbers person, you may be successful using Microsoft Excel®-like spreadsheets to present requirements. Accountants see the world as rows and columns, so if you can present your requirements in a similar format, an accountant will be more likely to review them and is more likely to help you spot errors and holes.

An SME who is a marketing person may like to see colorful graphs, pie charts with percentages, or high-level slogans. This SME is more likely to review a requirements document that is pictorial, maybe colorful with clever icons.

Most BAs don't have much time to tailor a requirements package to each individual's fancy. Of course, BAs are always balancing the time constraints of all of their decisions. Remember that the whole point of requirements documentation is to communicate. If you can't get an SME to look at a requirements document, you have wasted time creating it and you are going to lose very valuable feedback at a critical point in the project.

Another approach to consider is giving an SME small chunks of requirements to review, one at a time. This helps the SME feel less overwhelmed and allows him or her to focus on a particular area. Eventually you can put all of the pieces together and remind the SME that he or she has already reviewed this document piece by piece. One advantage of this approach is that as you are preparing and reviewing each section, you can ask follow-up questions and get clarification as you go. The SME will also see value in your documentation as it helps you both find missing pieces. It also helps the SME see progress on the project and become aware of how much work the project really entails.

Some SMEs enjoy writing their requirements themselves. They may prefer to write down their requirements instead of spending time talking with you. This is a tricky situation to manage because often the requirements that an SME documents do not meet the criteria for excellent requirements. The good news is that these documents give you a lot of information about the SME. The level of detail in the document tells you how much complexity the SME sees in his or her processes. Many SMEs do not realize the complexity in their business area because they are doing the work every day and it is simple to them. It also shows you their priorities because the most important issues are likely to be mentioned numerous times.

Case in Point

One marketing SME wrote a description of a data query that she needed: "Select all of the people in the database who live in the United States and have attended a class." This sounded simple enough, but after many iterations of this query, the actual requirements were more like:

- Include people with a valid mailing address (meaning there was data in the street address, city, state, and zip code fields)
- Exclude people with a country code other than United States
- Exclude people who had requested no mail (*do not mail* indicator is on)
- Include people who had attended a class in the last three years
- Exclude people who had registered for a class and then canceled their registration
- Include people who are currently registered for a class in the upcoming six months
- List each person's preferred address (there were two mailing addresses for each contact, a primary and alternate)

When I told the SME that this query was very different than what was originally requested, she did not agree: "Of course it should only include valid mailing addresses. Who would select invalid ones?" In her mind, there were several "requirements" that were so obvious that they did not need to be written down. She did not understand how queries are written—specifying every necessary field requirement. The most important lesson that we learned from this exercise was that when this SME requested a query, we had to ask many questions about her assumptions before we even guessed about whether or not we could create it!

Developer Preferences

Developers are stakeholders also. You need to think about how best to communicate with developers as much as you think about communicating with the business people. Understanding how developers think is similar to understanding how accountants or marketers think. You need to learn about their job and get an understanding of what they do and how they do it. The better you understand the work of developers, the better you will be able to communicate with them. Developers usually prefer short, concise, visual requirements (see the section on communicating with developers in Chapter 5).

Project Manager Preferences

Project managers (PMs) are focused on developing a plan to get the project done and then sticking to the plan as closely as possible. The PM wants you to understand the business area just enough to be successful. No more and no less. He or she wants you to present requirements to stakeholders in a format that will allow for quick and painless approvals and quick and efficient development. Usually, the PM doesn't have a stake in what types of diagrams or models you use. The most important thing that you can do for the PM is to estimate how long you will

BABOK Connection	
Knowledge Area	**Task/Technique**
Business Analysis Planning and Monitoring	Communicate Requirements Analysis

need to accomplish your work on the project. The best way for you to develop this estimate is to think through all of your work and develop a detailed plan. This includes a requirements communication plan and list of requirements deliverables (see the section on business analysis planning in Chapter 7).

Standards

Setting standard analysis techniques and deliverables is difficult. Projects vary greatly, and the analysis necessary differs in quantity, perspective, and level of detail. Organizations should be careful when setting business analysis standards. Requiring a particular requirement deliverable for every project seems like a good way to introduce consistency into requirements but may result in wasted work for projects for which the technique is not appropriate. New BAs need guidance when choosing techniques. Ideally, this guidance is provided by a mentor rather than a set of standards. There is a benefit in trying to use the same set of presentation formats (e.g., decomposition diagram, ERD) on most projects because stakeholders will become accustomed to them and become efficient at reviews.

Case in Point

One organization with which I was doing some consulting work had a standard list of required requirements deliverables. The BAs were complaining because the time required to prepare these deliverables slowed down their projects and they felt many of the deliverables were a waste of time. I was asked to review the list and give my opinion. I was surprised to see two diagrams right at the top of the list which are both used to show the scope of an analysis area: the context-level DFD and the IDEF0 context diagram. These two analysis techniques are very similar, but they were developed from two different software development approaches. They are both excellent techniques, but my question was "Why do both?" The answer was that the manager who had developed the list preferred the IDEF technique (she had used it successfully at another company), while other analysts were familiar and successful with the context-level DFD. So they were both included!

My recommendation was simple: require one of the two diagrams but not both. Allow the analyst to choose the appropriate technique for each project. My recommendation was not immediately accepted. Management's concern was that the analysts would not know which diagram to use. Flexibility in standards requires the BA to understand the differences in the techniques and make intelligent decisions about which one to use. Experienced BAs must be given flexibility to choose requirements deliverables that clearly communicate specific project needs. Newer BAs should discuss deliverable selection with their mentor or manager. Having a rule that requires the same deliverable to be used for every project creates unnecessary deliverables and wastes valuable time.

Tables 6.7 and 6.8 show examples of guidelines for deliverables for different types of projects and different audiences, respectively.

AS IS VS. TO BE ANALYSIS

When eliciting, analyzing, and documenting requirements, the BA must always be aware of the *state* of the business environment he or she is capturing. There are two states: the current state of the business, commonly referred to as the *as is,* and a potential future state of the business, commonly referred to as the *to be.* It is very easy to forget about this difference and allow requirements to include both in a confusing mix in a single diagram. This is an easy mistake because when business stakeholders talk about their work, they will often tell you (1) what they currently do, (2) why they see a need for a change, and (3) their recommendation for a change. An experienced BA listens carefully for these three very different pieces of information and dissects them into their components. For example:

I log in to our accounts receivable system to enter the customer purchase information and make sure that the information is correct. Then I have to log in to our customer relationship management (CRM) system to enter the customer profile. This is a waste of time because I have already entered the address into accounts receivable (AR) and I have to type it again. The AR system should send this information to the CRM system to save me time.

TABLE 6.7.   Deliverables to Project Matrix

Deliverable Artifacts	New Development	Software Maintenance	COTS[1] Purchase	Process Re-engineering	Data Warehouse	Business Modeling
Cost/benefit analysis	○	○	√	√	○	
Project initiation	√	√	√	√	√	√
Business (logical) data model[2]	√	○	√		√	√
Conceptual class diagram[2]	√	○	○			○
Essential process model	√	○	√	√	3	√
As is workflow	○	○	√	√		√
To be workflow	○			√		○
Use case model	√	√				○
User interface layout	√	○				
Test case/procedure	√	√	√			
Security requirements	√		√			
Performance requirements	√		√		√	
Quality requirements	√					
Physical data model	√	○			√	

Key: √ = required, ○ = optional.

[1] Commercial off-the-shelf.

[2] Conceptual class diagrams and logical data models may or may not be used on the same project to document data requirements.

[3] Data warehouses often use "ETL" concepts: Extract data, Transform data, and then Load data elsewhere (the warehouse). By definition, a process transforms data, so some data warehouse projects will need to document some essential processes.

TABLE 6.8. Deliverables to Audience Matrix

Category	SDLC Phase[1]	Deliverable	SMEs	Executive Sponsors	Quality Assurance[2]	Network Architects	Regulatory Agencies	IT System Architects	IT Developers	IT Security Architects	Database Architects	Legal	Business Analysts	Project Managers	External Customers
Business	1	Cost/benefit analysis	R	A									C	A	R
Business	2	Project initiation	A	A	R			R				R	C	C	R
Business	3	Business (logical) data model	R		R			R			A		C	A	R
Business	3	Conceptual class diagram	R		R			R			A		C	A	
Business	3	Essential process model	A		R			R			R		C	A	R
Business	3	As is workflow	A		R			R	R				C	A	
Functional	4	To be workflow	R		R			A	R				C	A	
Functional	4	Use case model	A		R		R	A	R	R	R		C	A	R
Functional	4	User interface layout	A		R			A	R	R	R		C	A	R
Functional	4	Test case/procedure			C				R				R	A	
Non-funct.	4	Security requirements	R		R	R	R	C		A	R	R	C	A	
Non-funct.	4	Performance requirements	R		R	R		R	R		R		C	A	
Non-funct.	4	Quality requirements	R		R		R	R					C	A	
T	4	Physical data model			R	R		R	R		A		R	A	

Key: A = approve, C = create, R = review.

[1] SDLC phase: 1 = planning, 2 = scoping, 3 = elicitation and analysis, 4 = design.

[2] Note that quality assurance should have review or creation responsibilities in almost all stages of the project, since the creation of test cases and procedures is a process that is synchronized with the software development life cycle.

The BA must be careful to listen for the facts vs. opinions or ideas in this discussion. The current process (as is) was described briefly, but the speaker got distracted by describing his or her problem and recommendation. Did the BA get a clear, complete description of the current state? No. The BA needs to ask more detailed follow-up questions:

◆ What specific data items are entered in AR to process the payment?
◆ How is the information validated?
◆ What if the payment information is not correct or is incomplete?
◆ Is the CRM system still updated?
◆ What specific information is entered into the CRM system?
◆ How many fields are entered into both systems?
◆ Are the fields named the same?
◆ Why does the procedure require this double entry?
◆ What if this customer is already in the CRM system?
◆ Is the profile updated?

Business analysis professionals must be very careful not to jump to conclusions or recommendations without understanding the as is state. If solutions to business problems were extremely obvious, they probably would have already been implemented. An analyst wouldn't be needed in such situations. Rarely are good-quality solutions that obvious or simple. There are a whole complex set of parameters that impact the problem and situation, and all must be considered before a solution is proposed.

Do you need to document every detail of the current state when you know that it is going to change? This is a judgment call that the BA and team must make. The current state needs to be understood and considered carefully, but it does not always benefit the team to create detailed, presentation-quality documents that describe it (see the discussion in Chapter 4 on learning the current system).

Every project and situation within a project must be evaluated individually. Depending on the reason for a project, the BA will determine the type of documentation that is appropriate. Returning to the AR example, why are you learning about the as is procedure? Is the goal to document the current procedure because new employees will be hired and must learn this job? Has the BA been asked to look for possible process improvements or streamline the efficiency of this task? Is a new AR software package being installed that will change this procedure? Is the organization considering building an interface from AR to CRM? From CRM to AR? This reinforces the importance of understanding why a project was initiated (see the section on project initiation in Chapter 3).

If a project was initiated as a process improvement project, understanding the current system is very important when making recommendations for changes. If you will be proposing a change, you will probably be asked to present your reasons for the recommendation. Showing the current process next to the proposed process is a great way to articulate the improvements that you anticipate. In addition, when planning for the change itself, it is important to know where you are starting from to build a detailed change plan. In other words, if moving from A to B, you need to know where A is to make the move.

If a project was initiated with a solution already selected (e.g., a new AR package), recommendations will be limited to how to best utilize the new functionality. In this case, it may not be necessary to formally present the as is state because the organization has already decided that it is

BABOK Connection	
Knowledge Area	**Task/Technique**
Enterprise Analysis	Determine the Gap in Capabilities to Meet the Business Need

inefficient or not appropriate. In this situation, the BA needs to understand the as is state to the extent that important tasks are covered by the new system and to write conversion requirements, but may decide not to create any documentation about the old procedures or processes. The as is state is *old* because the organization has already decided on a *new* process.

PACKAGING REQUIREMENTS

How Formally Should Requirements Be Documented?

One of the skills of an experienced business analysis professional is the ability to decide how formally to document each requirement. The main reason why many organizations don't spend as much time as necessary on requirements is because there have been a lot of projects where analysts have created large volumes of documentation, most of which was never read. The agile development approaches represent a backlash against this formal documentation.

Part of the attraction of the agile approaches to software development is the erroneous concept that the team doesn't have to document requirements. Generating a lot of documents is not the goal of any business analysis professional. BAs seek to understand business needs and clearly communicate requirements to the solution team. There are an infinite number of ways to accomplish this goal. This is the excitement and challenge of

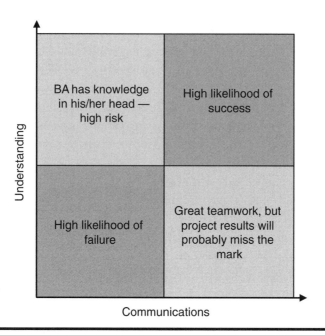

FIGURE 6.9. The Importance of Understanding and Communications

the business analysis profession. BAs are constantly asked to balance understanding of complex processes, clear communication, and time. Figure 6.9 shows the expected results as understanding and communications improve in quality.

What Is a Requirements Package?

In traditional methodologies, the concept of a requirements package was developed as a way of organizing and presenting all of the requirements information. The package was presented to the sponsor and SMEs for approval before the development team moved on to start building the proposed solution. It is called a *package* because analysts recognize that requirements may be contained in various documents, diagrams, forms, etc. A requirements package may include a table of contents, executive summary, and reviewer instructions. It may also contain links or references to electronic requirements such as simulations. Putting all of this important information together into a *package* organizes the information and allows it to be reviewed by others. The same concept is used in many financial organizations: a *loan package* includes the application for the loan, income verification documents, collateral documents, underwriting notes, etc. and allows everything about a loan to be presented together. In the medical profession, a patient's file contains lab results, medical history, prescription information, etc. When a "package" contains a lot of different documents from different sources in different media, automation is difficult. This is why many requirements management tools are not used. Most requirements management tools support one format (mostly text) for requirements but have a difficult time storing, retrieving, and organizing different types of deliverables.

As organizations move to a more iterative and incremental style of development, the use of a complete requirements package is giving way to smaller, more incremental presentations of requirements. Specific requirements deliverables are presented to SMEs for review and revision in each iteration. Packages may still be created for ease of presentation and delivery, but a package may include just a portion of the requirements and/or rough drafts of some deliverables.

The idea of waiting until requirements are *finished* before they are *packaged* and presented is an unrealistic and detrimental approach. The sooner requirements are reviewed, even in a rough draft form, the more likely it is that major flaws will be found and corrected.

When a package is created, it should be tailored to its intended audience and reviewed carefully before being distributed. All diagrams should be clearly labeled. Long textual requirements should be organized under major and minor headings. The package should be as clear and easy to review as

BABOK Connection	
Knowledge Area	**Task/Technique**
Requirements Management and Communication	Prepare Requirements Package

possible. It should use terminology consistently and contain a glossary. A customized cover page can be added to each package indicating the pages or sections on which an individual stakeholder should focus.

Case in Point

I worked on many projects using the waterfall development methodology. On one project, we spent several months eliciting and documenting requirements. We also spent many hours preparing the requirements package. At completion, it filled three very large binders and had dividers for chapters on internal and external design, screen layouts, report layouts, database design, etc. Every business and functional requirement was included in excruciating detail. The first page of this tome was the sign-off page and listed the names of the sponsor and key stakeholders. We delivered the package to our sponsor (using a rolling cart!) with great pride and then we waited.

We gave the business stakeholders a deadline for reviewing and approving the requirements and warned them that no development work would be done until they had signed off. I feel confident that no one in the user group read this package from cover to cover—we didn't give them enough time! Under political pressure, they signed and returned the tome to us, authorizing work to begin.

We diligently began coding and within a few months were ready to begin testing and showing our work to the users. Suddenly problems began to surface. As users looked at our product, they immediately began pointing out problems. Screens were missing key pieces of information, screen flow was not intuitive, and data entry was awkward. We had a well-documented change control process, so we started filling out change control forms for each change. But the IT director would not approve the changes. He pointed out to the sponsor that the requirements had been approved and that our product met the requirements. In answer to a change request, I remember telling one user: "That screen was on page 348 of the requirements package and you approved it." Allowing changes at this point in the project would have delayed implementation. The IT director, who was relatively new, was determined to get projects done on time (a frequent complaint about the prior director was that projects were always late), so we implemented our system on time, according to the requirements as planned.

A success story for IT? Not really. The business stakeholders were not satisfied and yet couldn't complain because their signatures were on the tome, approving it. Their frustration lasted a number of years as the change request forms continuously flooded in, and we eventually evolved to a system that really supported the business.

Generating large requirements packages that are difficult to review and use doesn't work. The business analysis work is to understand and communicate requirements. Find the communication approach that works best for your stakeholders. Presenting requirements in sections, conducting requirements walkthroughs, and offering to sit down and discuss the detailed deliverables are just a few of the approaches to consider to guarantee effective requirements communication.

Request for Proposal Requirements Package

An important use of packaging is in creation of a Request for Information or Request for Proposal (RFP). These packages are formal documents because they are sent outside an organization and are used to make decisions that lead to legal agreements with vendors. When creating a requirements package to include in an RFP (see Chapter 3), there are some additional considerations and components. When the package is going outside of the company, information is typically presented more formally and confidential information is only included if absolutely necessary (along with a confidentiality agreement).

Business requirements should be included in an RFP. Some functional requirements may be included when a COTS package can be customized for workflow or screen design. Business data requirements should be included in an ERD or data dictionary list. Vendors must include individual data element support in their responses. Business rules should be included so that vendors can report whether their applications can support each rule. The deliverables included in an RFP may be a subset of those used internally. For example, you may choose not to include the list of project objectives or risks.

An important section of an RFP is non-functional requirements. Limitations and constraints of an organization's technical environment must be detailed. Security and user access requirements are also important because the vendor will not know how

BABOK Connection	
Knowledge Area	**Task/Technique**
Solution Assessment and Validation	RFI, RFQ, RFP

many or what type of users will be accessing the software. Quality and reliability requirements should clearly communicate an organization's expectations for the quality of the product.

Characteristics of Excellent Requirements

The characteristics of excellent requirements have been understood for a long time (Wiegers, 1999). Unfortunately, many requirements still do not meet the criteria. Why? Because the criteria are very difficult to achieve and requirements are very complex. As discussed earlier, the business analysis profession does not even have clear agreement on what a *requirement* is. If the definition of the term is not solid, it is difficult to assess its quality.

Wiegers' characteristics of excellent requirements are:

◆ Complete
◆ Correct
◆ Unambiguous
◆ Verifiable
◆ Necessary

TABLE 6.9. Sample Data Requirement

Data Name	Data Type	Length	Allowable Values
CUSTOMER EYE COLOR	Text	10 characters	BLUE GREEN BROWN HAZEL UNKNOWN

◆ Feasible
◆ Prioritized

Just looking at the first characteristic points out a challenge. Can an individual requirement ever be complete? When you break requirements down into components and show their relationships to other requirements, completeness is difficult to assess.

Table 6.9 shows an example of a requirement for a data element. Is the requirement complete? It could be considered complete if it was completely described. However, in terms of using the requirement to solve a business problem, a data element alone is probably not complete. There is likely a process that needs to use CUSTOMER EYE COLOR, a business rule around when the value UNKNOWN is used, possibly a screen prototype where CUSTOMER EYE COLOR will be entered and displayed, etc. Thus, a requirement's "completeness" is determined by not only its description but also its relationships with other requirements.

The same can be said for all of these characteristics. To adequately evaluate excellent requirements, you need to look at the entire requirements package. Within the defined scope of the project, the package should be complete, correct, unambiguous, verifiable, feasible, and prioritized.

BABOK Connection	
Knowledge Area	**Task/Technique**
Requirements Analysis	Verify Requirements

Getting Sign-Off

Sign-off is an important milestone in any project. The sign-off is an official approval from the project sponsor and business stakeholders that the project is moving in the right direction. A project of duration longer than a month or so should have multiple sign-off points. Ask for sign-off for individual deliverables as they are reviewed. Be sure that the stakeholder understands what he or she is signing. The more you ask for approval and receive it, the more buy-in you will have from the business stakeholders. It is also easier for them to give their approval if you don't wait too long or ask them to approve too much at a time. The sign-off can be the BA's best friend.

A BA should work with his or her PM at the beginning of a project to set the project sign-off milestones. If you anticipate that your requirements package will be longer than 10 pages, consider how difficult it will be to review this in one session. An ideal method for getting sign-off is to have a

BABOK Connection	
Knowledge Area	**Task/Technique**
Requirements Management and Communication	Formal Requirements Approval

formal review session where the business stakeholder can ask specific questions about the requirements. In an open environment, business stakeholders will feel that you are all one team and they will be anxious to give their approval to move forward.

Requirements Tools, Repositories, and Management

Few excellent requirements tools are available to BAs. As vendors learn about the needs of BAs, more flexible requirements tools will be developed. Vendors must be aware of the requirements components and the importance of traceability and impact analysis. A requirements tool that does not allow an analyst to break down requirements to their lowest level or link them together is no more useful than a simple drawing tool or word processor.

A repository is a place (physical or conceptual) where "things" are stored. A requirements repository is the place where project requirements will be stored. They should be stored in a permanent repository for reuse on future projects.

Requirements may be stored only in the minds of the project team members. They can be communicated verbally and never written down. This is not recommended because relying on people's memories is dangerous. Document requirements in any location or format available. The re-

BABOK Connection	
Knowledge Area	**Task/Technique**
Business Analysis Planning and Monitoring	Plan Requirements Management Process

quirements repository may be a series of flip charts hanging in the project room. It may include index cards with user stories. The repository may be a directory on a server which contains many files (Microsoft Word documents, Excel spreadsheets, Visio diagrams, etc.). An organization may use virtual or shared document management software. On the most formal end of the spectrum, there are commercially available requirements repositories that manage and maintain requirements in very sophisticated database management systems (e.g., IBM Rational Requisite Pro®, IBM/Telelogic DOORS®).

SUMMARY OF KEY POINTS

Every business analysis project requires the use of analysis techniques. An analysis technique provides a structured, thinking approach to help the BA understand a business problem, opportunity, and requirements from different perspectives and different angles. BAs should be able to use many techniques and know when each technique will be most effective.

◆ The core requirements components of data, process, business rules, and external agents must always be considered. There are analysis techniques that focus on one particular component (e.g., data modeling) and techniques that identify multiple components at the same time (e.g., use cases).

◆ BAs must be aware of the difference between business requirements, solution requirements (functional and non-functional), and technical requirements or specifications.

◆ BAs use analysis techniques not only to understand the business needs but also to communicate them to all of the project stakeholders.

◆ Business stakeholders must feel confident that the analyst understands their true needs and will represent them accurately to the solution team.

◆ The solution team stakeholders need clear direction on software functionality to be built.

◆ The SQA and testing team need an understanding of the proposed solution so that they can design effective tests.

◆ BAs should work with their PMs to determine the formality of requirements packages and milestones for stakeholder approvals.

BIBLIOGRAPHY

Ambler, Scott (2005). *The Elements of UML 2.0 Style.* Cambridge University Press.

Bittner, Kurt and Ian Spence (2002). *Use Case Modeling.* Addison-Wesley.

Chen, Peter Pin-Shan (1976). The entity-relationship model—Toward a unified view of data. *ACM Transaction on Database Systems.* Vol. 1, No. 1 (March).

Cockburn, Alister (2000). *Writing Effective Use Cases.* Addison-Wesley Professional.

Cohn, Mike (2004). *User Stories Applied: For Agile Software Development.* Addison-Wesley Professional.

Gottensdiener, Ellen (2005). *The Software Requirements Memory Jogger.* GOAL/QPC.

Jacobson, Ivar (1992). *Object Oriented Software Engineering: A Use Case Driven Approach.* Addison-Wesley Professional.

Lauesen, Soren (2002). *Software Requirements: Styles and Techniques.* Addison-Wesley.

Martin, James (1986). *Information Engineering.* Savant.

Martin, James and C. McClure (1985). *Diagramming Techniques for Analysts and Programmers.* Prentice Hall.

Page-Jones, Meilir (1988). *The Practical Guide to Structured Systems Design.* Second Edition. Prentice Hall PTR.

Pande, Peter S., Robert P. Neuman, and Roland R. Cavanagh (2000). *The Six Sigma Way: How GE, Motorola, and Other Top Companies Are Honing Their Performance.* McGraw-Hill.

Ross, Ronald (2003). *Principles of the Business Rule Approach.* Addison-Wesley.

Simsion, Grame C. and Graham C. Witt (2005). *Data Modeling Essentials.* Second Edition. Morgan Kaufman.

van Duyne, Douglas K., James A. Landay, and Jason I. Hong (2006). *The Design of Sites: Patterns for Creating Winning Web Sites.* Second Edition. Prentice Hall PTR.

von Halle, Barbara (2003). *Business Rules Applied: Building Better Systems Using the Business Rules Approach.* John Wiley & Sons.

Wiegers, Karl (1999). *Software Requirements.* Microsoft Press.

Yourdon, Edward (1988). *Modern Structured Analysis.* Prentice Hall PTR.

Yourdon, Edward and Larry Constantine (1979). *Structured Design: Fundamentals of a Discipline of Computer Program and System Design.* Prentice Hall.

7

INCREASE YOUR VALUE

One of the great things about business analysis is that you can increase your value to an organization by learning new techniques and continuously improving your skills. A business analyst (BA) initially learns the foundational skills of communications and requirements techniques and then builds on that foundation, maturing as he or she gains more and more experience. A business analysis professional has unlimited possibilities for career development and expanding responsibilities. The skills used in business analysis work are prized by organizations and offer BAs the opportunity to move into management and executive positions if interested.

Many of the skills used in business analysis work are also used in related disciplines. Project management, quality assurance, business management, and strategic planning professionals all share skills with business analysis that are never really perfected, but rather enhanced.

There are numerous ways to improve your skills: read books and articles, practice new techniques and skills, and learn from other BAs. You also improve your skills when you teach other people. Join a business analysis community like your local International Institute of Business Analysis (IIBA™) chapter or your company's business analysis community of practice, help the group schedule meetings and find speakers to improve your leadership skills, volunteer to mentor new BAs, and give presentations to share your knowledge. Join other industry groups focused on IT, process improvement, or your industry. Sharing your experiences helps other BAs and improves the professional as a whole.

The skills and techniques presented in this chapter are not learned in any particular order. They are grouped into the following general sections:

◆ Build Your Foundation
◆ Time Management
◆ Build Your Relationships and Communication Skills
◆ Keep Learning New Analysis Techniques
◆ Continually Improve Your Skills
◆ Business Analysis Planning

BUILD YOUR FOUNDATION

Skill: Get Started

One of the hardest skills for a new BA is getting started; when first assigned to a project, a new BA can easily become overwhelmed by the complexity of the business and the sheer volume of information that is not understood. If you are a new BA, try to find an experienced BA who can act as a mentor and help you through some of these roadblocks. Every BA gets overwhelmed occasionally, but with experience you can learn to structure your work and manage the volume.

Think about how you would put a puzzle together. Most people start by finding the pieces that will form the edge and trying to fit them together. The edge is like the boundaries or scope of a project. You must first determine what will be inside the project by finding the edges. This can be accomplished by asking a lot of questions about which business processes should be analyzed. For example, if you are working on a project in the human resources area, you could start by asking fairly broad questions like: "Will anything in the payroll area be involved? Is the hiring process to be included? Will we be talking about employee benefits?" As you receive answers, you are beginning to frame the puzzle. Mentally line up all of those edges and they will start to fit together.

When you are feeling overwhelmed, the best thing to do is to *do something*! Pick one piece of the business and start asking questions. Start writing down the answers you hear even if you don't completely understand them. Pick an area that you do understand and work at its edges to increase your knowledge by building on what you already know.

Another reason why the puzzle analogy is so appropriate is that when you get frustrated with or stuck on one section of a puzzle, you get up, walk around, and then work on another section. You may have the same experience with business analysis. When you feel stuck in one area, leave it alone and work in another area. You will probably continue to make progress, and when you go back to the area in which you were stuck, it may suddenly seem clearer.

The following approach is useful for new BAs. It outlines a generic list of steps that are usually performed in business analysis work. This approach should work for any type of project and with any software development methodology. BA work rarely is this straight-forward, but this gives you a general direction to get started. Make sure that you truly understand the business and its needs before designing a solution. Sometimes you may be asked to do research pre-project, to help the group decide if a project is warranted (see the discussion on business case development in Chapter 3). This research may also be compiled around high-level requirements components.

1. The executive (project) sponsor and business stakeholders put together an initial project request. Review all available project initiation documentation (the BA may be involved before, during, or after this step).
2. Begin asking high-level questions to find your analysis boundaries and get a high-level view of the project (see the section on asking the right questions later in this chapter).
3. The BA and project manager work with stakeholders to document the project scope (see the discussion on project initiation documentation in Chapter 3).
4. Meet with stakeholders to verify and validate the project scope. Get sponsor sign-off (see the section on requirements reviews later in this chapter).
5. Plan the analysis work (see the section on business analysis planning later in this chapter).
6. Elicit detailed requirements (see the discussion on how a BA learns the business in Chapter 4).
7. Identify and document core business components (see the section on core requirements components in Chapter 6).
8. Create a comprehensive glossary of terms (see Chapter 6).
9. Double check for missing requirements by linking data to process requirements (see the discussion on the CRUD matrix in Chapter 6).
10. Once business requirements are complete, work with the business subject matter experts and technical team to design a solution (see the discussion on making recommendations for solutions later in this chapter).
11. Elicit and document functional and non-functional requirements.

Skill: Think Analytically

Training yourself to think analytically requires practice. Some people do it more naturally than others. To learn to analyze, train your mind to break down problems and complex systems into small, manageable pieces. Breaking down complex systems is not easy and requires practice. The analyst must learn to look for business patterns and significant facts (some of the information an analyst will hear and read is insignificant) and must learn to discern the relevant from the irrelevant.

Take the opportunity to practice whenever possible. There are problems and complex systems everywhere in the world. As you order breakfast at your local coffee shop, think about the steps necessary to get a cup of coffee to you. What questions would you ask if you were learning about the business? Which facts would be important? Is the flavor of the coffee relevant to the process? Is the country of origin of the bean? Does the price of the coffee affect the process?

Try using a variety of analysis techniques on the same problem to see what new information is exposed. Don't ignore tried-and-true techniques (e.g., data flow diagramming) just because they have been around for years. Many analysts still use these successfully on their projects. Every technique you learn offers another opportunity for you to expand your analysis skills. Newer techniques are often developed from the older techniques, so understanding an old technique makes it easier to learn a new one. Even if you never use the older technique, you are using your brain to learn it, and using your brain is what keeps it working well.

Learning a new tool or technique doesn't mean abandoning the old ones. It just adds another skill to your repertoire. Imagine that you are a musician learning to play instruments. If you play the flute and then learn to play the clarinet, you don't

BABOK Connection	
Knowledge Area	**Task/Technique**
Underlying Competencies	Analytical Thinking and Problem Solving

suddenly forget how to play the flute. The more tools and techniques with which you are comfortable, the easier it will be to learn new ones.

Skill: Note Taking

It is critical that a BA develop strong note-taking skills. When a BA is asking questions and listening carefully to answers, he or she must be able to accurately record the answers as they are provided by stakeholders. There are a number of methods for effective note taking:

- ◆ Shorthand or handwritten notes
- ◆ Diagramming/modeling using an analysis technique
- ◆ Having a BA partner record answers while you ask questions
- ◆ Outlining/mind mapping
- ◆ Video or audio recording of the elicitation session

Note taking during elicitation sessions is critical for two reasons. First, effective BAs make very good use of their stakeholders' time and as such should not make stakeholders repeat any of their requirements unless clarification is needed. Few people can remember everything that is said during an elicitation session, so note taking is critical to increase the likelihood of remembering the requirements accurately. Second, it would be rude not to take notes when interviewing a stakeholder. If the answer to a question is important, you need to make sure that you record it. If it is not recorded, you are giving a non-verbal message to the stakeholder that his or her answer is not important.

New BAs may want to use a standard template for recording notes (see Chapter 6 for examples). Mind mapping is another useful technique (Allen, 2002). Jot down requirements by the core components (data, process, business rules, and external agents). Make notes on a copy of the existing system documentation or the existing requirements document from a prior project. Try different techniques and learn the ones that work best for you.

Every time a BA begins learning about a business area or a requirement, he or she needs to decide what to do with the information. Does this information need to be turned into a reviewable presentation-quality document? Not always. It is critical that

BABOK Connection	
Knowledge Area	**Task/Technique**
Elicitation	Document Results of Elicitation Activity

business analysis professionals learn to think ahead about what the information will be used for and who will use it. Thinking ahead about why particular information is being collected will help to determine how much detail is needed and how formally the information needs to be presented.

Technique: Brainstorming

Brainstorming is used as a tool to generate creative ideas in a group session. The technique has become popular because it helps participants think outside of their current procedures and generate new innovative ideas. Brainstorming is often used when trying to streamline an existing process, resolve a complex problem, or develop a new business opportunity.

Brainstorming encourages group members to contribute all of the ideas that come into their minds without filtering them. Ground rules should be set for the session: no idea is bad, one person speaks at a time, do not evaluate any ideas during brainstorming, and do not eliminate or organize ideas during the session. For shy groups, try the *round robin* approach of asking for an idea from one person at a time.

When a team is experiencing *groupthink,* brainstorming can help the BA break through. Groupthink occurs when a group works together well and members have affection for each other. Sometimes the team members value the team more than the development of a quality solution. They are hesitant to disagree with each other or point out flaws in recommended solutions. To break groupthink, conduct a formal brainstorming session to generate as many different ideas as possible. You may offer a small reward to the person or team that comes up with the largest number of new ideas.

Brainstorming can also be used by a BA working alone on a project. Allow yourself to imagine possible solutions to a problem that initially seem outside the realm of possibility.

BABOK Connection	
Knowledge Area	**Task/Technique**
Elicitation	Brainstorming

Skill: Work with Complex Details

Frequently, business analysis work involves complex details. A BA must be able to elicit and document these details accurately. Think carefully about the details that must be captured. Missing a data element or business rule in the requirements may result in significant costs during software testing or after implementation. Having the patience to keep track of very detailed requirements is critical to project success.

Case in Point

When my company was purchasing and customizing its customer relationship management (CRM) system, we decided to build an enterprise data model and perform gap analysis (our data needs vs. a commercial off-the-shelf database). We didn't have a data modeling tool available, so I drew the entity relationship diagram in Microsoft Visio® and put the attributes with their characteristics into a Microsoft Excel® spreadsheet. The spreadsheet included columns for the corresponding data element name in the CRM package so that my gap analysis was in the same file as my data needs. As the data model evolved and we learned more about the CRM system, attributes were added and updated. I added color to the spreadsheet to highlight the fields which were to be customized. I added a notes column to make annotations along the way. I also added a couple of columns specifying the conversion fields and algorithms from the old system.

This spreadsheet became very large, so I split the attribute list into separate worksheets to make it easier to find things. This was a very detailed file to maintain, and sometimes I wondered if it was worth the trouble.

But as I was updating these detailed requirements (almost daily), I would invariably see a hole and develop another question to ask the business stakeholders or the vendor. These questions helped us discuss and resolve issues before implementation. Because the spreadsheet never became a formal deliverable, I didn't waste time making it neat or printable. It was a reference or repository for me to make sure that we didn't miss anything.

The end result of all of this work was a smooth implementation with very few missing pieces of data. Once the conversion of the old database into the new was complete, the CRM system met our data needs immediately. It was almost a year before we identified a needed data element and this was related to a new business need. The detailed documentation paid off in productivity and data integrity.

How Much Detail? Just Enough!

One of the great characteristics of BAs is that they love details. BAs love to learn about details, talk in detail, document details—BAs just can't get enough details. This strength has a corresponding weakness: When is the detail *detailed enough*? An experienced BA periodically asks himself or herself: "Am I getting too carried away with details?" This is an important question for all BAs to discipline themselves around. Pull your head out of the details periodically and make sure that your time is being spent on the highest value task.

Case in Point

This BA challenge became very obvious to many of us when the IIBA certification committee released the application for certification. The application asks BAs to document their business analysis experience by project and by knowledge area. Since 7500 hours of experience is needed, this documentation process is significant. Also, since the application form and process were brand new, it was not a tested, streamlined process.

I spoke with many BAs and helped them with advice on their applications. Applicants spent hours compiling lengthy descriptions of their project work. Many broke down their work into very small, individual task descriptions. Some built spreadsheets with cross-references to the knowledge areas. I observed a common BA challenge: some applicants got so entrenched in the detailed documentation that they forgot the purpose of the work and lost perspective on how it would be used. The IIBA certification applications are reviewed very carefully to assure that candidates have sufficient BA experience, but the reviewers do not need to understand the specific projects on which an applicant worked. This is a good example of a situation where a BA must periodically remind himself or herself of the level and type of detail which his or her audience needs.

There really are two challenges here for the BA. One, recognize when you are getting into too much detail or detailing something which your audience does not need. Second, determine how to document in as little detail as appropriate. This is the real challenge. Many people tend to engage in "all or nothing" thinking, which means that if they can't go into all of the details, they don't want to bother with any! Learn to document "just enough" detail. Just enough detail means that you have gotten enough information to conduct a thorough analysis and have given just enough detail to stakeholders for them to make decisions and grant approvals as needed. "Just enough" should be the BA mantra when getting too far into the details. So the next time that you struggle with whether or not to include a particular detail in your requirements document, think *just enough!*

TIME MANAGEMENT

Skill: Understand the Nature of Project Work

Take a look at how typical BAs or IT team members work each day. They start the day by reviewing all of the project tasks that have been assigned to them. Often, they are assigned to more than one project, so the tasks vary from project to project. They must use the information provided by management and the project manager about priorities and dependencies in order to decide which of these tasks should be attacked first. Many of these assigned tasks are large; one task may actually represent 80 hours or 2 weeks of work to complete. There will also be tasks that have been started but are on hold because more information is needed (e.g., a BA may need the list of valid codes to finish the requirements for the drop-down box on a screen).

Having to prioritize work and make decisions about how to spend one's time is very different from a first-in, first-out task list that is common in other business areas. Individuals who have always worked in IT or in a project environment can't imagine working any other way, just as individuals who have worked in a reactive environment can't imagine doing project work. Most BAs go home every day knowing that there is work waiting to be done. Their desks are never empty. On the other hand, most of the time there is not a task that absolutely has to be done on a particular day (i.e., a task for which someone is waiting). This gives BAs the ability to: (1) be flexible in planning their work, (2) set their own working hours, and (3) vary their work tasks to prevent boredom or monotony.

Of course, there are many workers in most industries who work in an environment that requires them to do both—reactive work and also work on projects. This balance is very difficult. This is the reason why most IT departments separate their maintenance staffs from their new development project teams. If you have both project work and customer support work to do, the customer support work always comes first and projects get delayed.

A project by its very nature usually involves more than one person and more than one day of work. In addition, most IT projects are unique units of work, never having been done before and never to be done again. This is why many IT estimates are wrong. Business analysis professionals must be aware of project priorities and their dependencies on the overall project plan. Choosing the appropriate task on which to work each day is critical.

Skill: Work on the Most Important Work First (Prioritize)

BAs always have more work to do than time to complete it. The more effective you become, the more this will be true. Organizations recognize valuable employees and consultants and assign them the most important and difficult work. As you master business analysis, your time will become more valuable and learning to prioritize your time becomes critical. You have probably worked with people who are always busy and yet don't meet deadlines because they focus on the wrong tasks. Deciding where to spend your time is prioritization, and it is a critical BA skill.

Prioritizing one's time and the organization's resources is one of the most important benefits a BA contributes to the bottom line. How many times have you been in a meeting or working on a task and you suddenly think: "This is such a waste of time!" Those *ah ha* moments are when you need to stop and rethink your priorities. The BA should raise the awareness of the team to help everyone else prioritize their time correctly. One of the most effective ways of doing this is to ask a series of questions, beginning with the *why* question:

◆ Why are we doing this activity?
◆ What is this activity doing for the project?
◆ When do we expect a payoff from this activity?
◆ Is the payoff bigger than the effort that we are expending?

Prioritizing work is a skill that requires practice and diligence. One habit to embrace daily is looking at your to-do list (which is always longer than you will ever accomplish) and identifying the most important tasks. Some of these tasks will be quick and easy to complete, and these are often the most attractive. You might think: "I can get that out of the way this morning and be done with it!" But don't leave the larger, more difficult tasks until last or they will never get done. Often, those more difficult tasks are related to long-term strategic projects which are very important to the organization.

Case in Point

Imagine you have been assigned to two projects. One is to add a new field to an existing screen so that marketing can track an additional characteristic of each customer. This is important for marketing and sales of future products to specific customers.

The second project is an enterprise-wide initiative to restructure customer service and streamline order processing activities. This project requires that you interview stakeholders from several departments, ask detailed questions, and develop current and future workflows to design new processes.

To which project would you allocate your time during the day? Since the first project is small and fairly straightforward, your tendency will be to get it done. It is easier because you already know how to update a prototype, define a data element, and communicate a change to IT. The second project is less structured. It requires planning and scheduling. You will need large chunks of quiet time to think about the issues. It is easy to put off.

If you spend the majority of your day on the first project, the second, strategic project waits. In addition, the next morning there will probably be another small, easy task on your desk that will get in the way of the bigger project. The natural tendency is to put off more complex tasks.

A useful technique when working on large projects is *divide and conquer.* A successful BA must understand how to manage a large task by breaking it into small manageable tasks, putting them in a logical order, and doing them one at a time. Take a basic project management class or read a project management book if you have never been introduced to the work breakdown structure. Using this approach will help you break down your work into smaller, easier to manage tasks. These smaller tasks can be scheduled into your day, balancing work on large projects with smaller assignments.

Another skill that most experienced BAs have recognized and refined is their ability to work unconsciously on a project. This is actually a common human ability that is really amazing. Do you ever come up with a great idea while you are in the shower? Does the solution to a problem come to you suddenly as you are driving home from work? Do you wake up in the morning with an approach to deal with a sticky situation? These are all examples of the subconscious at work. The human brain has an amazing ability to be doing one thing consciously (like driving, showering, or watching a movie) and working on a problem in its subconscious. When you realize that you have this ability, it gives you a great advantage over those who do not. You can read an e-mail request without acting on it, and the next day the answer will be at your fingertips. You can interview a subject matter expert, make some notes, and then let your subconscious work on the issue for a day or so. When you come back to it, you will have great insights into the business needs and will have come up with several follow-up questions.

Technique: Understand the 80-20 Rule

It is a well-established fact that BAs spend 20% of their time eliciting 80% of the requirements. The other 80% of analysis time is spent gathering 20% of the requirements. This occurs because the majority of requirements (roughly 80%) are fairly straightforward and can be elicited fairly quickly. An experienced BA can interview business stakeholders briefly and immediately begin to understand the high-level requirements. An analyst can quickly get the "big picture" and then fill in all of the details. Some of these details will also be straightforward and fairly easy to document. Then there are the rest of the requirements. Every business area has at least a few processes, business rules, or data needs that are very complex and difficult to understand. These may be the 20% that take the most time to find and are the most important because they are complex. Try to determine whether the most important requirements are in the 80% (straightforward) or the 20% (complex). The difficulty and complexity may be related to industry specifics or they may result from a business area where policies and procedures have never been clearly articulated.

The most important (highest priority) requirements should be elicited as early as possible. Be careful not to become preoccupied with complex *unimportant* requirements. These requirements are often concerned with business transactions or

BABOK Connection	
Knowledge Area	**Task/Technique**
Underlying Competencies	Analytical Thinking and Problem Solving

situations that rarely occur and require human intervention. Don't spend time designing a sophisticated piece of software for an infrequent business need. A BA can easily spend 80% or more of requirements elicitation and analysis time on these complex areas of the business.

Technique: Timeboxing

A useful technique for analysis is timeboxing. Timeboxing acknowledges that some types of tasks are difficult to finish because the end state of the deliverable is subjective (e.g., is a screen design ever "right"?). This technique is used in software development when the time frame is set and the deliverable is negotiable. Timeboxing gives the worker a specific amount of time within which to complete a given task. The task must be completed by the specified date and time, with the goal of getting as much done as possible in the allotted time. Timeboxing is difficult because it forces the analyst to prioritize the most important work first. If time allows, lower priority items can be addressed. Timeboxing is valuable for people who tend to be perfectionists and tend to overcommit.

Imagine you have been assigned a small project for which you need to write a complete requirements document by a specific date and there are four high-level business requirements. The tendency would be to take one high-level requirement at a time, elicit the detailed needs, and prepare the requirements document. Using this approach, the time allocated might be used up on the first two high-level requirements. Timeboxing would recommend that you initially spend some time on each requirement to learn a little about it, its priority, and its risks. By working on each requirement for a short period of time and then moving on to the next one, you will get an overall view of the deliverables requested and be able to determine how much can be done in the time available. Talk with your project manager and sponsor frequently to provide a status update and confirm your plans for utilization of the time.

If all four requirements are needed, break the total time available into four time slots and get as much done as you can on each. Acknowledge that you may not be able to completely detail everything and your requirements package may not be a professional-quality deliverable. Keep track of risks and outstanding questions as you go along. At the end of your timebox, you will have an overall understanding of each requirement and at least a rough requirements deliverable. You will also have a list of risks and outstanding questions.

These risks and outstanding questions should be reported to the project manager and sponsor. They need to decide if more time should be allocated to resolve these items or if they are willing to accept the risks and move forward. Timeboxing must include risk assessment because, by its very nature, the technique acknowledges that the work will be rushed or squeezed into a smaller than ideal time frame. Analysts must be able to best utilize this time and report the risks of the shortened schedule.

Timeboxing is a great technique when the deliverable is a written document like a requirements package or training manual. Writers can edit and rewrite over and over again, never getting the sentences perfect. But most documents used internally in organizations don't need to be perfect—they need to communicate the important messages to their audience.

BUILD YOUR RELATIONSHIPS AND COMMUNICATION SKILLS

Skill: Build Strong Relationships

Building relationships is an important skill of a successful BA. Every day you interact with other BAs and your current and potential stakeholders, you can be practicing this skill. It is important for people in the business analysis role to build strong, solid relationships both in and out of the office. There are two key reasons why you should always be working on building relationships to improve both personally and professionally:

1. **Knowledge and experience**: "No one lives long enough to learn everything they need to learn starting from scratch. To be successful, we absolutely, positively have to find people who have already paid the price to learn the things that we need to learn to achieve our goals"—best-selling author Brian Tracy (www.briantracy.com). You can't know and experience everything. What you *can* do is be connected with people who have the knowledge and experience you need at any moment.

2. **Access and openness**: Your project is the number one priority for you, but it may not be for the subject matter experts (SMEs) and other stakeholders from whom you need time. Having strong relationships with those stake-

holders prior to and during a project will help open the necessary doors and encourage them to give you their time. As previously discussed, trust is a big part of a good relationship. SMEs will be more open and honest with you during a project if they trust you. There are many great references on the power of building relationships and how to go about it. Take a look at *Never Eat Alone* (Ferrazzi and Raz, 2005).

Skill: Ask the Right Questions

An important analysis skill is developing good questions. A business analysis professional should always be thinking of more questions to which an answer is needed. For initial meetings and interviews with stakeholders, use broad questions and elicit answers that describe an overall view. Subsequent elicitation sessions will require more detailed, clarifying questions. When an analyst listens to an answer, he or she first hears the message, then determines if the answer is complete, and asks follow-up questions. When stakeholders tell you how they perform a task like accepting a customer order, follow-up questions include things like:

◆ What if the customer's payment is not approved?
◆ What type of payments do you accept?
◆ What are the typical dollar amounts of these payments?

A master BA will ask detailed questions around each process, piece of data, and business rule. Some of the questions may be slightly out of scope, but the BA knows that he or she needs to make sure nothing is missed. Strong questions are open ended and encourage the stakeholder to talk at length about the requirement. Often, a stakeholder provides information over and above the answer. This additional information may prove relevant.

New BAs can use the development of questions as a planning and organization technique. When you are having trouble getting started, write down all of the questions that you can think of. Use open-ended questions to evoke a response that is more than just yes or no.

Use the journalist model to think through the *who, what, where, when, why,* and *how* (the *why* question will be further discussed later in this chapter). Each of these question starters will generate many specific questions for a particular project or business area. Formulating a list of questions is something that any BA can do, at any point in a project, working alone or in a group. Creating and reviewing this list exposes the analysis work that needs to be done.

Sample questions include:

◆ Who performs the process?
◆ Who manages or approves the process?
◆ Who provides the input to the process? Who receives the output?
◆ What data, materials, forms, or software are used?
◆ What constraints, policies, or procedures guide the process?
◆ What problems occur with the process?
◆ Where is the process performed?
◆ When is the process performed? On a regular basis? After a triggering event?
◆ Why is the process performed?
◆ How is the process performed?

Once you have a list of questions, look at each question and think about:

◆ How could you best elicit this information?
◆ How will you best record it when you receive it?
◆ How critical will the answer be?
◆ What type of requirement component will be found in the answer?
◆ Who would have the answer?

As you are formulating questions, you should think about who would be able to best answer each question. Most projects involve many stakeholders, each one able to provide unique information or pieces to the puzzle that you are putting together. It is important to think about which questions you will ask each stakeholder before your scheduled interviews. Stakeholders from different departments and at different levels of an organization will be able to provide different information. It is important to ask the right questions to the right people so that stakeholders don't feel incompetent or ignorant.

Typically, the *why* questions are best asked to higher level stakeholders. Executives and managers often see the bigger picture and know the reasons for the organization's decisions. Middle-level managers and supervisors can answer questions about *who* does *what*, *where* activities are performed, and *what* the goals of each activity are. Business workers will be able to answer specific, detailed questions about *how* work is accomplished and *what* specific activities are related to others.

This is communication planning at its most basic level. If you ever feel a bit overwhelmed on a project, take a moment to sit down and make a list of questions. Then note for each question which stakeholders you would ask. You have just developed a simple communication plan. Understanding and documenting what you don't know gives you a better sense of what you do know.

Case in Point

Imagine you have been assigned to create a new financial report for your chief financial officer (CFO). He wants to see consolidated profit and loss numbers for all of the company's product lines. Even though you have only been given a two-sentence description of this project, you should be able to generate a long list of questions. For example:

- What is the name of the CFO? What is his phone number and e-mail address? What type of communication does he prefer? What are the best times to contact him? What is his availability?
- Where is the CFO located? In what time zone?
- When is the report needed/expected?
- What do existing profit and loss reports look like?
- How are these reports created?
- What are the product lines? How many are there?
- What should the format of this new report be? Should it be the same as existing ones?
- Are the product line financials all managed by the same software?
- If not, how do accounts map from one product to another?

No matter how little you know about your assignment, you can always develop questions!

Skill: Listen Actively

Listening well is an important skill for all people and especially for people performing business analysis. Eliciting requirements involves asking excellent questions and listening carefully for responses. Listening is very difficult. Most individuals have never been formally taught how to listen. Listening is an active, conscious decision that is made during a conversation. The BA must *decide* to listen and be actively involved in the listening process.

Becoming an excellent listener brings the BA many benefits. People enjoy talking to good listeners and really appreciate the attention given. Good listeners are able to help resolve disagreements and conflicts by finding common ground and clearly articulating the opposing viewpoints. Listening carefully allows you to make decisions based on solid facts.

Studies show that as much as 55% of a message is received non-verbally. Consciously watch body language and facial expressions. When a business stakeholder is telling you about a task, watch for signs that will indicate how he or she feels about the task. Is it enjoyable? Is it tedious? Does he or she see value in it or is it just busy work? Is he or she interested in helping to improve the process? You can gather valuable information about a business area by listening with your eyes and your ears.

Communicate interest and curiosity through your tone of voice and body language. Since 55% of a message comes not through the words that you speak but through non-verbal behaviors, be aware of the non-verbal messages that you are send-

BABOK Connection	
Knowledge Area	**Task/Technique**
Underlying Competencies	Communication Skills

ing. When you are engaged physically with a stakeholder, by actively leaning toward the person, concentrating on his or her answers, making notes, and being honestly interested in what he or she is saying, you encourage the individual to give much more detail and elaborate on unclear points. If you are disinterested, sarcastic, condescending, demeaning, or negative in any way, the stakeholder may shut down and not be willing to provide important requirements.

Barriers to Listening

There are many barriers to listening. These barriers prevent the listener from accurately interpreting the intended message. Identify your barriers and work to eliminate them. One barrier is *filters*. An individual's brain processes each new piece of information through filters that have developed since childhood. You may not be aware of the filters that influence your ability to hear an intended message. Filters are based on prejudices, beliefs, values, attitudes, past experience, interests, and fears. For example, if you have had a bad experience with a person of a particular nationality, you may be predisposed to anticipate negative experiences with other people of the same nationality. Become aware of your filters. Try to determine how they were developed and how they influence your thinking. Improve your communication skills by recognizing your filters and their effect on your ability to listen. In addition, be aware that other people also have filters. Listen for these and be aware of their impact on your intended messages.

Another barrier to listening is *lack of interest.* When a BA is not curious or interested in learning about an SME's business area, his or her body language and behavior will reveal the lack of interest. Lack of interest by the listener is interpreted by the speaker as a lack of interest in him or her as a person. Determine why you are not interested. Are you feeling tired? Are you distracted by unrelated problems? Do you think that you already know what the speaker is telling you? Once you determine why you are not interested, you can correct the problem. Listening is committing. Decide you will get something of value out of the conversation.

Preconceived ideas can also be a barrier to listening. Preconceived ideas and thoughts are almost always present when dealing with a familiar topic or person. The tendency is to selectively listen for what you *expect* to hear. You may screen out information that doesn't meet your expectations. If you have worked in the business area being analyzed, you risk missing important information because of your preconceived ideas. Although having some previous knowledge of the business is helpful, it can also be a hindrance. You may not reconfirm specific information because you think that you already understand it. You may also fail to probe for differences between what you already know and what the SME is telling you. Keeping an open mind rather than relying on preconceived ideas is critical to eliciting requirements that are clear and complete.

Be careful not to *formulate responses or follow-up questions* while an SME is still talking. When you allow your mind to jump ahead to your next comment or question, you may be missing valuable information. Try to stay open and actively listen until you hear the entire thought. Paraphrase the message back to the SME to be sure you heard it all. Actively take notes on the information being provided. Once the SME has finished, take a few moments to compose your response and follow-up questions. The SME will appreciate the fact that you were focused on listening while he or she was talking.

Another barrier to listening is *finishing statements for others.* This will diminish an SME's desire to continue to communicate with you. Finishing other people's sentences is a habit that can be broken. If you become aware of this habit, work to break it by listening for periods and question marks from the SME. The SME will pause when he or she finishes a thought, and this is the opportunity for you to respond. If you have a hard time keeping silent, drink water while the SME is talking. Try to count to three once the SME has paused

TABLE 7.1. Phrases That Lead to Requirements

Words or Phrases	Possible Requirements Component
If . . .	Business rule
Sometimes . . .	Conditional business rule
Of course . . .	Assumption
It would be nice . . .	Unnecessary or low-priority requirement
Hopefully, envision, imagine, would like	To be solution possibilities/ideas
Existing, current	As is procedures and processes
Only when . . .	Business rule, possibly a security issue
Quickly	Performance requirements
Not	Business rule
Always, never	Mandatory business rules
When . . .	Business rule
Save, store, capture, write down	Data

to ensure that he or she has finished and allow yourself to gather your thoughts before responding. Use body language like nodding and eye contact to help the SME finish his or her thought.

Dispersed teams may amplify these communication barriers. Refer to Chapter 2 for suggestions on working with dispersed teams.

Listening for Requirements

There are common phrases an analyst can listen for to find requirements. Table 7.1 lists words and phrases to listen for and the possible requirements components that will be discovered.

Skill: Write Effectively

Business analysis professionals communicate and present information to stakeholders verbally and through the written word. The ability to write clear, concise, unambiguous sentences is highly valued. BAs should be careful with all of their written communication: e-mail, memos, meeting agendas, meeting minutes, and most importantly requirements deliverables. Clearly communicating requirements in text is very difficult. Experienced analysts use diagrams and models as much as possible, but this does not eliminate the need for textual descriptions. Models, diagrams, and tables are all supported by definitions and detailed descriptions which can only be documented with text.

New BAs should focus on using consistent terminology and developing strong definitions. Have others review your writing as often as possible to learn about your areas for improvement.

Case in Point

Growing up, I did not receive a strong foundational education in English language structure. Formal writing skills were not emphasized in my schools, and when they were, I was not particularly interested because I didn't understand their importance. My college had a requirement that every student had to take a writing exam and pass it before graduation. The writing exam really scared me. I realized that this missing piece in my skill set could prevent me from graduating and achieving any of my goals. I was a bright, hard worker, but I didn't have the knowledge required in this fundamental area.

The college held writing workshops for students like me. They gave us very practical advice about organizing and planning an essay before writing. They taught us to use the first sentence of a paragraph as a topic sentence. They taught us to write our introduction and summary paragraphs after the essay was complete. I learned a lot of valuable lessons about writing and was able to pass the essay exam on my first try. I began to think more about writing as a skill and worked to improve this skill when I could. Since then, I have purchased reference books on writing, taken workshops, and paid more attention to the writing styles of authors whose work I read. I have practiced writing and exercise my skill almost every day. And now I have written a book! This shows that new skills can be learned at any time in your career.

This experience is not uncommon. Two of a BA's most important skills—listening and writing—have not been emphasized in formal education. This is unfortunate because these two skills are needed for almost every type of work, not just business analysis. Spend some time thinking about your personal skill level in the area of writing. Do people usually understand your e-mail messages and documents on the first reading or do they come back with a lot of questions? Have you been invited to write for committees, your manager, or other departments because they like what they have seen from you? Are your thoughts well organized? Do you rush through a document just to get it done even though you know you could do better if you took your time? Does it take you too long to create a document because you agonize over sentence structure? *Like all of the skills needed to be a successful BA, you can learn and practice to improve the clarity and quality of your writing.*

Skill: Make Excellent Presentations

One of the communication skills used frequently in business analysis is presenting information. BAs are constantly presenting information, formally and informally, to stakeholders. BAs present:

- ◆ Business cases with cost/benefit analysis to executives to get approval for recommendations
- ◆ Work plans and time estimates to project managers and sponsors
- ◆ Business requirements to business stakeholders to confirm that they clearly understand the business
- ◆ Business requirements to the solution team stakeholders to jump-start design meetings
- ◆ Functional requirements and design ideas to business stakeholders to get feedback on the ideas

These presentations vary in formality and audience size but are always important opportunities for the BA to increase the success of the project.

Formal presentations must be carefully planned and practiced. For some, delivering a formal presentation is one of the most frightening human experiences. Confidence in speaking comes from knowing your topic well and practicing. Give yourself opportunities to practice with community groups, your church, your children's PTA group, etc. Start with short presentations and work up to longer, more involved lectures.

When you are preparing for a formal presentation, be sure that you understand the reason for the presentation: Are you making a recommendation? Are you notifying management of implementation plans? Are you informing business workers about how their jobs will change with the implementation of the solution? Be sure to communicate the main points concisely and clearly and allow time for questions and answers. Be positive, even when you have to deliver bad news.

Some BAs are a bit introverted. This is common because introverted people tend to listen more than talk, be very good thinkers, and focus on details. But if you are introverted and shy, this may hold you back in terms of talking with stakeholders and presenting important information. Work to increase your comfort with initiating conversations. Get comfortable making formal and informal presentations.

BABOK Connection	
Knowledge Area	**Task/Technique**
Requirements Management and Communication	Requirements Presentation

Skill: Facilitate and Build Consensus

Every business analysis professional needs to master the skill of facilitation. To facilitate is "to make easy." This skill is used in almost every interaction, not just in formal requirements workshops. BAs are constantly helping stakeholders to easily express their needs, their problems, and their preferences. *It is common to hear IT people complain that the users don't know what they want. Often, they just don't know how to articulate their wants and needs.* A business analysis professional knows how to ask questions, discuss answers, and provide suggestions: to *facilitate* or make it easy for users to explain what they want. This is a valuable skill in any profession and in personal relationships. The ability to listen carefully, interpret unclear statements, ask clarifying questions, and help to bring people to a common understanding is a skill worth developing. BAs working on agile-style projects facilitate on-the-fly in their team workrooms.

To improve your ability to facilitate, first concentrate on your active listening skills. Second, improve your verbal presentation skills. Speak precisely and concisely, and be direct and honest. One of the difficult aspects of facilitation is enforcing session rules and pointing out inaccuracies. Use a non-judgmental tone. You will know when your skill is improving because co-workers will begin to ask you to help them resolve issues between other people.

A facilitator helps a group build *consensus* or agreement so the participants will all support the decisions or ideas generated by the session. During a facilitated session, many ideas are recorded or discussed. It is the group's responsibility to narrow those ideas down and come to an agreement that meets the objective of the session (see the section on facilitated sessions in Chapter 4).

While narrowing the ideas, the group may want to review the list and eliminate some of them. Once the list is narrowed down to real possible solutions, the facilitator helps the group make a decision.

BABOK Connection	
Knowledge Area	**Task/Technique**
Elicitation	Requirements Workshop
Underlying Competencies	Interaction Skills

TABLE 7.2. Types of Group Decisions

	Consensus	Unanimity	Majority Vote	Compromise
Definition	100% support	100% agreement	51% wins	Halfway point for all
Pros	All members will support	All members will support	Majority will support	All will support partially
Cons	Time consuming	Unrealistic	Creates win/ lose scenario	Creates win/lose scenario
When to use	Support is needed	Clear-cut issue	To narrow a list	Need breakthrough
When not to use	Short time frame	Complex issues	To make a final decision	Support is needed

Consensus is a collective opinion arrived at by a group of individuals working together under conditions that permit open and supportive communication, such that everyone in the group feels he or she has had a fair chance to influence the decision. Participants in consensus agree to decisions even though they may not personally prefer them. A facilitator's goal is to help the group achieve consensus if possible. The facilitator creates the environment to foster these conditions. Be aware of the potential results of a group decision when consensus cannot be reached. Table 7.2 lists types of group decisions.

Skill: Conduct Effective Meetings

Business analysis professionals are often responsible for scheduling and leading meetings. This is a core skill that every BA should develop. Many of the activities and behaviors used to run an effective meeting are simple and straightforward. The trick is to remember to use them consistently.

There are many reasons why a BA may decide to schedule a meeting. Examples include to consult with a group of stakeholders on the business analysis plan, to develop or confirm the scope of the analysis area, or to brainstorm on solution alternatives. It is important to define your objective for a meeting. Without a strong reason for getting people together, you may waste their time. Think about whether your goal could be accomplished in a different way. If you are simply giving stakeholders the status of your progress, would an e-mail message work just as well? If you need help getting started with your requirements document, could you meet with a senior BA to get that help? If you need requirements from one department, is there one key stakeholder who could answer the majority of your questions? Any time that you can accomplish your goal without holding a meeting, you have saved your company valuable time and money.

When you have decided that a meeting is the appropriate forum to accomplish your objective, take a little time to plan the meeting. Select the appropriate attendees, develop an agenda, conduct the meeting efficiently, and follow up after the meeting is over.

Prepare for the Meeting/Select Appropriate Attendees

The leader or organizer of a meeting should prepare himself or herself and the participants for the meeting in order to be effective. Clear objectives are necessary to describe specifically what the meeting is to accomplish. The leader should create an agenda and estimate the time required for each topic or activity in the meeting. Based on the objective of the meeting, select participants who will contribute to the objective. Be sure to only include necessary participants. The more people in a meeting, the greater potential to waste time. Other interested people may be informed about the meeting and sent the meeting minutes.

Determine a time and location for the meeting that best meets the needs of the participants. Since all of your participants are necessary to accomplish your goal, aim for 100% attendance. If a key stakeholder is unable to attend, reschedule the meeting.

Meeting Agenda

The meeting agenda should be prepared in advance and distributed to the participants. This allows everyone to adequately prepare for the objective of the meeting. New topics added during the meeting should be noted and scheduled for future discussions unless the group agrees to adjust the agenda. An agenda should include the following items:

- ◆ Objective of the meeting (including the expected outcome)
- ◆ Date and start and end time
- ◆ Location
- ◆ Meeting participants

- Topics, with estimated time for each topic
- Person assigned to lead or present each topic

When the BA spends a few minutes thinking through the meeting agenda, a meeting is more likely to be well run and effective. Although not all meetings will proceed as planned, having a plan sets everyone's expectations and clearly shows when the discussion is getting off topic (Brassard and Ritter, 1994).

Conducting the Meeting

The BA or meeting leader should be constantly alert and focused on making the meeting successful. Meetings have become known as time wasters to many people because they are not well planned or well run. A BA will demonstrate his or her value to the organization by running effective meetings. As your reputation for being prepared and well organized grows, people will be more willing to attend and participate in your meetings. People will arrive at your meetings on time with an optimistic attitude. Your success will breed even more success.

Tips for Conducting Successful Meetings

- Always start on time; invite latecomers to stay after the meeting to hear what they missed.
- Consider scheduling meetings to start 15 minutes after the hour instead of on the hour. This gives participants time to travel from their last meeting to yours.
- Introduce participants to each other and explain why each was included in the meeting. This lets everyone know the role they are expected to play and encourages every attendee to participate.
- Introduce the meeting objective and review the agenda; ask for suggested changes or clarification before getting started.
- Walk through the agenda, one item at a time, making sure that all attendees feel each item is complete before moving on to the next. Post outstanding items and issues on an issues list for follow-up.
- Be sure to watch the time and keep the group focused.
- End the meeting on time (even if the agenda items were not completed). When necessary, schedule a continuation or follow-up meeting while the group is together.

◆ Assign outstanding items to appropriate team members, along with expected completion dates.

◆ Thank participants for attending and emphasize the value of the work that was accomplished. Make participants feel good about how their time was spent.

Follow-Up/Meeting Minutes

Meeting minutes serve a valuable purpose in business analysis work. They provide a written record of decisions that were made and confirm consistent understanding of the agreements made during a meeting. Requirements can be ambiguous and easily misinterpreted, especially during a discussion with several people. By writing out the meeting results, the BA shows the participants his or her understanding of the discussion. If the BA misunderstood, a correction will be identified immediately. Follow up with meeting minutes and/or any deliverable produced during the meeting. Send these to attendees as soon as possible to verify everyone understands and agrees on the work product.

Follow up on any issues that were not resolved during the meeting. If a participant volunteered to get back to you with answers, make sure that he or she does. Let the entire group know when issues are resolved outside the meeting. Following up

BABOK Connection	
Knowledge Area	**Task/Technique**
Elicitation	Confirm Elicitation Results

on loose ends demonstrates thoroughness and a concern for quality. These attributes contribute to the respect given to the business analysis profession.

Skill: Conduct Requirements Reviews

A requirements review is a formal working session where participants ask questions, make suggestions, and improve the quality of the requirements being reviewed. Requirement deliverables are naturally very complex and difficult to perfect. Rarely would an analyst be able to capture all of the requirements correctly and completely for a project without the help of a review. Reviews are also referred to as *walkthroughs, peer reviews,* and *inspections.*

Every study of the failure rate of IT projects shows that missing or poorly defined requirements are the main cause. Having requirements reviewed before using them to develop a solution is the best way to mitigate this risk. One missed requirement discovered during a review could save the project team hundreds of hours of work later in the project during testing or after implementation. In addition, having your work reviewed helps you learn and produce improved requirements for the next project.

Analysts must encourage others to review their work as frequently as possible and must be open to suggestions. This requires a courageous analyst. You must be open to constructive criticism.

BABOK Connection	
Knowledge Area	**Task/Technique**
Requirements Management and Communication	Requirements Review
Requirements Analysis	Validate Requirements
Solution Assessment and Validation	Structured Walkthrough

How to Conduct a Review

All of the recommendations for conducting effective meetings also apply to reviews. To make the best use of participants' time and have an effective review, there are specific steps that you should follow:

1. Decide on the purpose of the review
2. Schedule time with participants
3. Distribute review materials
4. Have participants review materials prior to the session
5. Conduct the review session
6. Record review notes
7. Update material
8. Conduct a second review if necessary

This review process should be incorporated into every project plan and become a regular practice in your organization. It is supported by all of the major quality initiatives (i.e., CMMI, ISO) as the best method for "testing" the requirements for quality.

Step 1. Decide on the Purpose of the Review

Any deliverable can be reviewed in a formal review. The more requirements deliverables for which you conduct reviews, the better the quality of your project solution.

- ◆ Reviews can be used for project initiation documents to confirm understanding of project scope and gain approval to move forward.

- ◆ Reviews conducted for business requirements are opportunities for the business SMEs to carefully review the results of elicitation sessions and verify that their core business needs are articulated, clearly and correctly.
- ◆ Technical requirements and specifications are great candidates for reviews because they lay out the "blueprint" for IT work. Any questions or inconsistencies found in these blueprints help to improve the foundation upon which the software is built.
- ◆ IT teams often conduct reviews of programs to ensure standards are met and that software will be easy for other developers to understand and maintain.
- ◆ Test plans and test cases are also good candidates for reviews. Reviews can compare the tests against the requirements to make sure that all requirements are covered by the testing plans.
- ◆ Implementation requirements should always be reviewed with both the business stakeholders and solution team. A smooth implementation depends on a well-thought-out plan, including the concerns and issues of all stakeholders impacted.

Step 2. Schedule Time with Participants

Determining who will participate in the review is an important step in making the review successful. The *author* of the material being reviewed must always be present. The author, usually the analyst for requirements reviews, best understands the intent of the material and can answer questions from the reviewers. The author also needs to hear suggestions for improvement so that they can be incorporated into the material.

Some review teams use a *recorder* to take notes during the session. Other teams have the author take notes. This decision should be made by the author. If the author would feel more secure with another person taking notes to be sure that nothing is missed, then another BA is often a good choice for a recorder.

Some review teams also have a participant act as the *facilitator* or *moderator* of the session. This person conducts the session and makes sure that the rules are enforced. The larger the group of reviewers, the more important this role becomes in making sure that each participant is heard and that the group stays focused on the topic of the session.

The mandatory participants are the *reviewers*. They are people who understand the purpose of the requirements and are interested in making the requirements as accurate as possible. A helpful reviewer for requirements is another BA. A BA peer understands the work that was done by the author and can look for holes or inconsistencies even if he or she is not involved with the particular project or knowledgeable about the business area being analyzed.

The most essential reviewers are the SMEs for the requirements. They have provided the requirements to the author and now need to make sure that the author really understood their needs.

Other important participants are solution team stakeholders. These stakeholders will be using the requirements to design and build solutions and will have good questions as they imagine how they will implement the requirements.

Another great resource for requirements reviews is quality assurance. A quality assurance analyst will look at each requirement and think about how it could be tested. If a requirement is too vague or ambiguous to be tested, it needs to be further defined or described.

One caution when inviting participants to a review: *Ideally,* managers should not be included. There are a couple of important reasons for their exclusion. Since a review is intended to be a discussion about a deliverable, a participant's title and position in the organization should not have any importance during the session. The review is *not* a discussion about the author's productivity or proficiency. It is a discussion about a product. It is *not* an employee review. This is why managers should not be invited.

When the author's manager is a participant in the session, the author will be reluctant to admit any mistakes. As participants point out inconsistencies or ambiguous requirements, the author may become defensive, refusing to acknowledge the criticism or accept any suggestions. This destroys the whole point of the review.

When a reviewer's manager is a participant, it is possible that the reviewer may, consciously or unconsciously, "show off" for his or her boss by pointing out a lot of errors and giving a lot of suggestions for improvements. Some of these suggestions may be for aesthetic changes to the document with little substance because the reviewer is trying to impress his or her boss. This participant may also monopolize the session, wanting the manager to know how smart and prepared he or she is. Unless the manager is a critical SME, find a better way to keep him or her in the progress loop. Send the manager a copy of the review findings or a summary of the results of the review.

Steps 3 and 4. Distribute Review Materials and Have Participants Review Materials Prior to the Session

The most critical success factor for a review is having the participants arrive at the session prepared. This means that each participant has read the material and made notes about his or her questions. Participants who are not prepared will not be useful members of the group. Since people read and review at different rates of speed, it is not productive to have everyone read the document at the beginning of the session. It is also more beneficial if the participants have had time to think about what they read. The subconscious mind can find problems while the conscience mind is engaged in other activities. By reviewing the requirements at least a day before the review session, the participants will be best prepared to contribute to a meaningful discussion.

Point out areas that are critical for each participant to review (when everyone does not need to review the entire document). The author should deliver the requirements document to the participants far enough in advance of the session to give them adequate time for a quality review. Participants are responsible for committing to this work and telling the author when they need more time.

Case in Point

Early in my career, I learned the value of review firsthand. Although these were program reviews, the lessons learned directly apply to requirements reviews. When I was a developer in a manufacturing organization, I was transferred to the group that maintained the parts inventory system. The group had designed and built the system a few years earlier, and it was considered one of the most well-run and successful IT projects in the division. One of the reasons for the success was the emphasis placed on program walkthroughs. Every new program and program change was reviewed by at least two other developers for correct processing, conformance to requirements, standards, ease of readability, maintainability, and error-free logic.

This review philosophy was so deeply embedded in the culture of the group that new employees coming into the group were required to write a program based on a fictional specification and practice conducting a program walkthrough. There were strict rules, enforced by my peer group, not management. A developer was not allowed to test a program before a walkthrough. The program was delivered to the reviewers at least 48 hours before the review session, and they made their individual review a high priority. If a participant was not prepared for the review session, the review session was postponed and the group informally "shamed" the participant who had caused the delay. I was pretty nervous before my first review because this seemed like a tough group. I concentrated on writing a great program and reviewed it carefully myself before handing it out to the group. Everyone teased me the day before the review session, saying "Are you ready?" As we sat down in the conference room and everyone laid my program on the table, I glanced around and saw a lot of red marks, yellow highlights, and notes scribbled in the margins. Everyone's copy of my program was covered with writing and notes. I gulped as I realized that they were about to tell me all of the things that I had done wrong.

A senior member of the group explained to me that I would be leading the discussion and that this was an opportunity for quality improvements and learning. I was to read the high-level paragraph names (this was a COBOL program) and ask if anyone had comments before moving on to the next paragraph. I took a deep breath as I read the first paragraph name and looked around the room to see who would speak first. A developer I didn't know well started off by suggesting that I give a more meaningful name to a particular data field. Her tone was calm and objective. There was no judgment in her suggestion. She also noted that she liked the way I had documented the reason for the paragraph. A compliment! I hadn't expected that, but what I came to learn in that first session, and in subsequent review sessions, was that this group of people was truly focused on quality. The people in the group were dedicated to helping each other produce the highest quality work, learn new techniques, and maintain the outstanding quality of the system that we all supported. I was amazed at what a great working environment these reviews fostered. Developers were constantly asking each other for advice on complex coding strategies and complimenting each other on solving tough challenges. The result of this dedication to quality was that the software rarely had problems. We joked that we were like the Maytag repairman in the TV commercial. We were sitting around waiting for a problem and then argued about who would get to solve it! If I had any complaint about working in this group, it would have been that sometimes I was bored because things went so smoothly! My prior experience had been in a group that supported a system with constant problems. Every morning there were abends (abnormal ends) from the programs that ran the night before, and we spent half of our time fixing critical program problems. This new group was like a utopia—mainly due to the consistent use of quality reviews.

Step 5. Conduct the Review Session

When participants come prepared, a review session is easy to run. Set the ground rules first, especially when new participants are involved. Allow the moderator or author to lead the discussion through the document, focusing on one section at a time. Comments, suggestions, and criticisms must all be directed at the document, not the author. Notes are recorded, along with any issues that cannot be resolved by the people in attendance.

At the end of the review, the group will decide whether enough changes have been found to justify a second review. Finally, participants in the review are instructed not to disparage the author.

Rules for a formal requirements review include:

1. All participants must have reviewed the deliverable before the session.
2. Critique the deliverable, not the author.
3. All participants carry equal weight during the session (leave titles outside the room).
4. Make suggestions and ask questions to improve the quality of the deliverable.
5. Stay on topic.

Steps 6 and 7. Record Review Notes and Update Material

Changes, questions, and issues are documented by the author or recorder. In some organizations, these notes are formally distributed to the participants after the session, but in most groups the author simply makes the suggested changes and distributes the updated document to the participants for rereview. If the purpose of the review was to get approval of the requirements, the approvers will decide whether to approve before or after the changes are made.

Step 8. Conduct a Second Review If Necessary

If the group decides that significant changes were found, it may request a second review. The subsequent review is conducted in exactly the same way as the first one, or a second review may involve new participants to get other opinions on the requirements.

Requirements reviews use valuable time of stakeholders and the analyst. To get the most value out of that time, reviews must be supported by functional management and project management. Time for reviews should be built into every project plan. Reviews must be held consistently for requirements deliverables. If they are not performed consistently, analysts may feel that they are all not being treated fairly. In addition, it is critical that reviews are not sacrificed when a project has fallen behind schedule. In the frenzy of a looming deadline, it is easy to start cutting corners and skipping tasks, but skipping quality reviews will almost guarantee project failure. Mistakes in requirements cost anywhere from 10 to 1000 times more to fix when they are found after development (National

Institute of Standards and Technology, 2002). Review, review, review. This is a guaranteed method for improving the quality of your requirements.

Typical Requirements Feedback

Corrections

Rarely will anyone write a requirements document that is 100% correct, especially on the first or second draft. Finding errors and correcting them is the goal of requirements reviews. But even though a BA knows that the document cannot be perfect and wants others to identify problems, it can still be deflating to have someone point out errors. Leave your ego outside the room and be open to all suggestions.

Missing Requirements

Rarely will a requirements package be complete. Missing a requirement is very common and does not indicate a character flaw or any personal weakness. Because it is difficult to discover and document every requirement, BAs must always welcome questions and suggestions about missing requirements.

Unclear Sentences

Ambiguous sentences are easy to write. The more the BA understands the requirements, the less clear the requirements may be. The BA may skip important details or make assumptions about what the reader knows. Written descriptions should lead the reader from a high-level description down to a more detailed level. This requires very careful sentence and paragraph construction. Each sentence explains the concept or requirement in a little more detail and leads the reader to the next sentence, which will give more information. This is referred to as funneling. Imagine the words and the concepts circling in a funnel, only getting through the end when they are small enough pieces to go through one at a time.

Scope Creep

An important observation during a review is that the analyst has gotten outside of the project scope. This *scope creep* is natural when the BA is curious and has asked many questions. The value of a review is to help keep the analyst and the entire project team from increasing the size of the project. Ask reviewers to keep the project objectives in mind when reviewing the detailed requirements (see Chapter 3 for more information on scope creep).

KEEP LEARNING NEW ANALYSIS TECHNIQUES

Technique: Avoid Analysis Paralysis!

Many BAs have experienced *analysis paralysis* at least once in their careers. This phrase describes the situation when you keep thinking about and analyzing a problem, doing more research, documenting it, and then repeat. Think, research, document, think, research, document. It is the BA's equivalent of an infinite loop in programming. You get stuck in this cycle and can't seem to get out. Why does this happen and what can you do to get out of it?

Why does this happen? There are a couple of common reasons for analysis paralysis. First, when you started the analysis, you thought that you knew the answer, but your research shows something else. You keep looking for more information that would support your original theory because it is human nature to prove ourselves right. Also, if you are wrong, you want to make sure that you are really convinced because you will have to convince others about the new direction.

Another common reason for analysis paralysis is that the answer you are coming to will not be one that your boss is going to like. In this case, it is a good idea to make sure that you have really done your research and thought through this carefully because you are going to be the bearer of bad news.

Finally, analysis paralysis may be caused by a lack of confidence in your work. New BAs may not be sure that their conclusions or recommendations are correct, so they continue to prove the same point using different techniques or approaches. This will be solved with experience and is very common with new BAs.

Stop, take a step back, and think about how you are spending your time at least once each day:

- ◆ Have you gotten off track?
- ◆ Have you wandered down a path that is very interesting to you but is really outside the scope of your task?
- ◆ Are you spending time detailing a requirement that will never be automated because its complexity requires the human mind to manage?

◆ Are you looking for something that you may never find (i.e., a software package that meets the user's exact need)?

◆ Are you overanalyzing how the work is currently done when your project will be changing that procedure anyway?

◆ Are you brainstorming about better ways of operating the business when you should be focused on understanding the core processes?

Whatever you are spending time doing, is it the very best use of your time at this point in the project? If not, stop and change direction. A busy analyst doesn't have time to get distracted.

One of the best ways to get help with this perspective on your work is to talk with your project manager. Many project managers conduct weekly status meetings because they want to make sure that their team members are not getting too far afield of the project goals. Project managers are very good at getting things done. Don't hesitate to give your project manager a description of what you have been working on for the past week and see how he or she reacts. BAs are very good at reading body language, so even if your project manager doesn't say it directly, you will be able to tell if he or she winces and fears that you are off track.

How do you stop analysis paralysis? First you must learn to be aware that you are doing it. This is often the most difficult part. BAs must "look up" from the details periodically and make sure that the work they are doing is the most important work to be done at that moment for that project. This is a good reason for leaving a task incomplete at the end of the day and giving it a fresh look the next morning. In the light of a new day, after a good night's rest, the problem may suddenly appear clear or less important. Do you ever hear yourself say "Why did I spend so much time agonizing over that?"

Ideas to get unstuck include:

1. Ask a fellow BA or co-worker (or any friend) to listen to you talk about the problem; just talking about it out loud sometimes helps you to see why you are stuck.
2. Give yourself a time limit: "I am going to work on this for one more hour, and then, wherever it is at that point, it will be done."
3. Sit down with the SME and review the work that you have done so far; explain that it is a draft and ask for help to find the missing pieces.
4. Sleep on it.

5. If you have time, put it aside for a few days; this is the best way to get perspective.
6. Try a different requirement technique to represent the situation (e.g., if you are using a swim lane diagram, try an entity relationship diagram).
7. Know the 80-20 rule.

An important fact about business analysis work: *The requirements will never be 100% complete and will never be perfect.* If you are a perfectionist, be prepared to feel a little frustrated. Hugh Prather, an inspirational speaker and writer, once said: "Perfection is a slow death."

When you are stuck in the details of a problem (analysis paralysis), you lose perspective. Change your perspective so that you can see it differently to get unstuck.

Technique: Root Cause Analysis

Root cause analysis is a technique used to assess the symptoms of a problem and find the ultimate cause. Often, problems are not clearly studied and inappropriate solutions are recommended. An analyst should not make a solution recommendation until he or she understands the underlying cause of the problem. Finding the *root cause* is the first step in solving a problem. The fishbone diagram (see Figure 7.1) is one visual technique for structuring root cause analysis. Major categories of possible causes are connected to the "backbone" of the fishbone diagram. Brainstorm in each category and document the causes in each category. Another technique for root cause analysis is the *five whys*.

The Five Whys

The *why* question is one of the most valuable tools in the BA's tool kit. It is used to help dig down to the root cause or underlying reason for a problem or opportunity. The *why* question can be used at any point in analysis work and is often used to help a business or IT stakeholder better explain their requirement. The five whys technique recommends that the analyst ask *why* in response to reasons five times to get to the root reason. Sometimes the root cause is found after only a couple of *whys* (GOAL/QPC, 2000).

Case in Point

"I want a red Ferrari!" Why? "Well, it looks good." But why? "Because I would look good in it!" But why? "My friends would be very impressed if they saw me driving it." Why?

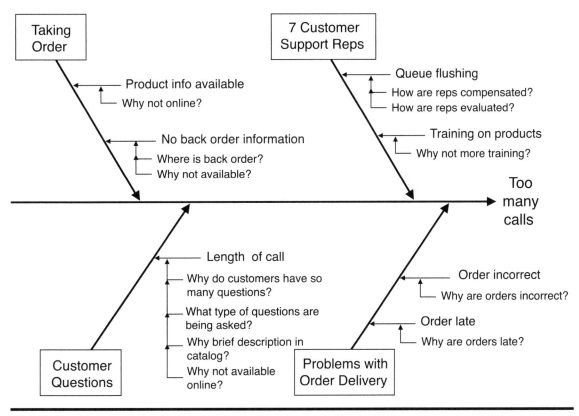

FIGURE 7.1. Sample Fishbone Diagram

"Because it is a very expensive car so, they would know that I must have sold a large number of books!" Why is that important? "If I sold a large number of books, then my book must have contained some really important information, so I must be very smart!" So—you want a Ferrari so that your friends will know that you are very smart? "When you put it that way, I don't want the Ferrari so much anymore."

Although the *why* question is very powerful and useful, you must use it carefully. It can be very annoying to keep asking the same question over and over again. When you ask the *why* question the first time, you need to listen carefully to the answer. Does this answer seem to be the true reason? In many cases, the question needs to be asked only once to get to the correct answer. If you feel there is more information, you need to elicit using different words (for example, "For what reason do you . . .?") or pose a scenario question ("What would happen if . . . ?"). Varying the type and format of questions will be less tedious for stakeholders. Explain the technique to the stakeholders to help them understand your line of questioning.

Uses for the five whys include:

◆ Get to the true reason/objective for a project
◆ Get to the root cause of a problem
◆ Get to the true reason for a requirement
◆ Find the true essential business process (see Chapter 4)

The following two scenarios are projects where the monetary justification may not be initially obvious. The five whys will be used to get to the root cause of the *project*.

Scenario A

Project Statement of Purpose

The purpose of this project is to upgrade our XYZ payroll software from version 1.0.3 to version 1.1.0. This upgrade is being undertaken because the vendor of the XYZ software will discontinue support of version 1.0.3 at the end of the calendar year. All customized screens and reports that are currently available must be available in the new version. New functionality must be analyzed and considered. If any new functionality will be implemented, user procedures must be updated and users must be trained. (See Table 7.3 for the why questions and answers.)

Ah ha! It only took four whys to "find the money" in this case. Although undertaking this project is going to cost the organization some money, the expectation is that if the project is not funded, the organization will spend more money on developers. Thus the underlying justification for the project is to save costs.

Notice that the project is not being done to provide more functionality or better usability. Understanding and remembering that this project is focused on saving money are critical. It may be tempting to add functionality or improve usability "while we are making this change anyway," but those tasks do not support the fundamental objective of the project. Always remember the reason for project initiation.

Teams sometimes try to add features and functionality that were not requested. The phrase *gold plating* was used by McConnell (1996) to describe this behavior. This is not

TABLE 7.3. Five Whys for Scenario A

	Question	**Answer**
Why #1	Why do you think the organization is funding this project?	The software vendor is discontinuing support of the current version of the software.
Why #2	Why does it matter if the vendor discontinues support?	Because if the vendor does not support the software, it will have to be supported internally or another software package must be purchased and implemented.
Why #3	Why not maintain it internally?	No internal developers (current employees) are familiar with the underlying architecture or the development environment.
Why #4	Why not hire experienced developers or train internal developers in this technology?	Because developers with this experience are rare and very expensive. Training developers would also be expensive and time consuming.

a positive activity for an organization. Deliver on business needs as quickly and inexpensively as possible.

Scenario B

Project Statement of Purpose

Convert the customer database from the ABC DBMS to the XYZ DBMS. This conversion will not have any impact on the user interface to the application software. The change should be transparent to the software users. (See Table 7.4 for the why questions and answers.)

After asking why five times, the BA uncovers the true reason for the project: increase sales. "Buy more products" translates to receive more revenues, which translates to more profit! If you go back to the statement of purpose, you won't see anything about increasing sales, but this is the underlying

BABOK Connection	
Knowledge Area	**Task/Technique**
Enterprise Analysis	Problem Analysis

TABLE 7.4. Five Whys for Scenario B

	Question	Answer
Why #1	Why do you think the organization is funding this project?	The XYZ DBMS is a more current technology.
Why #2	Why do we want to be using a more current technology?	Because we want our systems to be state-of-the-art.
Why #3	Why do we want our systems to be state-of-the-art?	Because we don't want customers or outside competitors to think that we are using old technology.
Why #4	Why don't we want customers or outside competitors to think that we are using old technology?	Because we want to be perceived as being on the leading edge of technology.
Why #5	Why do we want to be perceived as being on the leading edge of technology?	Because if we are perceived as having leading-edge technology, our customers will buy more products from us.

business driver. You may consider revising the statement of purpose when you discover the true "why."

Skill: Intelligent Disobedience

Intelligent disobedience refers to the skill of being able to disagree with an organizational decision without jeopardizing one's career or relationships. The decision may be a mistaken solution strategy or a missed opportunity for the organization. It is important for business analysis professionals to get comfortable with intelligent disobedience because occasionally a BA will see that a proposed solution is not appropriate for the business need. If a solution has been proposed before the root cause of the problem was identified, the solution may be less than optimal. If the BA determines that the proposed solution is not the best, he or she utilizes the skill of intelligent disobedience to bring this problem to the attention of management.

Intelligent disobedience is not difficult. It simply requires three components: (1) get your facts together, (2) present the facts without emotion, and (3) be willing to accept the decision and move forward. One additional component that is very useful is having an alternate plan. These components allow the business analysis professional to communicate the mistaken decision objectively and offer the highest likelihood that the mistake will be corrected.

Some would say that the business analysis professional has an obligation to bring these types of problems to the attention of management. As an employee of or consultant for an organization, a BA is committed to facilitating the best solutions possible for the business. When a BA knows that a proposed solution is not the best, he or she must alert the organization to the mistake. The earlier the problem is identified and addressed, the less costly the mistake to the organization.

Get your facts together, either formally or informally. Use your business case skills to help show management why the proposed solution will not provide a good return on investment or will cost more money than it saves. Be prepared to answer detailed questions about why your argument is correct. Be aware of who originally proposed the solution against which you are arguing. If you can, go to that person directly, one on one, to first discuss the facts that you have discovered. If you can get the person to change his or her mind, the two of you will have an easier time convincing management. Be aware of how much time and money have already been spent on this solution. The more an organization has invested, the more difficult it may be to get the group to change direction. The money already spent is considered "sunk cost" according to accounting principles and should not be factored into any decision going forward, but it is human nature to want to complete the original project and not *waste* the time and money already spent.

The next person with whom the BA should talk is the project manager. The project manager is a great sounding board for your facts and business case. If you can convince the project manager of your discovery, the two of you can work together to communicate the issue to the project sponsor and senior-level stakeholders. As mentioned earlier, talk with the originator of the idea if possible. Also identify any strong advocates for the solution and work to gain their support for your case. Be persistent in convincing people on your team to recognize the situation. This is bottom-up work in an organization. Use the official (and unofficial) chain of command to communicate your concerns.

Present the facts without emotion because an emotional case will probably not be accepted. Be careful with your choice of words. Don't say "I don't *feel* that this is a good idea." Don't give the impression that you dislike the project or don't want to tackle it. Such impressions will lead your manager to think that you are arguing against the work because you are not willing to do it. Instead, provide very objective, factual statements to show that you have carefully considered the issues and concluded that the solution is not the best. Be prepared to face emotion from the people with whom you are communicating. Members of management may be vested in the idea or may be reluctant to reverse the decision. They may not want to address the issue with their management. Making major changes to project priorities and direction can shake up an organization, and most managers will be reluctant to do this unless they really see a compelling reason.

Should you ever go over a manager's head to a higher level manager? This would only be recommended in rare cases where the mistaken design will cause great harm to the organization or there is an immediate threat to customers or employees. If you feel strongly about changing the direction of a project, use the same approach with higher level managers. Assemble your facts, present them objectively, and accept the decision. Few will appreciate your behavior, so be sure to be prepared for negative consequences.

Finally, be willing to accept the final decision, no matter what it is. Your responsibility is to alert the organization to a possible waste of resources. If management decides to go ahead anyway, you must be willing to get on board and work on the project enthusiastically. This is extremely important for your long-term credibility. When your organization views you as someone who objectively provides honest opinions and also acts as a team player to get things done, you will be highly valued. Those in management will be more open to your opinions in the future because they will feel confident that you will accept the final decision with grace and commitment. Bob McGannon of Mindavation (www.mindavation.com) has spoken eloquently on the topic of intelligent disobedience.

CONTINUALLY IMPROVE YOUR SKILLS

Learning will never end for a BA. People are drawn to this career because they love learning new things. This love of learning makes BAs very effective because when gathering requirements, you are learning. When you are asking questions, you are learning. You are learning how the business makes decisions, how the business gets work done, why the business does its work, and how the customers are satisfied by the business. This education continues on every project. There is always more to know even if you have worked in the same industry or in the same business area for your entire career. You will never know everything and you may never gather the perfect requirement. Businesses change constantly, and BAs must keep up with the current standards, policies, product offerings, and market trends.

Staying up to date on trends requires the business analysis professional not only to learn about new techniques and concepts but also to be able to apply those concepts to the existing organization. Understand how pieces fit into the whole. Step outside the boundaries of your current organization's thinking and see how a new concept might work in your business.

Skill: Make Recommendations for Solutions

BAs are skilled in understanding problems and developing solutions. They also see approaches for taking advantage of business opportunities. They should make recommendations for solutions because they truly understand the business problem and can imagine many possible solutions. BAs also have the skills necessary to evaluate possible solutions, looking at feasibility and cost vs. benefits to determine the best solution not just for the business area but for the entire organization.

The following three components are essential for making excellent recommendations:

1. Understand the problem
2. Imagine possible solutions
3. Evaluate solutions to select the best

New or junior-level BAs need to be careful in making recommendations when they don't truly understand business requirements and technical options. This is a value that an experienced BA can provide to a business. New BAs should learn to "float" ideas, asking questions like: "What if we created a screen to allow you to capture that information?"

On many projects, the solution has already been selected before the BA has even been assigned. Maybe the person who initiated the project has already decided on the solution and is just bringing on the BA to help facilitate the transition. In these situa-

BABOK Connection	
Knowledge Area	**Task/Technique**
Solution Assessment and Validation	Assess Proposed Solution

tions, an experienced BA will still perform root cause analysis to understand the problem, brainstorm on possible solutions, evaluate each solution, and make a recommendation. As the BA, you may make a recommendation that is not the one for which the project was initiated. Use intelligent disobedience to step forward and let the project sponsor and project manager know that there is a better option. In these situations, the BA really has to make sure he or she has carefully thought through the solutions and can adequately explain why a change to the project is in order.

Understand the Problem

Understanding the business problem is the main job of every BA. If a business just wanted the quickest, easiest solution, it would not have invested in a BA. A technology person can always come up with a quick idea for how software and/or hardware can improve the business without investigating the cause of the problem. An experienced analyst will thoroughly analyze the problem and consider possible solutions before jumping to a software fix.

Imagine Possible Solutions

The second step is to brainstorm about possible solutions. Experienced BAs will be imagining possible solutions constantly throughout the requirements elicitation process.

One of the challenges of being a BA is learning not to recommend a solution too early in a project, except during a feasibility study. Although an obvious solution may immediately present itself, many times the most obvious solution is not the best. Also, the most obvious solution may have already been tried. If the answer was that easy, a BA would not really be needed! As you begin to learn more about the business, its people, its processes, and its deliverables, you will see more and more possible solutions. As you learn more, some of your earliest ideas may prove to be inadequate, or you will find yourself refining your ideas, working to find the perfect solution. This is a natural activity for most BAs. BAs refuse to believe that there is a problem that can't be solved.

Experienced BAs have learned to keep their initial ideas to themselves and focus on listening and learning. Work on your ideas alone; don't present an idea until you feel confident that it will work. This ability to keep quiet and wait makes a BA more valued in the organization. How annoying

BABOK Connection	
Knowledge Area	**Task/Technique**
Enterprise Analysis	Determine the Recommended Solution Approach

is it when someone walks into your area, listens to your problem for five minutes, and immediately gives you the answer? The message that comes across is that your problem must be very simple, and you were not smart enough to solve it as quickly as someone else did. BAs who solve problems before understanding them will not be welcomed back into business areas. This quick-fix mentality is not appreciated.

Case in Point

Suppose a medical insurance company's claims processing area is having trouble handling the volume of claims. Customers and providers are complaining because it takes too long for a claim to be approved and paid. Even without knowing much detail about this organization or this problem, we can imagine several possible solutions:

◆ Add more people to process claims. It may be that the processes are very efficient and streamlined and just need to have more people available to perform them.

◆ Improve the training of the existing claims specialists so that they can do their job faster.

◆ Decrease the number of claims or the amount of work required for each claim. This is a less obvious solution but should be considered. Could individual charges be combined into a single claim? Would that save time? Could policy guidelines be changed, allowing small claims to skip the approval process?

◆ Buy or merge with another insurance company that has a stronger claims processing system.

◆ Outsource claims processing to an organization that specializes in this work or to a location/workforce that is cheaper.

◆ Automate or more fully automate the process of receiving claims. Are they still coming in on paper? Could they be electronically transmitted? Could they be scanned?

◆ Automate or more fully automate the approval process. Create a business rules engine or decision support system that could make approvals based on a set of guidelines.

◆ Automate or more fully automate the payment system. Send funds electronically or combine small payments into a few large ones.

◆ Purchase a claims processing software package that manages most or all of the entire process.

An experienced BA will not let himself or herself get tied to any particular solution too early in requirements elicitation and analysis. He or she recognizes that any solution idea may be eliminated at any time as more information becomes available. In the above example, the BA may learn that the people approving claims are highly trained medical professionals who use their extensive knowledge and experience to determine if the treatments recommended are appropriate and should be paid. This highly specialized task cannot be automated, even by the most sophisticated software. This quickly eliminates one of the possible solutions.

Brainstorming about possible solutions is an important task that is often overlooked. Many times, the best solution turns out to be a combination of solutions. Maybe 50% of the claim approvals are very straightforward and could be automated, while the rest require highly specialized evaluation. Could the approvers be presented with a clearer, concise description of the claim components to help them more quickly make their decisions?

Maybe after the problem is clearly understood, there will be only one solution that will adequately solve it or other solutions will present themselves. Continue to be open to any solution as long as it is still feasible.

Evaluate Solutions to Select the Best

After extensive information gathering, observation, and analysis, there may be more than one possible solution. How do you decide which one to recommend? This is when a different flavor of analysis is required. Cost/benefit analysis, feasibility analysis, and business case development are

BABOK Connection	
Knowledge Area	**Task/Technique**
Enterprise Analysis	Develop the Business Case
	Feasibility Analysis

all names given to the activity performed by the BA to evaluate possible solutions. These techniques are often performed at the enterprise level but can be used on every project at any level of an organization (see Chapter 3).

Consider narrowing the solution scope. Sometimes you will imagine a very elegant solution to a business problem but can't convince anyone to give you the time or money to build it. Everyone wants a Mercedes when they can only afford a Volkswagen. The challenge is to solve a problem in a cost-efficient way. This requires creativity, brainstorming, and thinking outside the box with the business stakeholders and the solution team. BAs make recommendations, but the stakeholders, primarily the sponsor, make the final decision. Present each option along with its strengths and limitations to give the sponsor the information needed to make a good decision.

Skill: Be Able to Accept Constructive Criticism

Being able to accept constructive criticism (or any type of criticism) is one of the most difficult things for human beings to do. Hearing that you have made a mistake or missed an important requirement is never enjoyable. But being able to accept criticism and learn from it is a skill that will allow you to grow as a person and as a BA. It shows real self-confidence. People often make mistakes out of habit, and until someone points them out, they may never be able to see their mistakes. BAs should not only learn to accept criticism well, but should welcome it and solicit it. Ask people to tell you what you can do better! You may not always like what you hear, but you will definitely get some ideas for how you can improve your effectiveness. Some people may tell you something that is not really helpful or you may disagree with some of the descriptions of your weaknesses. If you ask a lot of people for advice, you will start to see consistent patterns and have great information for increasing your effectiveness.

If two people set out to write a description of the same process in English, what is the probability that they will write the same description? Zero! The flexibility and extent of the English language (and probably any modern language) are such that there are an infinite number of ways that a particular process may be described. This is why writing excellent requirements is so difficult. As a BA, no matter how clear your writing style, someone else will read your description and it will not be exactly the way they would have said it. Be able to accept constructive criticism and constantly work to improve your skills. If you are a person who does not like be questioned or challenged, you are probably not in the right career. Everything that you document with the intention of communicating to another human being will be scrutinized, dissected, interrogated, and criticized. It takes a strong, self-confident individual to listen to these comments without taking them personally.

As a successful BA, you not only accept these comments graciously, but can welcome them. Only by refinement will requirements be understood and accepted. There is nothing more valuable (and frustrating) than receiving feedback on your work. A successful BA will hear himself or herself react to criticism with an instantaneous "Thank you—that is a great help."

This skill has a corollary: give criticism graciously to fellow BAs when reviewing their documents. It is the golden rule: Treat others as you would like them to treat you. As you demonstrate the professional handling of corrections and improvements to the work of others, they will learn from you and the organization will improve overall.

Case in Point

I have not yet changed my reactions to criticism as fundamentally as I would like. When someone criticizes my work or makes a suggestion for a change, my first, gut reaction is still defensive. I think "How dare you criticize what I have done!" I have to pause, take a deep breath, and then force myself to say "thank you" with a big, sincere smile. Getting to the attitude of gratitude for criticism is a significant goal in itself.

One of the results of not being able to accept constructive criticism and amendments to your requirements deliverables is that you may miss important requirements, leading to a solution that does not meet the business need. You will have failed in your core BA task.

Skill: Recognize and Act on Your Weaknesses

As professionals who are always interested in improving skills, BAs should be constantly looking for suggestions for improvements. The challenge is that as anxious as BAs are to get these suggestions, they also hate to hear them. The suggestions that are the hardest to hear are the ones that you already know about but try to ignore. Everyone has weaknesses. Weaknesses are areas or behaviors that prevent you from being as effective in your professional (and personal) life as you would like to be. Most people are aware of these weaknesses but spend much of their lives trying to forget about them or cover them up. When someone points out a known weakness, it is like touching a tender spot. It is a reminder that no one is perfect.

To master business analysis, constantly try to improve your weak areas. Get additional training, participate in self-improvement programs, and practice the correct behavior or skill. Correcting and eliminating a weakness is a very difficult and time-consuming project, but it increases your value personally and professionally. Work on improving your weaknesses when you have time, and practice your new skills at every opportunity.

Weaknesses that impact one's ability to be a master BA include being critical or judgmental of others, jumping to conclusions, finishing other people's sentences, not listening carefully, talking too much, writing in an unclear style, being inflexible, and not being open to other people's ideas.

The best way to improve your skills as a BA is to look critically at yourself, when you are alone and not vulnerable to others. Ask friends, family, and trusted co-workers for honest feedback on your skills. It is always interesting to find out what others think about your strengths and weaknesses.

Once you have identified the areas that you want to improve, create a plan for yourself. It may be very simple or very formal. Just make a commitment to yourself to start working toward improvement.

Technique: Lessons Learned

Does your organization look at project results and "learn" from them? This is often referred to as *lessons learned.* Project managers are aware of the importance of learning from prior mistakes or missteps. BAs should also get in the habit of looking back at the end of a project to identify areas that could be improved. The post-implementation user assessment provides a formal pro-

BABOK Connection	
Knowledge Area	**Task/Technique**
Business Analysis Planning and Monitoring	Lessons Learned Process
	Plan, Monitor, and Report on Business Analysis Performance

cess within which to learn these lessons. As organizations form BA competency centers, lessons learned will be formalized and used to improve the overall business analysis process for an organization.

BUSINESS ANALYSIS PLANNING

Once you understand why a project has been initiated and is being funded, you must plan your part of the work. Planning is an activity which is very important to a BA. Planning may be done at any time: before a project has been officially initiated and scoped, after project initiation, or during a project to re-estimate for changes. Planning the analysis work involves identifying the people with whom you will be working and understanding their communication needs. It requires the BA to decide which requirements analysis techniques will be used and which requirements deliverables to create. It also involves estimating analysis time.

Technique: Map the Project

A useful analysis technique to help start the planning process is shown in Table 7.5. Mapping a project helps the analyst determine what type of analysis work will be needed in two dimensions: *what* vs. *how* and current vs. future. *Most projects require business analysis work in more than one quadrant. Understanding the type of analysis needed gives the team clear direction and helps to estimate the analysis time required.*

One of the reasons for thoroughly analyzing the project scope is to have the facts necessary to build a realistic plan. Project planning and business analysis planning are very

TABLE 7.5. Mapping the Project

	Current (As Is)	Future (To Be)
Business analysis (the "what")	Description of the current business area independent of how the work is done	New service or product for the organization
Solution/functional analysis (the "how")	The current systems/procedures used to accomplish the business processes	The design plans for a new or updated system or procedure to better accomplish the business processes

complex activities even when project objectives are well understood. The better the understanding of project expectations, the faster you will be able to develop an accurate plan.

The first dimension (the rows of the mapping quadrant) represents the *what* and the *how* of the business area. The *what* refers to business requirements.

◆　What are the core processes?
◆　What are the core data elements?
◆　What are the business rules?
◆　What are the goals of the business?

Generally, the *what* of the business does not change significantly over time. If an organization is a financial institution, the core business work of providing loans, servicing accounts, and managing funds will continue to be important goals of the business.

The *how* refers to the software, systems, procedures, and personnel that accomplish the business goals. The *how* of business changes frequently. Organizations are constantly trying to improve the efficiency with which they accomplish their goals. This is the area where most change takes place during projects.

Business analysis involves identification of both the *what* and the *how*, and it is important to differentiate between these two aspects of a business area. This differentiation helps to break down and plan the analysis work that will be needed. For example, in a business process re-engineering project, the team may be assigned to improve the *how* (procedures, systems, or personnel) of an existing business process without changing the *what*.

TABLE 7.6. Sample Project Map: Add a New Shipping Method

	Current (As Is)	Future (To Be)
Business analysis (the "what")	2. Perform root cause analysis ▲ and understand true business need	
Solution/functional analysis (the "how")	1. Analyze current system	3. Design change to system to meet need Plan implementation and conversion

What analysis is very different than *how* analysis. *What* analysis involves asking questions to *discover* the business needs. *How* analysis involves *imagining* possible approaches for accomplishing the business needs and then "testing" them out for feasibility and flexibility.

The second dimension (columns in the mapping quadrant) represents the current state and future states of the business. Determine if it is important to analyze/document the current business area before making recommendations for changes (see Chapter 4 for a discussion of the advantages of learning the current system). Some projects require a formal analysis and deliverable on the current state, while others do not.

When a project involves work in more than one quadrant, an arrow is drawn to show the planned sequence of the analysis work. Typically, the current analysis is done before the future. See Table 7.6 for an example of mapping.

Examples of Mapped Projects

Conversion of old software system to purchased package (COTS). If the business area is well understood and a business model exists, there is no need to perform *what* analysis, so the project is mapped to two quadrants: (1) As is analysis of existing technology is in the lower left quadrant (*how*). (2) To be analysis of the purchased package is in the lower right quadrant (*how*). Conversion requirements are also needed to implement the change.

Business process improvement project. These projects typically map to three quadrants: (1) Analyzing the current as is involves learning about the core business needs, which is the upper left quadrant (*what*). (2) To improve a process, you must understand *how* it is currently done, which puts you in the lower left quadrant. (3) The process redesign (*how*) is in the lower right quadrant.

BABOK Connection	
Knowledge Area	**Task/Technique**
Business Analysis Planning and Monitoring	Plan Business Analysis Activities

New business activity (e.g., new product for sale, new service). This project maps to two quadrants: (1) Understanding/analyzing the new business requirements is in the top right quadrant. (2) Creating a system to support this new business activity is in the bottom right quadrant. Analyzing a new business activity can be particularly challenging because the organization may not have any SMEs.

Skill: Plan Your Work

As in any profession where work is project oriented, planning your work is the best way to ensure a successful result. Even a new project that appears to be the smallest, simplest assignment that you have ever had requires planning. It is not necessary to write a formal planning document for a simple project. It may be that all the planning that is necessary is for you to sit for five minutes and think about what you are going to do, and then do it. This is still planning.

The goal is to realistically plan the amount of time needed to elicit, analyze, document, and communicate requirements. Traditionally, many project plans had one task for requirements gathering. Conventional thinking was that one or two meetings were needed to simply ask the users what they wanted and this task was complete. Actually, this one task represents *many* subtasks, and the BA should identify those individual subtasks for the project manager. Experienced business analysis professionals know what it takes to complete requirements. Be prepared to tell the project manager how much time is needed.

The first step in business analysis planning is to learn about the project. Review all existing project documentation to get an initial understanding of the work. Assess the current status of the project based on your research and by asking a few key questions of the project manager and sponsor:

◆ Is there a project charter or vision statement?
◆ Is there a project plan?

◆ Has the project been scoped?
◆ Have all stakeholders been identified?
◆ Are the project objectives clearly defined?

Once you know the current status of the project, you can plan your business analysis work. Any of the project initiation analysis that has not been completed goes to the top of your task list. Without clearly defining objectives and scope, successful analysis will be difficult. Assessing the project is the first step in the Business Analysis Planning Framework™ (B2T Training, 2008). Figure 7.2 provides an overview of the framework.

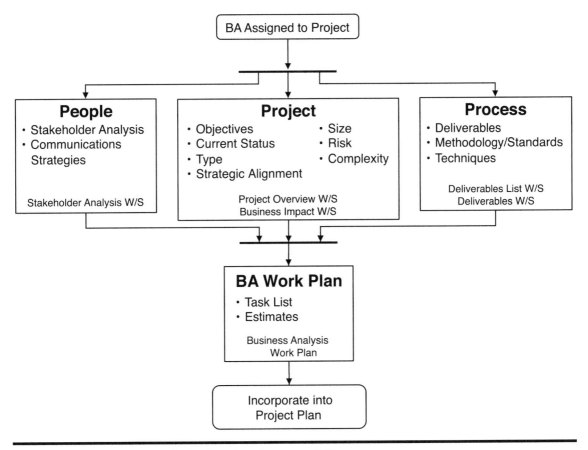

FIGURE 7.2. Business Analysis Planning Framework™

Technique: Assess Business Impact

Business impact is a measure of the criticality of a project to the business stakeholders and their work. Business impact describes the ramifications or effect of a project on the business environment. Excellent business analysis professionals are always aware of the potential business impact of a project. Being aware of a project's importance to the organization allows the BA to stay focused on the most important requirements and stakeholder issues. When a business case has been developed for a project, it probably includes a description of business impact. Business impact is an important characteristic of a project that must be understood as early as possible. The BA should determine the business impact of a project as he or she is planning for the work. Business impact is determined by looking at a large number of factors about a project. Although all of the factors may not be completely known at the beginning of a project, the BA should consider all that is known and make an assessment of business impact. Business impact is more than just risk. Risk should be considered when determining impact, but it is just one of many factors.

Many organizations use size to help determine the importance of a project and the structure that should be required for it. Small, medium, and large are common project categories. This is not the best way to categorize projects. There are some very small projects that have a huge business impact.

Case in Point

I once worked on a cash management system for a financial services company. We had one primary user of the system and only a few major business processes were involved. The solution was relatively simple. Everything pointed to categorization as a small or low-impact project. But the amount of money that was moved daily in this business area was huge. Decisions were made based on the output of the software, and a bad decision often meant thousands of dollars lost. I would categorize this project as having high business impact. Making a mistake here had huge consequences.

Projects that would traditionally be called *large* will also be assessed as having high business impact. If large implies a lot of people or a lot of time or complexity, the project will have a lot of costs. *High cost* typically translates to *high business impact*.

Factors That Determine Business Impact

Number of users: The larger the number of software users who will be impacted by a project, the higher the business impact. Software changes impact work flow and often disrupt productivity during the learning period, even when the changes mean more efficiency or more correct processing. Changes to software require users to learn new ways of getting work done. The more users who will be impacted by a project, the more user training and support that will be required. *Caveat*: One key user may indicate that a project has a high business impact.

Number of stakeholders (SMEs and working team members): The larger the number of stakeholders, the higher the business impact. Both the project manager and BA are responsible for communications with all team members. The project manager is responsible for overall communication of the project goals, plans, budget, assignments, and regular status reports. The BA's communication is focused on eliciting and communicating the requirements, along with implementation plans for the business. These communications become more complex as the number of people involved increases. When a BA has many business stakeholders from different departments, bringing the group to consensus around shared requirements takes more time and skill. This increases project risk and increases business impact. When a key stakeholder is a high-level individual in the organization, business impact is also high.

Level of stakeholders: This factor must be evaluated in combination with the others. Obviously, a lot of stakeholders who are at a high level in the organization (e.g., the board of directors) makes a project high business impact. There are a couple of reasons for this. When higher level stakeholders are involved, their time is more expensive, and as such, the true cost of the project is high. (True cost may not be formally measured/captured because few organizations ask their executives to record the number of hours spent on each project, but the BA should always be aware that time dedicated to a project by a business person always costs the organization money.)

Second, when a high-level stakeholder is involved or interested in a project, the project objectives probably are high visibility, high risk, and/or high potential financial benefit. These all make the project higher impact.

Case in Point

The CFO of a large retail company requested a very specific financial report and wanted it within the week. The results of the report were to be used in the board of directors meeting to make strategic decisions about future plans. This project immediately was recognized as having a high business impact because of the level of the stakeholders. In this case, none of the other factors driving business impact could make this a medium- or low-impact project.

Geographic location of stakeholders: The larger the number of geographic locations of the stakeholders, the greater the business impact. Also, the greater the time zone differences of the stakeholders, the greater the business impact. This is because of the obvious communication challenges that come with physical distance. Even a short distance between locations can increase business impact (e.g., stakeholders are in the same city, but travel between offices takes at least an hour because of traffic).

Business complexity: Increased complexity means higher business impact. More complex businesses require more time for BAs to understand and document the requirements, more coding time for the developers, and more testing time. Complex business areas typically have many business rules (i.e., insurance, government regulatory agencies) and/or involve processes that require high levels of knowledge and experience on the part of their stakeholders (e.g., financial securities trading, legal systems, chemical/pharmaceuticals). The requirements must be clearly and carefully documented so that the complexity will be handled appropriately.

Solution complexity: Increased complexity means higher business impact. More complex software, networks, and even manual procedures that require highly skilled workers increase the amount of analysis time that will be needed to design and develop functional requirements. Complex solutions must be carefully planned and studied for feasibility. The requirements must be clearly communicated to the development team and the quality assurance team so that the accuracy of the solution can be verified and validated.

Business risk: As business risk increases, so does business impact. Business risk is defined as the potential for significant business success or failure as a result of a project. For example, when a project involves the management of a large amount of money (e.g., cash management, large investments), the risk is very high. If the project solution/software contains an error, a large amount of money could be lost in a short period of time. Business risk is also measured in missed opportunities. If an organization wants to launch a new product but is delayed because the order processing system is not ready, customers may go to a competitor and be lost. The larger the potential for loss, the higher the risk and the larger the business impact. Managing risk is also the responsibility of the project manager. Once risks are identified, the BA and project manager should work together to manage them (see the discussion on project initiation earlier in this chapter).

Quality requirements/expectations: The higher or more rigorous the quality requirements, the higher the business impact. Quality or non-functional requirements include performance, reliability, security, etc. (see Chapter 6). Non-functional requirements increase business impact because they impose more constraints on the solution. If a particular user input screen must respond within 0.5 seconds, the technology team must create an architecture that can support that level of performance. This may mean a particular database management strategy (to speed data access), a particular networking structure, specific types of hardware, etc. The importance of these types of requirements to the solution design also points out that they should be elicited early in the project. Sometimes BAs let these non-functional requirements wait until all of the business requirements are complete, but that may be a mistake. Ask initial questions about quality requirements early—during project initiation—to help you decide if there are going to be some tough technological constraints. This is a good example of the importance of business analysis planning and assessing business impact. You may not know all of the details up front, but you get enough information so that you know which areas are going to require the most work and focus.

Firm due date: When there is an absolute firm due date for a project, business impact is probably greater. The due date may be driven by an outside (external agent) organization (e.g., government mandate). Make sure that you understand why the due date was set and what the ramifications of a delay would be. Often, IT people don't meet deadlines because they really don't understand the negative ramifications on the business. It is the responsibility of the project manager and BA to understand and articulate this time "requirement" to the team members to keep them focused on the goal. Projects with unmovable due dates must use "timeboxing" techniques (see the discussion earlier in this chapter) to get work done. Project managers and BAs may use their planning estimates to negotiate a smaller project scope.

Length of project: Long projects increase business impact. Long projects are less successful than short ones. Business requirements change frequently, so a long project may implement a requirement that is no longer valid. Project teams become less focused over a longer period of time—that's just human nature. Business stakeholders are impatient for solutions that are needed today but will not be delivered for a year or more. All of these problems are driving the move to more agile software development approaches with shorter, smaller deliverables (see Chapter 5). On the other hand, if a project with a large scope is scheduled for a short period of time, risk and potential negative impact increase.

Project budget relative to company size: The size of the project budget (number of employees, outside consultants, equipment, software, etc.) as a percentage of corporate revenue indicates the importance of a project to an organization. If the project budget is $1 million in a company with annual revenue of $10 million, the project is very important to the organization. The sponsor expects that the investment in the project will reap significant cost savings or revenue increases. The more money to be saved or made from the project results, the higher the business impact of the project.

Technique: Conduct Stakeholder Analysis

Stakeholder analysis is performed during planning because BAs need to think about all of the individual people involved in a project and analyze their needs. This is the second piece of the Business Analysis Planning Framework. Since a large part of business analysis work involves communicating with people, it only makes sense to plan these communications.

Ideally, the BA and the project manager will sit down during project initiation and discuss each stakeholder. Since the project manager is responsible for keeping everyone aware of project status and dealing with issues, he or she must also think about the best way to communicate with each stakeholder. The two can strategize about how to work with each team member and develop a cohesive and consistent approach. The most successful projects have a project manager and BA who are in sync with each other and always deliver a consistent message (see Chapter 2 for more on stakeholder analysis).

Technique: Plan Your Communications

At the beginning of a project, you should think about how and with whom you will be communicating. Obviously, you will be communicating with all of the stakeholders. A communication plan helps you think through how to *best* communicate. Always think through the *who, what, where, when,*

BABOK Connection	
Knowledge Area	**Task/Technique**
Business Analysis Planning and Monitoring	Plan Business Analysis Communication

and *why* of each communication. A little planning goes a long way in the area of communication. Everyone on the project team is busy, and no one has a lot of time to spend talking about the project and its requirements. You need to think ahead about how to best elicit and confirm requirements. Having a communication plan will also help you estimate the time required to complete your work.

With whom are you communicating? What is the individual's position in the organization? Where does he or she work? How much time does this person plan to devote to the project? How experienced is he or she in the business area? If you know the individual from previous work, what is his or her personality? Is he or she shy and quiet? Is he or she difficult to pin down? Does the person oversimplify complex tasks? Does he or she work well in a group or work better alone? What is his or her attitude toward IT and software? The more you know about each individual, the better you will be able to structure your communication and make the best use of your time and the stakeholder's time.

What information do you need from each stakeholder? Do you need to understand how work is currently done (as is)? Do you need to understand how one department works with another? Do you need to understand how one individual works with another? Are there complex business rules that you will need to document? What are the limits on your solution recommendations? Be sure to ask stakeholders for their ideas and suggestions for the solution. Plan enough time to develop questions, conduct elicitation sessions, conduct requirements reviews, etc.

How are you going to communicate? Business analysis work involves planning conversations, planning for interviews, and planning for facilitation sessions. Using a script may work well in these situations. There is a great book, not specifically written for BAs, called *Lifescripts* (Pollan and Levine, 2004). It suggests that when you must have a difficult conversation with someone and are unsure of how well the conversation will progress, you should plan the conversation. This fits well with requirements elicitation work.

The idea behind a script is that you plan each question or statement that you will say and then imagine the possible responses made by the person with whom you are speaking. In the context of trying to understand why a project is being initiated, imagine the entire conversation that you would have with a senior executive in your organization. Figure 7.3 shows the beginning of a sample script for such a conversation.

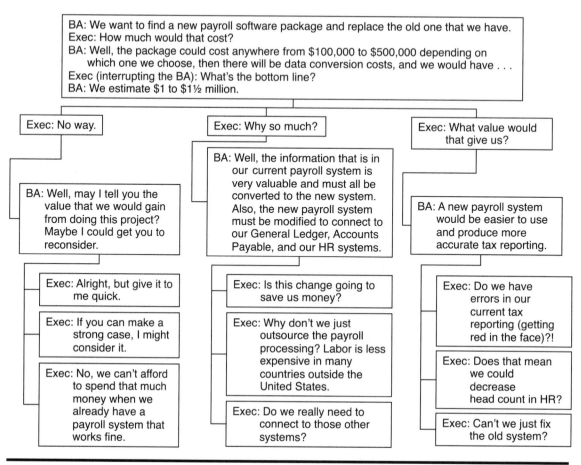

FIGURE 7.3. Sample Script

Where and how are you going to communicate? The ideal communication takes place when people are face to face to discuss project requirements. In a personal interview or requirements elicitation session, a BA gets non-verbal information in addition to the words that the stakeholder uses. Facial expressions reveal when you need to ask a follow-up question, paraphrase, or mirror a statement. If you can meet in person with a stakeholder, do so.

However, in many organizations today, face-to-face meetings are not always possible. When stakeholders are physically and/

BABOK Connection	
Knowledge Area	**Task/Technique**
Elicitation	Prepare for Elicitation
	Conduct Elicitation

or geographically separated, BAs need to be creative in designing communications. Take advantage of the options that are available to you. Table 7.7 highlights some advantages and limitations of common communication vehicles used in business analysis.

TABLE 7.7. Communication Options

Vehicle	Advantages	Limitations
Telephone	◆ Convenient, available almost every-where ◆ Ability to ask clarifying and follow-up questions	◆ No visual, non-verbal information ◆ Requires both parties to be available at the same time
E-mail	◆ Convenient for brief information exchange ◆ Communicators do not have to be available at the same time ◆ Can easily ask follow-up questions and follow the e-mail string	◆ No visual, non-verbal, or tone-of-voice information ◆ Does not build relationships
Instant messaging	◆ Convenient for simple questions ◆ Communicators do not have to be available at the same time ◆ Can easily ask follow-up questions and follow the e-mail string	◆ History is not saved by default ◆ No non-verbal clues
Face-to-face interview	◆ Great for very detailed requirements elicitation ◆ Allows for use of drawings, comparing notes ◆ Non-verbal clues are available ◆ Builds relationships between team members	◆ May be costly if travel is required
Online collaboration tools (Web conferencing)	◆ Great for group work and review of documentation ◆ Individuals can work at their convenience	◆ Requires a moderator/coordinator to review all feedback ◆ Need a common understanding of the goal/purpose of the document being created

TABLE 7.7. Communication Options (continued)

Vehicle	Advantages	Limitations
Teleconference	◆ Allows several people in different geographic areas to "talk" ◆ Good for reviewing documents or deliverables ◆ Low cost	◆ No non-verbal clues ◆ Facilities and scheduling may be difficult ◆ Requires a structured agenda and strong facilitator
Video conference	◆ Allows several people to see each other in different geographic areas to "talk"	◆ Facilities and scheduling may be difficult ◆ Effectiveness varies based on equipment and room setup—poor setup makes this distracting ◆ Requires a structured agenda and strong facilitator
Questionnaire, survey	◆ Good when information is needed from a large number of people ◆ Well-designed survey produces easily tabulated results	◆ Excellent survey design is time consuming and costly ◆ Only closed-ended questions are asked
Work observation	◆ Great way to understand business stakeholders' work environment and learn how processes are done ◆ Helps with usability design	◆ May be disruptive to workers if questions are asked
Facilitated sessions	◆ Efficient when there are several stakeholders interested in the same requirements	◆ Scheduling ◆ Requires significant planning ◆ Requires a skilled facilitator

Skill: Choose Appropriate Requirements Deliverables

The third step in the planning framework is process. A BA must decide how the business analysis work will be performed and presented. BAs have hundreds of choices for representing requirements, but most BAs only use a handful. Different types of projects will necessitate different analysis techniques and requirements deliverables. Take a few minutes to (1) think about which requirements components will be needed (described in Chapter

TABLE 7.8. Sample Requirements Needed by Project Type

Project Description	Requirements Package
New in-house software development project	◆ Entire requirements package
Update an existing application to utilize new technology	◆ Project initiation ◆ Technical requirements
Change in a business process	◆ Project initiation ◆ *Business requirements* for the process ◆ *Functional requirements* for the process ◆ *Technical requirements*
Additional business data needed	◆ Project initiation ◆ *Business requirements* for the data ◆ *Functional requirements* for data maintenance ◆ *Technical requirements* for the database
Select a software package for purchase	◆ Project initiation ◆ *Business requirements* ◆ Limited *functional requirements* ◆ Description of current technical environment
Infrastructure project (e.g., data warehouse, networking, intranet)	◆ Project initiation ◆ Limited *business* or *functional requirements* ◆ *Technical requirements*

6), (2) decide which requirements deliverables will be created (described in Chapter 6), and (3) develop an approach for creating each deliverable. The approach for creating each deliverable will lead directly to a BA task list that can be incorporated into the project management plan. Table 7.8 gives some examples of requirements needed for different types of projects.

Skill: Develop a Business Analysis Task List

Once you understand and decide on the project deliverables and a communication plan, you can create a task list for the business analysis work. This requires a careful look at each deliverable to determine exactly what work will be needed to get each one done. Use your experience and your imagination to visualize the development of each deliverable. For example:

◆ **Deliverable**: Process decomposition of the accounts payable area
◆ **Stakeholders**: Three key SMEs, all working in the same office

Brainstorm about the things that will need to be done:

◆ Decide how to draw the diagram (and make tools available)
◆ Draft a list of initial questions for SMEs
◆ Set up initial meeting—make sure white boards/flip charts are available
◆ Facilitate the initial meeting
◆ Draft the decomposition diagram based on information from initial meeting
◆ Schedule time with each SME for follow-up questions
◆ Meet with each SME for follow-up
◆ Revise decomposition diagram based on follow-up
◆ Schedule a review session with SMEs
◆ Prepare diagram for presentation and review
◆ Deliver to SMEs before meeting
◆ Facilitate meeting/take notes
◆ Finalize decomposition diagram based on review notes
◆ Distribute final diagram and get sign-off

As you can see, after just a single brainstorming session, at least 15 individual tasks have been identified as required to complete this requirement deliverable. This assumes that the SMEs are knowledgeable and available.

The level of detail of this list may be too much for the project manager, so you may want to combine some of these tasks when developing the project work breakdown structure (WBS). However, this level of detail is very helpful when you are asked to estimate your time requirements. It is

BABOK Connection	
Knowledge Area	**Task/Technique**
Business Analysis Planning and Monitoring	Plan Business Analysis Approach
	Replanning

much easier to estimate how long it will take to accomplish small tasks than large combination tasks. Estimate your time for these detailed tasks and then combine up for the

WBS. This detailed estimate will be useful for you to check yourself as work progresses to determine if you are falling behind schedule. Having this detail also helps justify your estimates if the project manager or sponsor wants to know why things are taking so long.

Skill: Estimate Your Time

There are two effective ways to estimate the time required to complete a task: (1) break down the task into small enough subtasks that you can estimate each subtask and roll up or (2) use past history of time spent on similar tasks.

Estimating is very difficult, but the good news is that you can become better at it over time. This is because much of the knowledge required to give good estimates is found in past experience. The best way to develop good estimates is to track the actual time that you spend on your tasks and use that knowledge base for future projects. This

BABOK Connection	
Knowledge Area	**Task/Technique**
Business Analysis Planning and Monitoring	Plan, Monitor, and Report on Business Analysis Performance
	Variance Analysis

explains why it takes time and experience to improve your ability to estimate. If you keep track of your actual time spent in interviews, in facilitation sessions, writing detailed requirements, conducting reviews, etc., you will gain a very good understanding of realistic time frames. You also will have very good backup documentation when the project manager or project sponsor questions your estimates.

Planning is an activity which is very important to a BA because business analysis work is very complex and detailed. Planning should be performed for every project, even though small projects will not require formal planning documentation. Planning for business analysis work involves identifying the people with whom you will be working, developing a communication plan, deciding on analysis techniques and requirements deliverables, and developing realistic estimates of the time required to complete these tasks.

SUMMARY OF KEY POINTS

Great BAs live their profession in their heart and soul. They are very intelligent, well educated, and have significant experience. But intelligence, training, and background are not enough. To be truly excellent, you have to love what you are doing. And loving business analysis means enjoying problem solving, working patiently with people, and being an advocate for the business. BAs enjoy learning new things and have a natural curiosity. In addition, they have a rare combination of the ability to see the big picture (conceptual thinking) while being very detail oriented. This combination of traits results in a very successful business analysis professional who is in great demand. Understanding the unique combination of traits required for successful business analysis creates an appreciation for the complexity of the role and helps to explain why the role is so difficult to master.

BIBLIOGRAPHY

Allen, David (2002). *Getting Things Done: The Art of Stressful Productivity.* Penguin.

Brassard, Michael and Diane Ritter (1994). *The Memory Jogger II.* First Edition. GOAL/QPC.

B2T Training (2008). Developing a Business Analysis Work Plan. Three-day instructor-led course. www.b2ttraining.com (planning worksheets are available from the Web Added Value™ Download Resource Center at www.jrosspub.com).

Covey, Stephen R. (1989). *The 7 Habits of Highly Effective People.* Free Press.

Ferrazzi, Keith and Tahl Raz (2005). *Never Eat Alone: And Other Secrets to Success, One Relationship at a Time.* First Edition. Doubleday Business.

GOAL/QPC (2000). *The Problem Solving Memory Jogger.* GOAL/QPC.

McConnell, Steve (1996). *Rapid Development: Taming Wild Software Schedules.* Microsoft Press.

National Institute of Standards and Technology (2002). The Economic Impacts of Inadequate Infrastructure for Software Testing.

Pollan, Stephen M. and Mark Levine (2004). *Lifescripts: What to Say to Get What You Want in Life's Toughest Situations.* Wiley.

INDEX